£2-20

Danny Mackay

3 J.MC Talman

Melness

D0272323

GANG
of
ONE

GANG
of
ONE

GARY MULGREW

HODDER &
STOUGHTON

First published in Great Britain in 2012 by Hodder & Stoughton
An Hachette UK company

2

Copyright © Gary Mulgrew 2012

The right of Gary Mulgrew to be identified as the Author of
the Work has been asserted by him in accordance with
the Copyright, Designs and Patents Act 1988.

Photograph of Cara Katrina © Gary Mulgrew

All rights reserved. No part of this publication may be
reproduced, stored in a retrieval system, or transmitted,
in any form or by any means without the prior written
permission of the publisher, nor be otherwise circulated in
any form of binding or cover other than that in which it is
published and without a similar condition being
imposed on the subsequent purchaser.

A CIP catalogue record for this title is available from the
British Library

Hardback ISBN 978 1 444 73789 9
Trade Paperback ISBN 978 1 444 73790 5
eBook ISBN 978 1 444 73791 2

Typeset in Nofret by Palimpsest Book Production Limited,
Falkirk, Stirlingshire

Printed and bound by Clays Ltd, St Ives plc

Hodder & Stoughton policy is to use papers that are
natural, renewable and recyclable products and made
from wood grown in sustainable forests. The logging and
manufacturing processes are expected to conform to the
environmental regulations of the country of origin.

Hodder & Stoughton Ltd
338 Euston Road
London NW1 3BH

www.hodder.co.uk

To Calum and Cara

This is a true story. However, some of the events and/or timing of events, together with the names of the individuals or gangs, have been changed to protect the identities of those involved.

CONTENTS

PROLOGUE

Texas, April 2008

I DON'T KNOW HOW TO EXPLAIN why I, your father, am sitting here in a dark cupboard, aged forty-six, alone. I don't know how to explain that it's my choice to do this, to prepare for what lies ahead. I don't know how, but I must. I must find a way.

It's 637 days since I last saw you, and tomorrow I start a three-year term in a Texas jail. That will make it even harder to find you, although none of it has been exactly easy since they extradited us here twenty-two months ago. It will also be so tough on your big brother Calum; he has endured so much already. He is twelve now and he still talks about you constantly. He misses you and he misses his mother, and he doesn't understand why she doesn't contact him – none of us do. No birthday cards, no Christmas cards, no phone calls, no letters; nothing. Julie is taking care of him now, giving him as much love as she can, but I wonder how he can cope with losing contact with his sister and his mother, and now having to watch his father go away.

Before I can get back to him, though, I have to get through this time in prison and hope that the American Government honours its promise to me; honours the shabby deal I made to get home; honours the deal I made so I could be with Calum again and find you before it's all too late.

But to survive this prison I have to conquer so many fears. And the first, the oldest and the biggest one is this fear of darkness. Will they lock me up in the dark? What happens when the lights go out? I can't bear darkness; it is my enemy and my tormentor. People keep telling me that I am so strong and so brave, but they don't know that I am frightened. I am frightened of the dark. I have been since I was four years old. Who wouldn't have been in that place?

I remember it as pitch-black, save for a small sliver of light from a narrow window at the top. Sometimes, when the moon wasn't out, it seemed to me to be total darkness. Nothing. I would sit on an old chest, one of the few pieces of furniture in that dismal place, a garage at the back of a children's home just outside Glasgow. It was full of old clothes that the Cottage Mother would get me and the other children to dress up in, to play our 'pretend family' games in. That's what you do in those places – you play the pretend family you don't have.

My bare feet would dangle from the chest, away from the concrete floor, so that the cold wouldn't start creeping up my legs and aching in my calves. But the real reason I sat there was to try to keep that chest closed. I worried about what might come out as I peered towards the window, hoping for light, for the reassurance that nothing was there. Darkness then and darkness now.

I can't count how many times the Cottage Mother stuck me in there to learn the error of my ways, how much time I spent sitting in terror in that garage. But I was in the Home for over two years, and by the time I was almost seven and returned to your grandmother (along with your uncles, Mark and Michael) my fear of the dark came with me. It has stayed with me, from then until now, and I'm once again sitting here in complete silence, in complete darkness. This time, the door is right beside me, I need only reach for the knob and turn it, but that would be failing you. That would make it less likely that I will see you again. I have to overcome this fear for your sake – and for mine.

We thought you might be in here in the US, in Ohio, and then perhaps in Paris, and now it seems like it might be Tunisia, with the man your mum married; a man we know only as Abdul. I hope he's kind to you. The Foreign Office call what's happened to you a 'parental abduction'; in fact there is a whole department dedicated to working on cases such as yours, but they say if you are in Tunisia it will be very hard for us to find you and bring you back into our lives. Very hard. But I will. I'll find you. Just as soon as I can get home.

Wherever you are, and whomever you are with, I hope they remember to cuddle you every day. I hope they know how to brush the curls out of your hair without hurting you, where exactly to put your hairclips and how to wrap you in your favourite bath towel, so you're snuggled up and warm. I hope they carry you to your bed wrapped in your favourite blanket, and sing to you every night and tell you stories of princesses and kings and ponies. And I hope somewhere deep inside you know that we never forget you or stop loving you and missing you, and that the road I am on will lead me back to you.

1

WELCOME TO AMERICA

I TOOK THE TOWEL FROM THE foot of the cupboard as the light and sounds of another day in Houston started to drift in. Tomorrow I would surrender myself to Big Spring prison, just four hours from the Mexican border, in the middle of the Texan desert, and all this waiting and preparation would be over.

I looked at my grey suit hanging beside me in the cupboard. I fingered the material, as if the touch might soothe me in some way. There was a time when I had an array of suits to choose from. Now I had just the one – my court suit. The suit I'd worn when we lost the extradition hearings in England, the suit I wore when I changed my plea to guilty in America years later. It was a suit of setbacks and shame; a suit I wondered if I'd ever wear again.

Those last few days in England after the announcement of our imminent extradition had been chaos. The work of our friend Melanie Riley and her company Bell Yard had got us a level of publicity we probably didn't deserve or anticipate: front-page coverage in nearly every news-paper; Prime Minister's Questions, with Tony Blair under enormous pressure to postpone or cancel our extradition; a special debate in the House of Commons, with the result an overwhelming vote against the extradition, and then the unprecedented suspension of parliamentary business for the rest of the day. Then the suicide of Neil Coulbeck – a key witness against us – who rumours suggested had been so pressurised and hunted by the US Department of Justice (DoJ) that he'd taken his own life just two days before we were due to leave. Had he really been subjected to such pressures? Could we ever be that important to the Americans that a friend and colleague had to lose his life? It added a tangible sadness to what had until then had a surreal feel to it all.

Up until Neil's death, I hadn't paid much attention to the debates or looked at the newspapers and I had barely listened to whatever assurances Tony Blair was giving about how we would be treated. I'd lost hope some time before, and besides, I had more important things to do. I was by now a single father, living alone with Calum, and I had to tell my ten-year-old son that I was leaving him.

I had to tell him that I had got it wrong, that I had failed him in the worst way possible; that two years after having to endure the split from my ex-wife, his life was in complete turmoil again. Tell him that the promises that they wouldn't 'get me' and that I would never, ever leave or abandon him, had all been empty and false. That I had failed at being his father.

How do you explain all of that to a ten-year-old boy? Where was the *Oprah* show that covers a single parent's extradition? What words do you use when your son begins to cry uncontrollably as the realisation of what he's being told begins to sink in? Who can prepare you for the rawness of how a ten-year-old can cry? No inhibitions, no misgivings, just a pure unfettered pain. How the tremors and convulsions of his little body reverberated through me as I tried desperately to hold him, more painful than any physical blows could ever be. How he shook and whimpered as he began to calm down, the enormity of my words finally sinking in – the destruction of his last bit of security.

Would I ever be coming back to him? Our English QC, Alun Jones, had painted a pretty grim picture of the US Judicial System and our chances within it, but that, I'd told myself, was just posturing for the extradition hearings, right? Surely the success rate of the Department of Justice couldn't actually be as high as 98% – with 95% of those indicted pleading guilty for a softer sentence? Even Soviet Russia wasn't that successful; and this was America – land of the free, and home of *Law and Order.* I'd been raised to know that the Yanks were the good guys, who would go out of their way to do the right thing with dashing, good-looking actors, high-tech equipment and an even higher set of morals. That's what I'd believed; at least I had until they came to extradite me.

Then the day of the extradition itself: media in helicopters, motorbikes and cars following us as we made our way to hand ourselves over to the Transport Police at Heathrow Airport. All that noise and chaos seemed to be happening around me, but not to me. By 7 a.m. I stood in a small waiting room with Giles and David – the other two members of the NatWest Three – and a plain-clothes policeman bemused by all the fuss. I was watching the live pictures on Sky News of our plane, sitting motionless on the tarmac, soon to be bound for America. I looked impassively at Giles, grim faced and stern, arms folded, listening to some 'expert' in the studio saying how if we lost we faced up to thirty-five years in prison, but most likely would only do about twenty. What a relief that was. David stood transfixed and smiling, correcting every factual error made, hanging on every word. Even now he was focused and working. I felt detached from them both, cut off from all of it. The commentator kept saying Enron. Over and over again it was Enron. We were heading to Texas because of Enron. We'd be going to trial because of Enron. We had defrauded Enron. Still that same basic mistake trotted out by supposed experts. We had sat through years of court sessions, of appeals, of judicial reviews, in which it was clearly NatWest I was supposed to have defrauded, not Enron. I had committed this act of fraud by breaching my employment contract, which was news to me and seemingly news to the newsmen – because still they went on about our role in the greatest corporate collapse in US history. By now it was a byword for greed and corruption – and that word was 'Enron'.

I watched on, a live broadcast of the worst day of my life on national TV. 'That'll be something to tell the grandchildren,' I thought, musing that they would be in university by the time I got the chance – if we lost. They replayed the tapes of me leaving my house over and over again, getting into the car with Julie, and my friends Vincent, Jane and Joe, heading towards Heathrow. It was about four o'clock in the morning and I had just briefly woken Calum to say goodbye. He'd said he wouldn't sleep unless I promised to do that. Thankfully he was drowsy and didn't start to cry again. He just held me tightly and I promised over and over again that I would see him soon, and that I would be back, even though I didn't know if that was true. I've never hoped for something so much in my whole life and I felt such affection, such a powerful bond, as I cradled him in my arms. Had I ever felt such pain as when I had to let him go, stroking his head and kissing him gently for one last time?

The TV switched back to the helicopter view of the plane. They were focusing in on the food carts being loaded up and speculating on whether we'd be handcuffed on board and discussing how the US Marshals weren't allowed to carry their guns with them. A brief thought of me escaping at 20,000 feet passed through my mind – replaced with the urge to scream at the TV, the anger, the frustration, the despair suddenly all welling up.

'Has the whole FUCKING world gone mad?' I shouted, much louder than I'd intended.

Giles looked at me and shook his head. 'I know, mate, I know,' he said, placing his hand on my shoulder.

David glanced sympathetically at me, then pulled up a chair and moved closer to the TV.

'Right lads, time to go,' the plain–clothes officer said. 'We need to hand you over to the Yanks, I'm afraid.'

Two US Marshals were assigned to each of us. They didn't introduce themselves or offer their names, as we were 'handed over' by the British Transport Police at the doorway to the plane. No fanfare, no speeches, just some paperwork and a few brief words, none of which I could hear.

As we boarded, the beefier of my two escorts took

my elbow. 'You have to turn right here. You won't be used to that,' he chuckled as we headed to the 'cheap seats' at the back of the plane. Apparently banker baiting was all the rage.

I was too depressed to make any reply. I sat at the bulkhead, the last seat on the plane, upright, impassive, and trying to be determined, while sandwiched between one middle-aged US Marshal and one young beefcake, chiselled type. In front of me was David, occupying a central seat with Giles in front of him, both trussed up between two marshals. David was talkative, confident and assured, and I took some comfort from that. The plane was full of journalists and some made open attempts to film us or to ask us questions, only to be brusquely moved away by the marshals. They wanted to know if we were handcuffed (we weren't) and if we had any final comments to make. They made it sound like a one-way flight to the gallows.

The plane seemed to taxi for an age and then sat motionless on the runway for another thirty or forty minutes. A last-minute reprieve, perhaps? Tony Blair saves the day? Foolishly, I let such tempting thoughts creep into my mind. Hope can be a dangerous thing, but it was soon extinguished. The rumble of the engines gathered pace and we began to edge forward and then to pick up speed. I was off. Gone. Finished. The bastards had done it. There was nothing except my own thoughts to mark that moment of betrayal, when my own country handed me over to another and we became a minor footnote in Tony Blair's sycophantic love affair with the US. I felt an acute sense of loss and momentary help-lessness, as if a key plank of my life had been stripped from under me and being British meant nothing. I wondered if it would ever mean anything to me again. I wondered if I'd ever come home.

Other than an uncomfortable trip to the bathroom, when the beefcake marshal wouldn't let me close the door (what did he think I was going to do?), I sat perfectly upright for the full ten hours and said and did nothing. My mind was still full of my goodbyes. Had I handled it properly with Calum? Could my daughter Cara, at five years old, understand? How would my girlfriend, Julie, be able to cope with Calum now along with her own children, Jamie and Issi, and then Cara if and when she visited? What were they doing now? I hoped they would be kept away from the TV; I didn't want them to see me taken from them like this. And the worst thought of all – when would I see them again?

The beefcake made a point of openly reading *The Smartest Guys in the Room*, a story about the collapse of Enron, replete with references to the 'NatWest Three'. He overtly earmarked certain pages – I guessed they must have referred to us, as he kept taking surreptitious glances while he folded the pages over. I think he felt good about doing his duty for America, bringing these bad guys back to face justice. Thankfully, he wouldn't be on our jury, although the book and the man's attitude confirmed to me the uphill struggle we were going to face in the States. We were going for trial when the history had already been written, the books published and the movies made. I should have seen the signs long before I got on that plane. Enron, a word synonymous with greed, was etched into the minds of all Texans. But I held onto the thought that I'd be alright if I told the truth.

When the plane finally taxied to a stop in Houston, the stewardess announced that there were some 'dignitaries' on board and that everyone else must remain seated until they were deplaned. Almost immediately, armed marshals appeared to help escort us 'dignitaries' off the plane and the existing six marshals were reunited with their weaponry. Still seated, I watched the curious relationship between American law enforcement and their guns. They seemed to relax visibly as soon as they were 'packing heat'. I noticed Beefcake pat his gun about four or five times and then subconsciously, I hope, he began stroking it. It occurred to me just how much he would enjoy using it.

I had no luggage, nothing, no change of clothes, not even a toothbrush. Our lawyer, Mark Spragg, had advised us that anything we brought to America would get 'lost', so I had entered a whole new level in travelling light. In some ways the lack of any possessions added to the surreal feel of the experience. Getting off the plane was awkward, because they wanted two officers in front of us, then one on each side, gently leading us by the elbow, and then two behind. In the confined space of the aircraft bulkhead, this became somewhat farcical, but eventually we stumbled the length of the plane, submerged in marshals. Strangely and movingly, the UK press corps sitting towards the front and the middle of the plane began to applaud. Some stood up. 'Good luck, lads!', 'Bloody disgrace!', 'Stay strong!' were among the shouts I heard. Hearing those distinct regional British accents – some Cockney, some Northern and Scottish – really affected me. Maybe I hadn't lost my country after all. I mouthed 'thank you' as I caught the eye of a reporter I recognised from a few articles he had written – there seemed to be genuine sympathy in his eyes.

When we reached the front exit of the plane, things became even more chaotic. We were told to wait just outside the plane door as suddenly shouts and instructions seemed to emanate from every direction. Out of the morass of bodies came one marshal, small and rotund with a ruddy complexion. He was carrying our handcuffs – the confirmation that our freedom was over; that we were theirs now and that they controlled our lives. He shook loose the first set and with minimal fuss clipped them straight onto David's wrists. I noticed he made no eye contact with David and didn't speak to him, turning his wrist one way then another, checking them quickly and brusquely to see if they were tight enough. No one else seemed to notice. Quickly, he moved onto Giles, as the shouts and noise continued around us. That was just in the background though; all I could hear was the rustle of the chains and a cricking sound as the second set of cuffs was attached to Giles's wrists. David still stood transfixed, head bowed, staring at his cuffs. His earlier confidence had evaporated; he now looked frightened and I worried he might start to crack.

Next minute the marshal came to me and clipped mine on. 'Hey, how was London, England?' he said – not to me, but to the older of the two marshals who had been escorting me. They kept talking as he turned my wrists around and checked the tightness of the cuffs, still not looking at or talking to me.

'Fuck you,' I thought, enjoying my height advantage over him. 'Fuck the lot of you.' But then I chastised myself. I couldn't allow myself to get angry or emotional. 'Cuffs not too tight, Mr Mulgrew? Sorry about all this hassle!' – that was the kind of polite consideration I still expected. But I should have known I wasn't going to get it; I had to get a grip on myself.

A huge officer grabbed David by his elbow and started jogging down a long walkway with him. He looked like a linebacker, at least 350lb, and dwarfed David, who was pretty small to start with. I noticed David swallow hard as he peered up at the officer so brusquely guiding him along, but then I could see him reasserting himself as he stood upright and jogged along at pace, his army training no doubt coming to the fore. We were all jogging now. Someone had my elbow, also pulling me into a jog and shouting, 'Clear, clear!' to anyone foolish enough to come close. I counted twenty-seven officers in total, all armed, some with FBI jackets, some with 'ICE' (Immigration and Customs Enforcement) jackets, some marked 'US Marshals' and some just in plain police uniforms. The officer at the front of this entourage was clearing a path through the stunned onlookers as we jogged on. I looked at my guide, a youngish marshal, blonde, blue-eyed and serious.

'Why are we running?' I asked, as he continued to lead me by the elbow. He looked shocked, as if no one had told him in the briefing that I might speak; that I was capable of speech. I thought he was about to respond but then he faced resolutely forward again, keeping pace with the gradually strewn-out entourage. Some of the overweight officers were already lagging and out of breath but everyone seemed caught up in the bizarre spectacle, jogging past the departure gates of Houston's George Bush International Airport, on a balmy Wednesday afternoon in mid July, 2006.

I caught the eye of one elderly woman. She was standing back in surprise, clutching her bag in front of her, her husband's arm stretched before her in a protective, tender gesture. What was she thinking? I thought I saw something in her eyes – fear maybe, or was it something else? Her husband was saying something to her; I turned my head and evenly kept her gaze while I was whisked past. What was he saying? I doubted it was, 'Oh look! That's those three guys who breached their employment contract with NatWest in London. That'll teach them.' He probably thought we were terrorists.

A number of turns later and we eventually came to a wing not open to the public, which was controlled by Immigration. Entering a large office, we were positioned in three seats placed against the far wall and sat in silence as the various parties recovered from their exertions. There was an air of real excitement in the room, as some of the officers bent over and tried to catch their breath. They were smiling, laughing and insulting each other about their relative fitness or lack thereof. My despair deepened with the realisation that on one of the worst days of my life, these guys were actually enjoying themselves.

'Who are these guys again?' someone asked, drawing attention back to us.

'The three Brits that collapsed Enron.'

'Wow, the Enron guys?' one, sweaty, red-faced FBI agent asked, looking at us intently as he approached.

'Yup,' said another, fitter specimen, joining him. You would think we were behind a glass wall and couldn't hear, like specimens in a zoo.

'How much did they get?' asked the red-faced agent, peering intently at us.

'Millions, hundreds of millions I think. They're, like, famous in Britain.'

'Wow,' the agent said, still staring. We didn't speak or move and the conversation continued as if we weren't there. 'What happens to them now?'

'We book them in, lock 'em up and then they have a bail hearing tomorrow,' interjected a silver-haired marshal, who seemed to be emerging as the leader of this rabble. He held a plastic bag with our three passports in it – our sole possessions.

'They can't get bail, can they Dave?' asked a hitherto silent man sitting behind a desk with a sea of paperwork in front of him. He wore glasses and peered over them as he spoke. He had a cardigan on and looked more like your favourite grandad than a police officer.

'Word is they're gittin' it,' responded the same marshal, Marshal Dave, the would-be leader, who was now edging towards us, eyeing us ever more closely. I started to get a fix on Dave: definitely in charge, angry, a gun-stroker no doubt, and a Southerner. He'd probably claim to have invested his pension, his life savings, his house, and his kids' school funds in Enron stock when he thought it was a sure-fire winner, just before it imploded. And now he blamed me.

'How do they get bail? Surely they get locked up?' the cuddly desk officer asked again, looking straight at Marshal Dave's back as he crouched in front of us.

'Nope, the Brits said it would be unfair.' Dave grimaced. He definitely didn't like us – probably invested some of his parents' life savings as well.

'But they ain't legal in the US. They don't have visas,' the desk sergeant continued.

'So?' said Marshal Dave, rising back up, this comment clearly catching his attention. He started thumbing through our passports. I definitely hadn't applied for a visa to facilitate any extradition. That was never on my to-do list.

'So if they are released by the judge, Immigration will have to pick them up and impound them,' said the desk sergeant. I sat up. This was getting interesting.

'And then we would have to process them,' added one of the immigration officers in the ICE jacket.

'What do you mean, process them?' asked Marshal Dave, as he threw the passport bag over to the beckoning desk sergeant.

'Well, since they don't have a proper visa, we'd have to deport them.' Bingo, I liked that.

The FBI guy chipped in again; he had a real slow Southern drawl. 'Hell, we took four years to git 'em here, we sure as hell ain't gonna deport them. They're fugitives, God dammit; we'd never find them again.'

Oh, how I wished one of our judges in the extradition hearings could have heard this farcical conversation. It was exactly as our expert witness had predicted, exactly what the judges had decided would never happen. David had an I-told-you-so look on his face.

By now the immigration officer had motioned to see the passports. 'Nope, they don't have visas,' he said, thumbing through our passports. 'These boys are illegals. Did you boys apply for visas?' he shouted over at us. We all shook our heads.

'So, if they get bail tomorrow, as soon as they step

out of that courtroom, we'll arrest them and lock 'em up for being illegals!' he said forcefully.

'They'll git bail, then go straight to jail,' the ICE officer summed up, delighted with his little rhyme, which threw the room into further turmoil. By now our passports, still in their clear plastic bag were being thrown around the room as the tussle between the various strands of US Law Enforcement continued.

'I'll hold those,' said the FBI agent.

'No, you won't,' responded Marshal Dave. 'Those are coming with us. We'll give them to the judge.'

'Oh, no!' interjected the immigration officer again, holding the bag over his head. 'These men are here illegally. By rights we should be putting them straight back on the plane.'

This level of organisation didn't bode well for our time in America. It might have been funny to see how the reality compared to the gritty, heroic and, above all, efficient picture of US justice delivered on our television screens. But these same people had taken me away from my kids. And if they got their way, they would keep me away until my kids weren't kids any more.

The show broke up when Marshal Dave turned towards me and shouted, 'You! Stand up and come with me.'

Expressionless, I rose from my seat and followed him and another marshal round the corner into a small side room. I immediately noticed it had no windows. The second marshal took up a position at the far end of this room with his back to the wall. Bizarrely, he was still wearing sunglasses. He was also chewing gum and wielding what seemed to be a truncheon.

'Turn around and face the wall,' Marshal Dave barked,

clearly still angry about the discussion with Immigration. He sighed heavily as he started placing keys and other equipment on the small table in front of him. This guy oozed danger and intimidation. I sensed he needed only the barest of excuses.

'Face me!' he said briskly. I turned around. He stood right in front of me. He was much shorter than me.

'Don't you fuckin' look at me. Did you fuckin' look at me?' he growled, as I quickly averted my eyes from his gaze.

'He fuckin' looked at you, boss,' offered the irritant in the corner, tapping his stick gently in one hand.

'Did you fuckin' look at me?' Dave asked again, moving ever close to me.

'No, er, yes . . . I mean, I didn't.'

'Don't fuckin' talk to me like that!' Dave screamed. What the hell was wrong with this guy?

'You answer me, "Yes, sir," or "No, sir." You got that?'

'Yes, sir, or no, sir,' repeated the parrot in the corner.

'Yes . . . sir,' I replied haltingly. I'd walked into the wrong TV show.

'Now,' said Marshal Dave, breathing heavily. 'Listen up and listen up good: here are the rules. Number one: you answer, "Yes, sir," or "No, sir," – nothing else. If you answer any other way I will deem that as an attempt to escape. You understand?'

'Attempt to escape,' murmured the parrot, as if the words tasted of chocolate.

'Yes, sir,' I said firmly, my eyes fixed to the floor.

'Number two. You . . . do . . . not . . . eyeball . . . me . . .' He stretched the words out for emphasis. 'If you eyeball me, that is an attempt to escape. Do you understand?'

'Yes, sir!' I barked, feeling like a new army recruit.

'Number three. You do not converse with me, or with anyone else. You speak only when spoken to, by me or another marshal. Otherwise that is also an attempt to escape. You got that?'

'Yes, sir!'

'Any attempt to escape will automatically result in a new indictment, the penalty for which is another five years!'

'Another five years,' confirmed his number two, almost salivating at the thought of an attempted escape, where-upon, no doubt, he would have the pleasure of clubbing me to death.

'Do you understand?'

'Yes, sir!' I shouted a little too vigorously.

I sensed Marshal Dave tensing. After a moment's pause, he spoke more softly than before. 'You playing with me?' he asked quietly, coming ever closer. This guy was menacing. He was standing way too close to me, close enough to feel his breath, and I had to suppress a sudden urge to head-butt him.

'No . . .' then more quietly, 'sir,' I responded, involun-tarily raising my head a fraction to look at him.

'Don't look at me, boy!' he yelled.

'Don't look at him!' repeated the parrot, getting ever more excited.

'Don't you look at me. I warned you!' he continued.

The room fell silent. I stared ever more intently at the floor. I could feel the marshal was waiting for a flicker, a reaction, anything. I didn't move. Bizarrely, I felt complete calm; not intimidated or afraid. Instead in my mind I had one thought – Calum. The pain on his face; the way his body shuddered and trembled as he cried just those few short days earlier when I told him I had to go. There was nothing these people could do to me, nothing that would compare to that agony and the guilt that coruscated through my entire body, my heart, my soul. Looking back, I think I would have welcomed it if they had hit me – perhaps that would have numbed the pain I felt at being separated from Calum and Cara.

Then Marshal Dave spoke again, calmly, methodically, carefully. 'Now, I'm going to ask you what you have on your person. Think hard before you answer. If you don't tell me about something and I find something . . . then that will be an attempt to escape.'

The sinister tone was amplified by the failure of the parrot to repeat this. This must be the key bit, I thought. The denouement. The bit where people trip up.

But what did I have in my pockets? I panicked, trying desperately to think if I had anything from the plane or elsewhere. I had a desperate urge to rummage through, but my hands were still cuffed, and anyway I was sure rummaging through your pockets would be deemed an attempt to escape and punishable by another five years' imprisonment.

'Now,' Marshal Dave continued, 'what do you have on your person?'

I hesitated before responding, 'Nothing, sir.'

'Nothing, he said nothing,' repeated the parrot, edging forward as if getting ready to start on me.

'You come all the way from England – and you have . . . nothin'?'

I didn't put anything in my pocket on the plane, did I?

I was panicking, my head spinning trying to think of anything I might have accidentally put in my pockets when I went to the toilet or toyed with the plane food.

'I am going to ask you one more time. Think carefully before you answer. If I find anything . . . any-thing,' Dave pronounced it slowly for emphasis, 'then you're in deep shit.'

'Deep shit,' repeated the extremely annoying parrot. I hadn't looked at him closely before, and couldn't look at him now, but in my imagination he had become a RoboCop from an action movie.

'Nothing, sir,' I firmly repeated, not entirely believing it myself now.

'Nothing,' Marshal Dave said softly. 'OK, I am going to uncuff you,' he went on, 'and you are going to remove each item of clothing as I instruct you. Do you understand?'

'Yes, sir.'

'When you have removed said item of clothing, I want you to turn around, face the wall, and place your hands up against the wall, while I search your clothing. Do you understand?'

'Yes, sir.'

'OK, I am removing the cuffs,' he said, and did it quickly. 'Firstly, I want your shoes, laces and belt. The latter two items will not be returned to you.' He'd done this before.

I made a mental note to wear slip-ons and elasticated trousers the next time I got extradited as I quickly removed each item.

'Remove your T-shirt, then face the wall.'

I duly obliged, the move to semi-nakedness making me feel suddenly exposed. Almost involuntarily, I puffed out my chest. I didn't want to look like some poncey, flabby wanker-banker. I didn't want to feel like Marshal Dave was dominating me.

'Git your arms up.' I lifted them up. 'Higher!' he barked.

What a twat! He was really annoying me. Better not think that way, I told myself. Don't show a chink in the armour; don't give these pricks the chance to do what they would clearly love to. I stared straight ahead at the wall. It all seemed so unnecessary, although I learned later this was just the standard fare – everyone extradited got to enjoy this experience. Although we had perhaps been the highest profile case, there was a conveyor belt of extradition cases from the UK to the US waiting behind us, and even then I wondered how Gary McKinnon, for example, a hacker with Asperger's, would ever cope with such a welcome.

'Remove your jeans.'

I removed them quickly, pressing the pockets as I did to see if I could feel anything in them. They felt empty. I turned again to face the wall as I listened intently to Marshal Dave working his way thoroughly through my jeans. All I could hear was his breathing and I grimaced as I imagined him finding a sugar sachet from the plane and suddenly shouting that I was trying to escape and beating me to the floor. But my pockets must have been empty as nothing happened, although the temptation to turn around and look was building and building.

I was starting to feel more self-conscious standing there with just my boxer shorts and socks on, facing the wall with my hands up in the air.

How far was this going to go? Hopefully not the whole way, I thought.

'Remove your socks one by one,' was the next instruction.

He seemed to take an age searching my socks as I stood naked apart from my boxers, facing the wall with my arms held high up on the ceiling.

'Right,' he began. 'I am now going to begin a physical examination.' The words plunged into me. I considered asking him whether he thought he'd find any documents up there, four years after my indictment. But my own jokes didn't amuse me at that point.

'Turn around, keeping your arms raised and look straight ahead.' I obliged; my arms were getting increasingly heavy, but I decided it was too risky to ask for a rest.

'Relax your arms and open your mouth.' He had a swab or something and had a surprisingly good rummage around. I tried not to look directly at him. He tussled through my hair and checked behind my ears and under my armpits. 'Turn around, remove your underwear and then raise your arms again above your head.'

'Oh God,' I thought, 'he's going for the bum.'

'Spread your legs apart!'

I heard the unmistakable snap of surgical gloves. Each finger, snap, snap, snap. One by one those snaps resonated through the room as each finger became silicone wrapped.

'Face the wall,' he barked angrily as I glanced back at him. It wasn't easy not to take a quick look in such circumstances.

The snapping had stopped, but despite listening intently, I couldn't hear the swish of the lubricant being applied. I surmised he was going in lube–free. In what was turning out to be a really bad day for me, this was yet another setback. I braced myself.

'Now, bend forward and slowly moving your hands back, clasp each buttock and spread your cheeks.'

I thought of England. Of Tony Blair. I remembered I had heard him saying how we would be well treated. How the magistrate and judges knew we would be well treated. I thought of my family, sitting at home wondering what was happening to me. Probably tuned into *News at Ten* by now, with some Labour puppet assuring everyone we were in the best possible hands. I wished they could switch over live from the studio to see exactly what good hands I was in.

I clenched my buttocks. Nothing happened. I was desperate to look round. I thought about what Billy Connolly had once said about how the prostate was like a doughnut and the doctor has to check it hasn't become like a bagel. Marshal Dave was taking his time checking out my bakery status.

'Lift your sac,' he ordered. I duly complied, thinking maybe it was impeding his attack. Then he said the magical words, 'Turn around and pull your foreskin back.' I never thought I would be so happy to hear those words in all my life. Not from a man anyway. I turned around gleefully – too gleefully.

'What the fuck are you smiling at?' he asked, tippy-toeing up to my eye level. The smile was instantly off my face. 'You think I'm funny, English boy?' he spat.

I decided it wasn't the time to point out I wasn't English, and quickly answered, 'No, sir.'

'You think this whole thing's a joke?'

'He thinks it's a joke, boss; he thinks it's a joke.' The RoboCop was back.

I made mistake number two by glaring at him.

'Don't you look at him, you hear me? Lookin' at him is an attempt to escape! You trying to escape, boy?'

This was turning out badly. He was mad and I was naked. Naked in front of a marshal with anger issues.

'No, sir; no, sir,' I repeated quickly.

Dave paused for a second, staring intently at me and I stood there, arms aloft, bollock naked in front of these two lunatics.

'Then I'll ask you again.' More controlled now, more menacing. 'What were you smiling at?' His voice was a sinister monotone. I had to tiptoe out of this one.

'I . . . I . . .' I began falteringly. 'I was relieved, sir.'

'Relieved? Relieved?' he asked, as if in disbelief. 'You're naked in a room with two marshals!? How the hell were you relieved?'

I hesitated. Put that way, it did seem kind of strange.

'Well?' he demanded.

'I thought, I thought you were going to put your finger up my arse, sir,' I blurted out quickly, then clenched my teeth waiting for the fallout. It was immediate.

'You what . . . you want . . .' he stuttered. 'You want my finger up your ass, boy?' Dave exploded. Thrusting his face right into mine. The parrot was positively beside himself.

'He wants your finger up his ass, boss. He wants it up his ass!' he hollered as if he had just won the lottery.

'You want my finger up your ass?' Marshal Dave screeched again.

'No, sir. No, sir,' I repeated again, my aching arms still thrust up in the air.

''Cos I can put my finger up your ass, boy, if that's what you're wanting,' he raged.

'No, sir,' I barked out. 'I don't want your finger up my arse!'

He stood very close to me. We were both breathing hard. I was still naked. I still had my hands above my head. My heart was pounding. I was desperately trying not to look at him or RoboCop in the corner. The silence seemed to last an age.

'Git your boxers back on, then git dressed,' he finally said, as he stormed towards the door, adding charmingly, 'Let's get these British faggots locked up.' Gratefully, I started to reassemble my clothing, minus my belt and my laces, my welcoming party to America complete.

On the eve of my incarceration, my extradition and those first few hours in the United States already seemed a lifetime ago. Marshal Dave never did have the pleasure of locking me up, a political fix between the Blair and Bush governments ensuring we had the dubious pleasure of spending the next twenty-two months on tag and curfew whilst restricted to a small area of Houston. Now there was only one night left before the next stage, the worst stage, of my journey would begin. I wondered if that first experience of American Law Enforcement would be typical, and the thought made me shiver. I looked at the grey suit once more in the cupboard and decided I would leave it there tomorrow. I couldn't eat and I didn't want to drink. I didn't want to call anyone at home in England or do anything other than just lie there and breathe. I closed my eyes to wait for tomorrow and tried not to think about how scared I felt.

2

THE PROMISE

M Y ALARM WENT OFF AT 4.30 A.M. I stumbled into the bathroom and looked at myself in the mirror. Good, four days of growth, just what I had calculated as the optimum level. Long enough to give me an unkempt 'hard man' look, but short enough so the grey parts of my beard didn't age me and diminish the impact. My hair was shaved very short – gone were the curls.

But who was I kidding? I didn't look intimidating. In for fraud and feeling like a fraud. I'd get devoured as soon as I arrived. What the hell would they do with a British guy? Why did I have to get the tough prison when Giles and David got easier time? I breathed out slowly. 'Come on,' I said out loud, breaking the eerie silence of the last few days. 'You can do this. You will do this.' It felt strangely comforting to hear my own voice and I played around with some facial expressions, trying to look tough.

'Fuck, who am I kidding?' I thought, as my fearsome look revealed something more like suppressed terror. 'They're going to eat me alive.'

I pulled on an old pair of blue jeans, no belt, a white T-shirt and some slip-on shoes, clothes I never expected to see again and which wouldn't reveal me for the banker I once was. The taxi would already be downstairs waiting for me. I looked again at the only things I would carry – my mobile phone and my wallet. I would call Calum for the last time before I went in; I didn't want to but I knew I had to. It was Wednesday today, so Calum, six hours ahead of me, would be sitting in a lesson at school in England. Gazing out of the window, perhaps? Thinking about this moment? I hoped not. What do you tell your son just before you begin a thirty-seven month stretch inside? Stay in touch? I won't be long?

At the end of the last of many trips he had made to see me, I'd told him I would definitely be going to prison for a while. Just eleven years old by then, he'd seemed so small, so fragile, as he boarded that plane to go home. That was the last time I'd seen him. So young, so innocent, so loving – it was all so unfair. His name was called first, being unescorted, and I walked him to the front of the British Airways check-in desk. The air stewardess smiled kindly at him and he turned to me, but didn't raise his head. Getting taller but still a wee boy, he buried his head into my chest and held me extra tight. I tried desperately not to cry. I wanted to say something to him but I just couldn't speak. I was too afraid my words would sound weak and that would frighten him more. I felt a small tremor run through him. Keeping his face pressed hard against me, he squeezed me harder still.

'Hey, you're getting much stronger there, kid,' I said, in the daft American accent we sometimes played with, feigning shortness of breath. He laughed a little. I put my arms around him and lifted him up. His face rested into my neck and I could feel the wetness of his tears.

'I love you, Calum. I love you more than life itself. Do you know that?'

'Yes . . . Dad,' he managed to say, squeezing me ever tighter. There were people milling around waiting to start boarding after Calum, but I didn't want to let go of my son. I knew Troy, the lawyer sent to escort me to the airport, would give us as long as we needed. He wasn't the most sentimental guy, but he understood the significance of this goodbye.

I gently lowered Calum down and lifted his chin so I could see his beautiful face. His sadness was crushing me, but I knew I had to be strong for him. Especially now.

'Listen to me, Calum. Look at me,' I said as he tried to turn his head, embarrassed by his own tears.

'Uh, huh . . .' he mumbled as he looked right at me. God, he was so young. Too young to have to deal with this. My heart was breaking.

'I promise you I will be back. I will come back to you, Calum, and I will be there to bring you up and to be your father, OK?' I said as emphatically as I could muster.

'Y . . . yes, Dad,' he managed, before he pressed his face back into my chest.

'I will come home to you, Calum. Nothing bad will happen and I will be back, I promise. I promise,' I said in a whisper, hoping against hope that what I was saying was true.

I rocked him back and forth for a few moments longer. He kept holding me tightly. After a few more seconds, his breathing began to ease. He had calmed down. I kissed him once more.

'You have to go, my little man,' I said. I held him out at arm's length and he smiled at me.

'I love you, Dad,' he said, and picked up his rucksack.

'I love you too, Calum,' I said, suddenly feeling completely alone as he stepped away from me. Taking the air stewardess's hand, he walked confidently down the tunnel to board the flight. With his little rucksack decorated with badges from all his trips, he looked so small and inconsequential. I wanted to run after him and wrap him up in my arms. Halfway down he turned again, more confident now. 'Love you, Dad!' he shouted, then made the little 'call me' sign we had played around with over the last week as he beamed his smile at me. I tried to shout back, but initially the words got caught. 'Love . . . ahem . . . love you too, kid,' my affected American accent sounding a little hollow as it bounced down the gangplank.

The tears surged up.

He was gone. I was alone.

Despite having held up the boarding, no one had bothered us – no one had said anything. When I turned round, four or five people looked away. One lady in a blue dress just smiled at me and another younger woman was sniffling. I gave a weak smile as people cleared a way through for me. One suited businessman had stopped talking on his phone and was looking downwards as I approached. I could see the sympathy in so many of their faces and that upset me even more. Then I saw Troy. He was crying.

'Jesus Christ,' he said. 'I had no idea.' He didn't finish as I walked past him, my own tears falling freely now and a physical, aching pain clutching at my chest.

The memory of this last goodbye still felt raw as I looked at myself one more time in the mirror. This was all so hard. Was this man in front of me capable of handling this? I had no idea, but it didn't look promising. I knelt down and blessed myself and did what I often had done during any crisis in my life. I prayed.

'God give me strength,' was all I said before I faltered once more. I hoped He would have been paying attention and would know the rest of it. I knelt in silence for a few more moments and tried to gather myself. Then I stood, turned, grabbed my wallet and phone and took one final look at the desolate flat that had been my pre-prison prison for the last twenty-two months. The grey suit hung silently in the cupboard where I would leave it; the rest of the flat was empty save for a few abandoned boxes. I had a flight to catch to Big Spring, Texas. My gaolers awaited, and God only knew what else.

3

IF THE SOAP DROPS . . .

THE LOBBY OF MY APARTMENT BLOCK was deserted and I looked up to check the wall clock at precisely 5 a.m. – an apt time, it seemed, to be hauling yourself off to prison. The cab was parked directly outside. I had to meet Reid, my lawyer, at his hotel and then catch the 8.20 a.m. flight to Midland/Odessa. From there it would be around a two-hour drive through to Big Spring, Texas; my new home.

'Where to, buddy?' the much too enthusiastic driver asked.

'Downtown Hilton, please,' I responded morosely. Houston was empty, and the quiet added to my isolation. I was trying to hold back wave after wave of fear. Part of me kept questioning why I was going through with this; why I wasn't fighting, screaming, doing something, anything, to avoid what was happening to me. It seemed bizarre to be calmly taking myself off to prison.

I thought about calling someone in the UK – it was nearly 11 a.m. there – but who would I call? What would

I say? 'I'm just off to prison,' or 'Don't forget to write?' I decided against it; I knew that if I called, then what little strength I had left would fail me. I had to face this alone.

The taxi arrived at Reid's hotel way too quickly. I stood for a moment looking down Lamar Street, now deserted and silent again, save for the taxi pulling away. It wasn't daybreak yet, and there were no birds singing, just the sound of the occasional car horn in the distance. I'd never known Houston this quiet during my enforced stay here. I had grown to love the city and its inhabitants, despite everything. The population was just over two million people, with an unfeasible number wearing cowboy boots and cowboy hats, none of whom seemed to be a real cowboy. Now there wasn't a cowboy hat in sight as I stood, my back to the hotel, reluctant to move. It was surprisingly chilly for Houston, even for late April, and I regretted not wearing an old jacket for warmth. I gave an involuntary shudder – was that the cold or the fear I wondered?

'Thinking of running?' It was Reid behind me, right on time as usual.

'I was thinking about it, but I wore the wrong shoes.' I turned round to face him. He was immaculate as usual: suit and tie; clean-shaven; perfectly polished shoes; Ivy League parting in his tidy, sandy blonde hair. He was in his early fifties, still fit and trim, with a style like an older Don Draper from *Mad Men*.

'You look like a lawyer,' I said to him, meaning it as an insult.

'Well, thanks!' he smiled, taking it as a compliment. 'I wasn't sure what to wear, to be honest.' We were both silent for a moment. 'You want a cup of coffee?' he asked finally. 'We've got plenty of time. I got you here early because I know what a nightmare you are for showing up anywhere on time!'

His smile was sympathetic, almost sad. Reid didn't have to come with me. He wasn't getting paid and had taken time off just to come with me as a friend. I'd tried to discourage him, but in the end I was glad he was there. Even though we'd lost, I'd never regretted hiring Reid, Kevin and David as my legal team – they had done their best for me.

We sat silently for a while in a cafe. 'Do you want to talk about it?' Reid eventually asked, looking up from his coffee cup. 'Or we can talk about something else.'

'No, it's fine, we can talk about it.' I realised he had something he wanted to say.

His question was frank, brutal and to the point. The lawyer in him had usurped the friend for a few critical moments; his icy blue eyes looked right into me. 'Are you afraid?'

He was very matter-of-fact now and I realised I'd liked it better when he was a hesitant, embarrassed friend. I paused for a moment. Of course I was afraid of going to prison and I was especially afraid of going to an American prison. I had seen all the television programmes; I'd watched *The Shawshank Redemption*, like everyone else. I knew that, as non-US nationals, we wouldn't be allowed to go to the low security relaxed, open regime of what the Americans term a 'Camp' – that it would be much tougher for us. Tougher still for a Scot who was part of a high-profile case. How true to life would those TV shows, those movies, be? How would I cope with the tattooed nutcases, the hardened criminals, the psychopaths? I'd had some very dark moments, where I felt deeply afraid.

It didn't help that to Calum, my family and close friends I had to appear relaxed, almost unconcerned. I had learned the hard way that showing my true fears to them was very damaging.

When I had originally been indicted – could it really have been six long years ago? – I had spent about a month openly 'catastrophising' to anyone who would listen. How selfish I was. Eventually, my Uncle Martin – having listened to me lament pathetically for a number of days – took me aside and spoke to me. He was a man's man, the quintessential working–class Scot, and the nearest thing I'd ever had to a real father.

'You need to get a fucking grip of yourself and stop acting like a fanny,' he'd growled at me. 'Can ye noo see the impact of what yur doin' on the people around you?'

'I . . . I haven't . . . I didn't . . .' I stammered back, realising in that instant that he was, of course, right.

'Aye, ye "hav'nae this", ye "did'nae that",' he said, mimicking me with real disdain, shocking me all the more because I knew how much he loved me.

'This is hard on all of us, and we all need you tae be strong. We all need ye . . . tae . . .' he hesitated, suddenly becoming very emotional. 'Well just get a fuckin' grip will ya?' With that he let me go and stormed away. I stood there rooted to the spot. I'd never thought Uncle Martin needed me as well – I'd never thought I had to be strong for him too – but now I understood. I understood how I had to be, for his sake, for my sake, for everyone's sake.

Reid was still waiting for an answer. 'I try not to think about it much,' I bluffed. 'Anyhow, if you've lived in Glasgow through the seventies, everything else is a cakewalk.'

'It's good you can joke about it,' Reid replied, solemnly. 'Because I would be terrified. I wouldn't be able to sleep thinking about all those gangs and nutcases there and how you'll stand out like a sore thumb and you'll . . .'

'Reid.' He stopped. 'Shouldn't we be going or something?'

We took a taxi to Bush International, and quickly boarded the 8.35 a.m. Continental flight to Midland/ Odessa. The plane was pretty empty and Reid kindly offered me the window seat. No one else looked like they were casually flying up to go to prison, and it felt distinctly odd to be doing this of my own free will. I sat with my head pressed against the window staring down at the runway as we took off. Each passing minute was putting me more on edge. Was Reid right? Had I prepared enough? Could I handle this? Would I get stabbed to death the first time I went to the showers – or maybe they'd wait till I fell asleep in my bed? I'd been angry with Reid for voicing his concerns, but only because they were my own.

Many years before, when I had been fighting the extradition and fearing the worst, I had signed myself up on a positive-thinking course called MindStore, run by a Glaswegian called Jack Black. Being run by a fellow Glaswegian gave the course an edge of realism I had failed to find in management or lifestyle courses run by Americans – Jack Black was down to earth, relating his coping techniques to everyday events in a 'normal' person's life. He didn't cover the topic 'What To Do If You're Being Extradited', but I took a lot from the course and the books he recommended. I'd used some of his ideas when preparing for prison in Houston. My mum had always taught me when you had a difficult decision, or something was daunting, to take a blank sheet of paper and write it all down. Jack Black had taken this to a whole new level, more a form of mind–mapping, not simple lines of positives and negative columns. He'd use shapes and colours, arrows, highlighters – anything that would help you get a 'feel' for the problem. And this was one problem I needed to get a feel for. So one day, a few months before that final journey to jail, I got up and chose to deal with the problem in front of me. The problem was: I was going to prison.

I sat in silence at my kitchen table in Houston with just blank sheets of paper and some coloured felt–tip pens. In the centre of the page, I wrote one word: PRISON. Using a red pen, I then wrote out all the words that held my deepest, darkest fears. I 'brainstormed' – or more accurately 'brain–dumped'. Not asking why or how I came up with these words, I just wrote them out in bold, clear, red letters as they came to me. First of all I wrote 'rape', my number one fear. I really didn't want to be raped. Then number two, 'buggery'; pretty much the same as number one, but a bit more specific. 'Shagged'. Very similar to number one and with a striking resemblance to number two, but these were just the words coming out and I went with the flow. Shagged, raped and buggered – decent scores in a Scrabble game, but not so great otherwise. And then number four: 'darkness'.

Would I be in darkness at night in the cells? How would I even begin to cope with that, especially if it came hard on the heels of an afternoon spent being raped, shagged and buggered? Then I wrote 'buggery' again (I'm not sure why), then 'violence', 'darkness', 'murder', 'extortion', 'blackmail', 'bitch', 'knives', 'death', 'gangs', 'gang rape'. The words just poured out, often repeated. I didn't know why, but each one more frightening than the last. I stopped and looked silently at the bright red pen against the pristine white paper. I was breathing heavily. A pretty depressing list, and yet it had helped to write it down. It was all there now, previously unspoken, but at least now acknowledged. And confirmation, if I needed it, that I was justified in being terrified.

Next, in blue, I wrote out the other problems I faced – not so life-threatening, but problems nevertheless. First came boredom, then loneliness, fear, discomfort, then loss of choice. I drew branches out from these in green and got more specific. Little or no contact with Calum, or with Julie, or with the rest of my family. How would I survive that? Further away than ever from Cara. Would I ever find her? I'd made so little progress on her case. Perhaps the trail would go completely cold? No visits. Infrequent and short phone calls, if any. Long periods locked alone in a cell. No exercise. Poor diet. Limited amount of food. Bunk beds. No pillows. Thin mattress, thin blanket. No tea or coffee (a big one for me). No TV. No savouries, no chocolate! Shared toilets. Hard toilet roll. No body products. Bic razors? (Oh, how I hated those.) I put a question mark because I didn't know how people shaved in prison. Would they seriously give some of these guys a razor? Cold showers. Prison clothes. Strip searches. Invasive strip searches. 'Humiliation', I added, as I thought of my old friend Marshal Dave.

For the positives I chose yellow – a brighter colour and one that I always connected with hope in my mind. Now, the positives. I paused. What were they exactly? Well, I wouldn't have to cook on my own. That was a good one, yes. Next. Erm . . . There must be some. Ah, yes: reading. So many books that I've wanted to read over the years, this could be my one and only chance. I scrolled down and wrote 'catching up on my reading' in luminous yellow. Pleased with myself, I sat back looking at the brightly coloured design on my desk. Even just beginning to note some positives was making me feel better already. I sat back and looked again at what I'd written and, as I often did on my own in that apartment, spoke out loud.

'So, on the downside we've got rape, buggery, murder, my pathological fear of the dark, and generally living in complete fear, poverty and deprivation for years, while the upside is . . . I don't have to cook for myself and I can catch up on some reading. Mmmmm . . .'

My hopeful mood evaporated. There must be more positives, I told myself. I would have time to think. Loads of time to think. Put it down. I could learn stuff, new stuff. Another language, perhaps. I needed to work on my Spanish, since so many of the US prisons were full of Latinos – particularly in Texas. I wrote 'improve my Spanish' down. I'd probably lose some weight. That had to be seen as a positive, surely. Then, of course, it would be interesting; terrifying, worrying, scary also, but even so, still interesting. And that was it. I had run out of positives. My map looked more balanced but, in truth, the reds dominated. Draw it out any way you wanted, but the overall conclusion would be the same. This was going to be hellish. Going to prison is shit.

I moved uncomfortably in my aeroplane seat. Reid seemed to be dozing. We were cruising now at 33,000 feet heading north-west towards Big Spring. I couldn't see much out of the window, so I closed my eyes and tried to think more about how I had prepared for this day, hoping it would give me some semblance of confidence. I had done everything I possibly could, right?

When I'd finished that brainstorming session in my soulless apartment, my next step had been to try to neutralise the negatives as much as possible. Looking at them again, they broke down into two distinct categories. After searching for something appropriate I labelled the first group BAD – things like poor diet, boredom, bad beds, no pillow, cold showers, shared toilets, no tea or coffee; basically a loss of all the little luxuries of life. The second heading covered murder, rape, violence, death, etc., so after some thought I named that group FUCKING CATASTROPHIC, as that seemed quite apt.

Strangely the BAD list didn't seem that bad when I kept glancing at the FUCKING CATASTROPHIC list, but I made the decision to deal with the BAD list first. I understood that prison attacks your self-esteem by taking away not just your freedom but your freedom to choose. It deprives you of things and that, in turn, leads to a further loss of esteem. So many times the problems and violence I'd read about were triggered by the simplest things: another cold shower, a blunt and uncomfortable shave or a spilt cup of coffee. So I made a decision. I

wouldn't allow the prison to deprive me of these things
– I would choose to get rid of them myself. Without
dwelling on it any longer, I stood up from the table and
the piece of paper, walked into my bedroom and stripped
the quilt off, leaving one thin blanket, and then after
hesitating for a second, I took off all the pillows. In the
bathroom, I stripped out all the toiletries except for
one bar of soap, some toothpaste and a toothbrush.
I would buy and use only Bic razors from here on in. I
would only have cold showers, no hot water and no
baths. In the kitchen, with some reluctance, I binned the
tea and coffee. That was going to be a challenge for me,
but I realised that these small steps would all help me
to feel mentally stronger and better prepared. Either that
or I was turning into a lunatic. I wasn't entirely sure.

Next, I disconnected the TV and cancelled my satellite
subscription. I packed away the stereo, but kept a small
radio as I figured I would still have access to one inside.
I looked at my small wine stack, but at that point my
will faltered. The wine was helping me. I was a bit worried
about how much I was drinking – about a bottle a night,
sometimes two – but I understood why. I was alone in
Houston. I didn't have my family, I didn't have my
friends. I was going to prison. I didn't feel my drinking
was out of control or a physical problem. Julius Caesar,
no less, had once said, 'Give me a bowl of wine. In this
I bury all unkindness.' If it was good enough for a man
in a short skirt, then it was good enough for me. So the
wine stayed and I comforted myself by throwing out all
the chocolates, biscuits and other treats that I doubted
would be available in prison. These were my attempts
to wrest control back from the prison – to make it my

choice to forego these luxuries; to avoid going 'cold turkey' on life's little pleasures at the same time as I faced those dangerous first few weeks in prison. Much of these techniques were management practices I'd used when dealing with big issues in business. I'd no idea whether they'd translate to the setting of a prison, but I had little choice but to try.

Having stripped away the simple things, that still left the major issues: the fears I deemed 'FUCKING CATASTROPHIC'. I had to grapple with them. At once it occurred to me that I didn't know if these things actually still did happen in prison. People obviously did get raped, but was this an unusual or a common event and surely there were steps you could take to minimise the danger? Murder and violence came under the same heading. Truth is, I didn't know enough about it – I needed to research it and analyse the reality of prison life. I had studiously avoided reading things on prisons in the US especially after Marshal Daye – it was too scary – but I realised this had to change; I would have to start reading everything I could and that extended to the topics I feared the most. I knew that prison gangs were prevalent in a lot of the US jails – not so much on the East or West Coasts, where I had originally hoped to be placed alongside Giles and David, but certainly in Texas. I decided I'd better learn about them fast: how they worked, and what the 'rules' were. Most of this info would be available on the Internet, I reasoned, but I had to have the courage to read it.

With regard to the violence I was sure I would face, I decided I needed to do a physical stocktake of myself. As far as being threatened, I had one advantage: I was big. Just over 6ft 2, and at that point around 190lb. In the UK, being from Glasgow was always an advantage – people always assumed you were hard, not realising in my case that I was anything but. My bashed–up nose (caused by an operation to rectify a deviated septum, not any vicious man–fighting) gave me the look of a boxer at times. I focused on the large number of scars on my arms (caused by operations to remove various cysts over the years) and thought that at least gave me a further 'tough man' boost. Then I had my thistle tattoo on my right arm over my bicep, and tattoos were meant to be tough, right? A few ticks in the right boxes.

I had actually worked as a bouncer in a Glasgow nightclub for four years while at university. This might be impressive stuff for any prison CV, although the reality was that my natural fear of being punched, nutted or knifed by the assorted head cases who frequented the club had meant I sailed through four years without getting involved in one fight (although I did once wrestle an aggressive girl to the ground to stop her punching her boyfriend on the head). While I hadn't actually exchanged blows with anyone, that and my time growing up in the tenements of Dormanside Road in Pollok – a housing estate that was Glasgow's seventies successor to gangland Govan – had given me an uncanny antenna for spotting potential violence or disturbed body language, and techniques for avoiding it. Avoidance was always the safest route. I felt this talent would be getting significant usage in Big Spring, and I looked at that experience now as being a positive.

The negatives I saw, as I stripped down naked in front of my bathroom mirror, were numerous. Number one: I was flabby. I was forty-six and the middle-age spread, while not being too pronounced, was definitely there. I had been a keen sportsman most of my life, but mainly football and golf. My upper body lacked definition, my arms lacked strength. I didn't look very intimidating. I realised, of course, that I wasn't entering a strong man competition, but this was all about my own self-confidence. As a bouncer, I had learned that in nearly all situations a calm, confident persona would defuse even the most psychotic Glaswegian. But you had to be confident in yourself and it helped if you looked tough. I looked more critically at myself in the mirror. The curly hair would have to go. I had a heavy growth, almost a beard and quite dark, so I'd keep that.

During all of this appraisal, without admitting it, my eye kept being drawn to my rear end, my rump. I hadn't really thought of it before, but I had a huge arse. It was much bigger than I could ever remember it and, horror of horrors, it started to wobble when I walked. When did this happen? I meandered up and down a couple of times naked in front of the full-length mirrors. It looked enormous. And it was out of proportion to the rest of me. It was a notably large arse. Not only that, but with the rest of me having become quite brown in the Houston sun, it was an especially white arse. This sent me into a tailspin of panic. My large, white arse would be like a beacon to every bum-rapist throughout the prison – I could become a prized possession. I had read once that they liked straight guys more and they saw it as taking your virginity – or was I thinking of *The Shawshank Redemption* again?

What would happen in the showers, the dreaded

showers? My carefully written out diagram was becoming a blur as I descended into panic. I remembered all the jokes about not bending down to pick up the soap. I looked at the bar of soap by the sink tap. Without thinking much more about it, I reached across to it and threw it down on the floor. 'Pick it up, Mulgrew,' I thought to myself. 'Pick it up, wobble bottom.' Slowly I leaned forward to collect the bar, while watching myself carefully in the mirror. 'Oh, my God,' I blurted out. Bending over seemed to make my arse look larger. My arse had expanded. I looked like a big light bulb, a neon sign saying, 'Over here boys!' This was a disaster. I replaced the soap and tried again, this time clenching my buttocks as tight as I could (harder to do than you would think). That gave my buttocks a shape and form I really didn't want them to have. Attempt three involved crouching to pick it up, which momentarily I thought was a winner until I realised my head was now at dick level and I was picking up the soap like a girl, all dainty and delicate. That sort of act could just encourage the crowd. Standing up, I kicked the soap across the room. 'Fuck it,' I thought. 'If the soap drops, I'll stay dirty.'

At least these reminiscences of me playing the fool made me smile a little as I shifted in my aeroplane seat. The flight to Big Spring would only take an hour and a half and we had already been in the air for thirty minutes. I felt the need for a drink, an alcoholic one even this early in the day, but I guessed they would be testing me when I got there and didn't want to have anything in my system. I'd need all my wits about me.

I looked out of the window and saw the brown

scrubland below; just an empty wasteland. I could popu-
late that emptiness with fear, or stick to my careful,
determined preparation. I forced my thoughts back to
all the work I'd done in the months before.

The fitter and stronger I felt, the less likely it would be
that I would be attacked; that was my core logic. So first
of all, I needed to go into training. It was not just a
question of stepping up my usual running and weights
routine, but also of learning self-defence and focused,
clear attack techniques. I hadn't suddenly gained an
upsurge of courage, but the soap sketch had been about
confronting one of my deepest fears and I wanted to be
in a position to defend myself if need be. My thinking
was: if I did get into an awkward situation and my fat
virginal white ass proved too much of an attraction, then
at least I wanted to be able to handle myself. After all,
Tim Robbins always gave as good as he got in *Shawshank*.

Kyle and Lucy, two Scottish neighbours in my apartment block had introduced me to Sergei, a Ukrainian
personal trainer who was to become a good friend of
mine, and as much a philosopher as a fitness coach. He
was in his late thirties and handsome – a cross between
Daniel Craig and Arnold Schwarzenegger. I approached
him to train me with a clear mandate to teach me to
fight, which he took to with some enthusiasm. We trained
almost every day, often double or triple sessions, and
my weight quickly increased as we mixed weights with
martial arts and boxing. At that stage I was waiting for
a letter to arrive to tell me when and where to report
to prison, which made going to the mailbox a daily
nightmare, my hand trembling each time it reached

inside, but which also gave my training an intensity and focus Sergei liked.

'Shit, Mulgrew, you seem more angry than usual today. This eez good!' he would exclaim in his heavily accented English, as he cuffed me around the ear and told me to keep my guard up. He would hit me quite often as our training progressed, 'To get you used to the pain and numbness; so it doesn't stop you from hitting back,' he explained gleefully. So we focused on hitting and moving away; hitting and moving away; getting down on the ground, then quickly back to my feet for a quick one–two combination, then flat on the ground again. It was exhausting, but exhilarating and I felt that if I had to, if I really had to, I could at least hurt the person trying to hurt me.

Sergei also talked to me throughout the training, encouraging me and reminding me: 'Everyone is scared. Remember that. Everyone is scared – always.' That made me feel better, but I wondered if it was true.

The plane started its descent and I looked anxiously over at Reid as he gave me another compassionate smile. The realisation that I was getting closer, and that I would soon find out if any of my preparations had counted for anything, made my stomach lurch. I felt ashamed, an idiot, when I considered the final part of my prepa-ration, the time I'd spent in the cupboard trying to control my fear of the dark; a coward, a boy entering a man's world. I rubbed the sweat off the palms of my hands as the plane touched down and my breath shortened. I leaned forward in my chair with my eyes closed, wishing I was somewhere, anywhere, but here.

4

BIG SPRING, TEXAS

WITH NO LUGGAGE AT ALL FOR the second time in my life, we were swiftly out of the airport and into the hire car Reid had pre–booked. Midland/Odessa seemed as dreary as I had imagined, a small town ten hours' drive from Houston and six from Dallas. Its claim to fame was that George Bush Jnr had lived there and by all accounts intended to return some time after his presidency was over. He was completely welcome to it. After a few minutes we were on the I–20 heading east towards Big Spring, around seventy miles away. If we had gone in the other direction, four hours west, we would hit Juárez on the Mexican border, just across the Rio Grande and by now the murder capital of the world. I thought of suggesting we head west to Reid, but my stock of jokes was wearing thin. We were getting closer.

We drove along the long, straight endless road in silence, my mood darkening. The landscape was bleak, desolate and unforgiving. Flat as far as the eye could see and hot, damned hot! 'What the hell am I doing here?'

I thought as I surveyed what looked to me like the end of the Earth. I'd lived the dream; now I was living the nightmare, and it kept getting worse. Nothing but tumbleweed and abandoned jack-hammers. I felt I was being taken to a place time had forgotten, a place you take people simply to punish them.

'I can't believe you're having to do this,' Reid said eventually, disturbing the silence.

'I can't either,' I murmured back, still looking out at the endless stretch of desert.

'I keep beating myself up that I should have been able to get you out of this, that I should have been a better lawyer,' Reid said, genuinely emotional as he spoke.

'This was the best I was going to get. We were always going to get extradited no matter what, and we never would have won at trial. I've been fucked for a long time, all this was inevitable.' I waved my hand lamely at the tumbleweed and emptiness as I tried to make him feel better, knowing that what I was saying was ludicrous – how could any of this ever be inevitable?

I looked out across the empty wasteland again; barren and desolate.

After a while the long road found a destination and the town of Big Spring shimmered into view. Population of 33,267 – not including the 1,500 inmates of the Federal prison or the 3,000 housed in the nearby immigration facility. The town's website had boasted that the sun shone uninterrupted on Big Spring for over 320 days a year, and this was certainly one of them. It was named after the 'big spring' in Sulphur Draw, a historical watering place for coyotes, wolves, and herds of buffalo, antelope and mustangs, but all I could see was run-down housing and abandoned trucks. The spring had supposedly been a source of conflict between Comanche and Shawnee Indians with hundreds of skirmishes over the years, until the white settlers came along and turned it into the paradise it now was. Looking up into the sky, I wiped my brow and peered towards the sun. There wasn't a cloud to be seen; always the saddest of sad sights for a Scotsman. It looked like it hadn't rained in months. We drove through the stretched-out town in silence.

'Jeez, even the prison has to be better than this,' I said to Reid as we surveyed the abandoned trailers and boarded-up houses at the sides of the road. Reid stayed silent.

Halfway up the main street, we saw a Rib Shack and parked in there. It was still only eleven o'clock, three hours before I was due to report. I had no intention of turning up early, although the state of the town was giving me second thoughts. Reid ordered some food and I stepped outside to phone home to say some difficult goodbyes. As promised, I spoke to Calum and tried to sound upbeat. I told him the prison looked nice, like a library, and the people looked pretty friendly. I joked that I hoped they wouldn't feel too intimidated when they saw me.

Actually Big Spring did look a bit like a library when I had searched for it on the Internet.

For two months I had been going to my mailbox every morning, waiting for the letter from the Bureau of Prisons to tell me when, and where, I had to report to prison. I tried to kid myself that it didn't matter, that I didn't care – a prison was a prison, after all – but the truth was my hand would shake every day as I felt for the dreaded letter. Sometimes my heart would be beating so violently as I approached the mailbox I was sure it must be visible to anyone walking past. I would struggle to breathe and it would take me twenty minutes or so to recover my composure once I'd found the mailbox empty.

In the end, as it happened, the news didn't come via the postman. I was at Dan Cogdell's house – David's lawyer – with him and David, when David called his pre-trial officer to find out where and when we were going. He called out his prison first (a reasonable facility on the Californian coast) then shouted, 'Big Spring for Mulgrew.' Dan's face went white – so white that I wished I'd waited for the letter after all. It didn't help when he stopped opening the bottle of wine he was uncorking, walked over, put his arm around me and said, 'Sorry Mulgrew. Unlucky. You lucked out.' I didn't ask why he was saying that; I didn't want to know. David also confirmed that I was going in first, in ten days' time, with Giles heading off a week later to somewhere on the East Coast and David another week thereafter. They couldn't have placed the three of us any further apart.

By the time I got back to my apartment, fear was gripping me, and I plunged straight onto the Internet to find out what I could about the notorious Big Spring. Surprisingly, they had put quite a flattering photo of it on the Bureau of Prisons (BoP) website. Without the barbed wire and the fences, the main building looked somewhat like a library – just as I told Calum. I even got excited when I first explored the site, because on the drop–down list on the left-hand side of the BoP home screen, alongside items like Daily Routine, Visiting Rules and Facilities, it had a section headed 'Conjugal Visits'. Despite my anxiety to find out about the prison, I ignored everything else and double-clicked straight onto that page. I'm not sure what I was expecting, but all there was to read was spelt out in bold capital letters: THERE ARE NO CONJUGAL VISITS. Oh how I laughed. Some bastard in the Bureau of Prisons clearly had a sense of humour, which was reassuring since I was checking in that afternoon for an extended stay.

The call with Calum passed quite well, and I surprised myself at how easily I managed to stay calm and assured. I didn't talk to him for long for fear I couldn't keep it going. Next I called my mum and found her in 'Politician Mode'. It was the stance she'd started to adopt ever since she'd been elected, a few years earlier, to the Scottish Parliament. She sounded strong and assured, only betraying her feelings briefly at the end as we said goodbye – I wondered how long for.

Then I phoned Julie, with whom I could be more honest. I reminded her that it might take two or three weeks to 'clear' my phone numbers with the prison authorities; maybe even longer in my case since all my phone numbers would be foreign. Even then I would only be able to speak for a few minutes each week, as the cost would eat into what little monies I was allowed or could earn in prison. Julie sounded very strong, as she always seemed to be, and promised me she would take care of Calum like he was her own. We finished the phone call quickly, both fearful of the strain and emotion of the conversation, and Julie ended by promising to tell me everything that happened back home in Britain – no matter how good or bad. We agreed not to say goodbye and I promised her for the thousandth time that I'd keep my head down and stay out of harm's way, and that I loved her.

My last call was to Jim Moonier, a great American friend who had travelled from Hawaii to be there the day I first arrived in Houston and had introduced me to two friends of his, Bob and Teresa Rose, who had helped me settle so much into a challenging new life in Houston. Jim had then dedicated a lot of his time to trying to help me track down Cara Katrina. He told me he had finally made contact with a private investigator who had experience of dealing with Tunisia and that he seemed confident that if she was there they could locate her, and make an assessment of what kind of life she was leading. They would look at whether she was going to school, her living arrangements and the family circumstances. When I had first arrived in Houston I had spoken to Cara just one time, when Laura had briefly put her on the phone about a week after I arrived. 'Love you daddy' were the last words I had ever heard her say. I'd quickly said 'Love you too Cara' but Laura had taken the phone back and although I knew it was a small thing I often wondered if she'd heard my words. I prayed she had, that they were the last words she'd heard from her father.

For years later I clung to the simple fact that she'd sounded happy. After that, the mobile number Laura had given me rang out, but was never answered and after a few more weeks I began to panic. Since Laura hadn't contacted Calum either, I was sure they had gone. My initial phone calls from Houston to the British Police had got me nowhere, with the police refusing to take seriously my concerns that Cara had disappeared. I could hardly blame them; by the time I had explained my circumstances and extradition their cynicism was understandable. I was, after all, a bad guy – no one really buys in to the concept of 'innocent until proven guilty', and anyway, a few weeks or months without contact didn't necessarily mean abduction.

Time, however, is always of the essence in a disappearance case – the trail goes cold very quickly. Eventually, frustrated by numerous phone calls where the police continued to refuse to give me a case number unless I reported the disappearance in person at a police station in the UK (slightly awkward given my circumstances), my step-mother Audrey and my half-sister Anoushka marched into a station in Sussex and refused to leave until I was given one. Without a case number, I couldn't begin the court process of seeking the phone records and bank account details that I hoped may provide some clue on where she might have been taken to. Their perseverance ensured we had some leads which in time pointed to Paris, then possibly Ohio in the US (it shares the same 216 telephone code as Tunisia and Laura, as a US citizen, had always liked the mid-West), then eventually to Tunisia, Abdul's birthplace.

My heart lurched when Jim said the investigator thought he might even be able to get a photograph of Cara. A photograph? Of Cara? How would she look now? Frankly, the idea frightened me. It would be a visual confirmation of how much time had passed since I'd last seen her. I couldn't imagine my daughter looking any different, although I knew she must. Still, it was very encouraging.

Buoyed by this conversation, I walked back into the Rib Shack where Reid was looking incongruous in his suit amongst the dozens of assorted truckers, bikers and rednecks. I ate my ribs with renewed relish, suddenly hungry.

'Wow, did Bush call and give you a reprieve?' Reid asked, surprised at my new-found energy.

'Not funny,' I said. 'No, Jim Moonier thinks he's found a private investigator that might lead us to Cara. He thinks he might be able to find out how she is. Maybe even get some pictures of her . . .' The words were catching in my throat; the thought of seeing a picture of my little girl again making me feel very emotional.

'He's some friend. You're lucky to have someone like him.'

'Yes, yes, I am,' I said, meaning it. And I realised that even on this darkest of days I could find some positives. All my calls had gone better than I expected, and then the good news Jim had given me about the investigator had boosted me further. But the thought of being that close to a breakthrough in finding Cara also added to my frustration. As if sensing the dip in my mood, Reid spoke.

'Look. You have to concentrate on one thing now – getting yourself home safely and as quickly as possible. When you get there, they will give you a Case Manager, and it's your right to see them within the first month you arrive. You need to put that in writing as soon as you can and hold them to the one month. There are probably only about three Case Managers in Big Spring for 1,500 inmates, so you might only get ten minutes with yours. At that first meeting you MUST put a transfer request in immediately to get a return to the UK. If you don't request it in writing, they won't process it. You will only get one ten-minute meeting with your Case Manager each year, so you can't afford to waste time discussing anything else with them – no matter what else may be happening to you inside.'

Ten minutes, once a year. I focused on it, like it was a chink of light.

'The papers covering your case and Cara's abduction have all already been sent to the prison and they may even give you them today or tomorrow. It's your legal right to receive them. They show the deal you did with the US Government to get you transferred home to England early, when you can properly search for Cara – but don't assume that your Case Manager will have the slightest knowledge about it or care anything about the fact Cara Katrina is missing. You need to push them on that point.' I smiled at Reid as he paused, grateful for all he was trying to do for me.

'Time is against you, Gary,' he continued, more solemnly than before. 'It's been two years already since you last saw her, and the longer it takes to get you home, the less likely it will be that you will find her again, or have any chance of getting her back into your life. That's just the reality. Whatever you do in there, keep out of trouble and don't get involved in other people's disputes. With luck you could be transferred out of there in a year . . .' He trailed off, not sounding too convinced it could be that quick. His little speech had helped me though, and I tried to focus on what the prize was – however far away. Even though I had the legal right to bring Cara back to the UK, I had to do what was right for her, and every day that she became more settled and comfortable in a foreign country increased the possibility that allowing her to remain there might be the best thing for her. It was always about her – about what was best for her. The problem was: how could I be sure she was happy there, that Tunisia was a better life option for her than England? Deep down I didn't think it would be, but without knowing exactly where she was and what her life was like, I could not be sure. These thoughts swirled through my head as we decided to make our way down to the prison and drive around the perimeter. Even though we were just killing time, I was, under-standably, still reluctant to go in early.

The facility was huge, wrapped in a twenty-foot barbed wire fence that stretched for miles around its perimeter. It sat on a slight hill and had panoramic views of the dustbowl of Texas on three sides. It was just after 1 p.m. now, the sun was at its most brutal, and all the resolve I'd built up in the Rib Shack quickly melted away. I hardly saw any inmates, but those I did see milling around immediately intimidated me.

We drove around a little longer, saying very little, until it approached 2 p.m. – my check-in time. We didn't speak as we approached an inauspicious-looking front door. It could have been a tax department or the place you went to pay your parking fines, apart from the sturdy crew of Correctional Officers milling about. I stood with Reid for a moment outside to say our goodbyes. It felt awkward, and I was anxious to get started; to get on with it and to get home to Cara and Calum. I hugged Reid again, gave him the $50 I had in my pocket, thanked him for the twentieth time and stopped him from saying sorry for the thousandth. I walked away and got ready to go in the main door. Reid was still standing there about ten feet away, just watching me.

'Dude!' (It sounded more like 'doood' in a Scottish accent.) I turned to face him. 'You need to bugger off back to Washington and let me get on with this.' I looked to the floor, unable to take the intensity of his gaze. Finally looking back up, I moved towards him then quickly hugged him one more time. 'Go!' I said, pointing towards his car and the highway to freedom. He went to speak, but said nothing, just gave me an apologetic tap on my arm, picked up his bag, and turned and walked away.

I turned around to be confronted by a large, bulky officer, standing in the doorway, grinning with anticipation.

'That sure was emotional now, wasn't it?' he twanged in a deep Southern drawl. 'Why me an ol' Butters here was nearly cryin'. Wasn't we, Butters?'

'Sure was, Malone,' said the tall, spindly Butters, with a grin. Malone had a small moustache and a squint in one eye, which made it look like he was simultaneously watching me and Reid as he made his way through the car park. What I took for his good eye was looking me up and down.

'Now who have we got here?' he asked to no one in particular. I went to respond but hesitated as he pulled out his clipboard. 'Let me see now – hmmm.'

God, it was hot. I desperately wanted to get in out of the sun, but the big guy was blocking my way. 'Mulgrew. Mulgrew, sir. My name's Mulgrew,' I finally said, desperate to get inside.

'What's that you say!?' he looked up. 'Mildew, Mildew you said? There ain't no Mildew . . .' he tailed off as he went down his list. The heat was brutal – worse even than Houston. Had this been some sort of administrative joke – sending a man from Glasgow to the desert?

'Mulgrew, Mullll–ggrew,' I said more deliberately, but feeling that it just made my accent stronger than ever. I hadn't imagined it would be so hard to get into prison.

'There's a MULGREW here. Is that what you meant to

say, boy? Is that your name?' He looked up, but seemed to be addressing his question far out into the desert.

'Yes, yes. That's me.'

'Don't want you getting in if you're not supposed to!' he chortled as he scrutinised his list again, still blocking the door. 'Now let's see . . .' I tried to cover my face from the sun with my hands. It was so bright. I'd never get used to this fucking sun.

'Oh!' Malone stopped suddenly and looked at me. 'Oh my. Well lookie here!' I tried to peer at his clipboard to see what all the excitement was suddenly about. 'He's the ENRON guy!!' Malone exclaimed.

'Fucking marvellous,' I thought. 'I'm going to prison and they still don't know what for.'

'Hey, Butters. Lookie here. We done got us the ENRON guy!!' Malone exclaimed gleefully. The previously semi-slumbering Butters moved over with surprising speed and looked at me like I was an alien specimen. They both peered for a few moments as the sun continued its relentless frying of my lily-white skin. A fly buzzed past while they looked me up and down.

'He don't look like nuthin',' was Butters' considered opinion after a moment or two. Butters didn't look much like nuthin' to me either: tall and gangling with protruding teeth and sparse clumps of light blonde hair around his chin, like he was growing a beard section by section. He reminded me of a cartoon drawing from the *Beano*, a comic I read when I was a boy.

'Mildew, the Enron guy,' Malone mused slowly, nodding his head. With them both blocking the doorway, there seemed little chance of me gaining access to their fine estab-lishment, and the sun was unrelenting. I took a deep breath.

'Can I come in? Please?'

Malone sprang into life. 'Oh! Can I come in pu-leese! Did you hear that, Butters? Can I come in, pu-leese! I think we got some fuckin' royalty!' He pointed to a seat in the corner and went off to fetch some keys, muttering to himself.

I was glad to get inside and sit down; even just a few minutes' exposure to the afternoon sun had drained me. There was air-conditioning of sorts inside and it provided some respite. I could see immediately that the reception area was as tired and dilapidated as the two people manning it, a realisation which added to my general sense of deepening despair.

Coming back over, Malone prompted me through the metal detector as a disinterested Butters emptied my pockets and checked my shoes. Suddenly very perfunctory, they started to 'process' me, speaking as if I was not there, save occasionally to tell me to sit, stand or to turn around. Eventually Malone clipped the cuffs on me. I heard that unique 'crick' sound, and remembered the last time I'd heard it – two years ago – at George Bush International Airport, when this nightmare began. And I still hadn't woken up.

I was placed in a small holding cell where I sat in silence for about an hour. I was glad of the solitude, and even more grateful for the cold stone bench and being out of the direct sunlight. I lay out on the bench, and awkwardly put my handcuffed hands behind my head and stared at the ceiling. The cold stone felt good against my back. I cocked my head to watch Malone mechanically filling in form after form, while Butters sat nearby, his arms resting on the table and cushioning his head as he slept soundly.

The stone bench was the only item of furniture other than an uncovered stainless steel toilet. I stared some more at the ceiling and thought about all the TV shows and movies I had watched over the years, where people were held in some holding tank like this until some smartypants lawyer rescued them.

Malone was soon on the phone to one of his buddies. 'Guess who I got here?' he asked excitedly. 'Nope . . . Nope . . . Nope . . .' Then a longer pause. 'Nope again!' Malone was clearly enjoying the suspense. 'I'll tell you. The Enron guy!' Obviously pleased with the response, he looked over at me as he continued. 'I'm looking right at him right now.' This wasn't strictly true, but I didn't want to be pedantic. 'He don't look like nuthin',' he clarified, still smiling. 'Millions,' he then said, in answer to the next question. 'Hundreds of millions, I think.'

'I heard it was like thousands and millions, or billions or something like that,' piped up Butters, awake again suddenly.

'Processing him right now. Come on up, take a look-see!' said a delighted Malone as he hung up the phone, seemingly anticipating a party. I sighed and stared up at the ceiling again and wondered about the number of desperate souls who must have occupied this cell. Did it matter if people didn't understand why I was in here?

My thoughts were interrupted again as Malone approached the cell. 'Time for your strip search, Mildew,' he said, with a smile that disturbed me.

I got up as he unlocked the cell and followed him over to a corner area, where a doctor in a white coat had just entered.

'This is the Enron guy, Mildew,' announced Malone proudly, as if he'd caught, tried and sentenced me himself.

'*Habla español?*' the doctor asked, ignoring Malone.

'No,' I lied, figuring it was safer initially if people didn't know I could speak some Spanish.

He looked up at me quickly. He was young, maybe mid twenties, Hispanic, with a small Colombian flag on his lapel, which I took as a good sign. All the Colombians I had met in the US had been kind and considerate, but this man looked jaded, tired like the building itself. I could understand why.

'Take your clothes off, then open your mouth wide.'

Malone de-cuffed me, then stood beside me, still grinning, and clearly not going anywhere. I stripped off quickly and stood upright, looking straight ahead and trying not to think of my last strip search with Marshal Dave.

The doctor ran quickly and professionally through his check. Mouth, hair, armpits, feet, soles of feet and then onto the mid-section. He had a quick rummage around my balls, with a delicacy that Marshal Dave could have done well to have learned, before he suddenly stopped, sat back, sighed and said quietly, '*Dios mio.* What is that?' He was pointing right at my willie.

Both I and Malone looked down simultaneously to see what the drama was about, Malone peering way too close to my private parts with his operational eye.

'Is that a foreskin?' the doctor asked – somehow combining surprise and resignation.

'What kind of a question is that?' I thought. 'Of course it's a fucking foreskin! You're the doctor! What's wrong with a foreskin?' I scrutinised myself closely in case I had some 'foreskin issue' I had hitherto not detected.

'Aye, er, yes, it's a foreskin, sir,' I said. I noticed Malone was looking at it, perturbed and shaking his head. 'Shit,'

I thought. 'Now I'm going to be the Enron guy with a foreskin!'

'Don't call me sir,' the doctor responded more kindly. 'I'm a doctor, not an officer. Malone!' he called – wafting his hand towards the guard as he turned back around in his chair to make some further notes.

'Ah yes,' began Malone tentatively. 'Pull the foreskin back, Mildew.' He jabbed his finger doubtfully towards it. Embarrassed and uncomfortable, I pulled it back while I looked straight forward. 'Flip it round and to the side,' Malone asked, a look of disquiet etched on his face. I flipped my foreskin about like a five–year–old who's just discovered it can move, while Malone scrutinised it closely for hidden contraband. It seemed it was the only time both his eyes focused on the same thing, or maybe that was my imagination.

The doctor kept his back to me and said, 'OK, that's fine.'

At another command from the doctor, Malone, his intermediary, instructed me to bend over and spread my buttocks. I sighed. *Here we go again.* I bent over for what seem like an age. 'Cough,' said Malone, and I spluttered, trying not to let the situation get to me. I could tell he was close behind me and having a proper look as I tensed my buttocks involuntarily. Fortunately, his cheeks never touched mine.

'Alright, Mildew, straighten up and put your clothes on,' Malone said.

'Can't be fun that job,' I thought.

'I need to re-cuff you, Mildew, then I'm taking you to see the shrink.'

'His name's Mulgrew,' the doctor said, spinning around from his desk.

'What?' replied Malone, surprised.

'This man's name is Mulgrew. Mulgrew,' he said, tailing off and shaking his head. I caught his eye and mouthed 'thank you' as he turned back on me again and resumed his paperwork.

'A'ight, a'ight. Mul-grew, let's go see the psych.'

Malone grumbled as he led me down a long narrow corridor towards another room. It was strange, but after preparing myself for all manner of insults and humiliations during that first day inside, in the end my defences had been pierced by the smallest piece of compassion. I wanted to go back and hug that young Colombian doctor, I really did.

As Malone and I ambled down the long narrow corridor, I already sensed that everything would be on slow time in the Big Spring Correctional Facility. The corridor had brown painted walls and no pictures or signs, other than one announcing the presence of the psychiatrist's office. The air-conditioning didn't seem to work here, so it felt claustrophobic and hot. I couldn't tell if it was just the influence of my mood and growing fear, but Big Spring had an oppressive, depressing atmosphere to it. The paintwork was peeling in many places and I noticed that most of the office furniture and equipment was old and in need of repair. It seemed a grim place to work – as if the staff were being punished as much as the inmates.

The interview with the psychiatrist only lasted about two minutes. She was a white, middle-aged woman, in a cramped office, with an old bleeping computer terminal and papers scattered everywhere; under-invested and tired, like everything else I'd seen. And yet the US managed to present itself to the outside world as cutting edge and dynamic, the greatest nation on earth.

My shrink didn't look up, just kept her face down, writing furiously.

'Take a seat,' she barked. A shrink with anger issues, I noted. 'Mulgrew, right?' she asked, still without looking at me.

'He's the Enron guy,' Malone put in, trying to fit his large frame into the small office. Now she looked up.

'Malone, you know you're not supposed to be in here. Wait out in the corridor!' He shuffled off dejectedly. 'Mulgrew, right?' she asked again, this time looking right at me. She had layers of poorly applied make-up, enhancing, rather than disguising the terminal tiredness of her face. Imagine living in a town like Big Spring, I thought, then coming here every day to work. Didn't she hope for something better?

'Yes, ma'am,' I responded, wondering whatever happened to her American dream. I switched into a perfunctory mode, anxious to get all the formalities done with, and get myself tucked up in a solitary cell, which I'd read was the usual process for your first few days. To be honest, I liked the sound of that – a bit of time alone to get used to things and prepare myself.

'You ever felt like harming yourself, Mulgrew?' she asked, head down, pen at the ready as she returned to her form. This was speed psychiatry.

'No, ma'am.'

'Ever felt suicidal?'

'No.'

'Ever wanted to commit self-harm?'

'No, ma'am.'

'Ever been sexually assaulted?'

'Nope.'

'Physically assaulted?'

'Nope.'

She sighed, clearly bored by the questions or my answers, or both.

'Have you ever attacked or sexually assaulted anyone?' she continued.

'Nope.'

'When did you last cry?'

Celtic's UEFA Cup Final defeat in Seville in 2003 sprang to mind . . .

'Can't remember.'

'Do you cry often?'

Like a baby that day.

'Nope.'

'Do you feel like harming yourself now?'

If you keep asking me all these stupid questions . . .

'Nope.'

'Are you a member of any of these gangs?' she asked, handing me an extensive laminated menu covering such luminaries as the Paises, Sorenos, Crips, Bloods, Aryan Brotherhood and a whole host of others I had encountered on the Internet, and was soon to meet more directly. Just reading about them had made me scared enough.

'No, ma'am,' I answered, as I handed the card back. Her eyes narrowed, as if I couldn't be telling her the truth. She paused, before playing her trump card.

'Have you ever been associated with or had an affiliation with any other gang or gang members?'

Now this was a tricky one. Technically, having been

brought up in Pollok, Glasgow's equivalent of Beirut, and more specifically within its epicentre, Dormanside Road, I was 'affiliated' with the 50 Krew. These were named, unglamorously, after the Number 50 bus terminus that sat at the bottom of our street, and their activities ran to glue-sniffing, boot polish inhalation, a wee bit of breaking and entering and the occasional GBH when they had drank too much – which was most days. They were altogether less sophisticated than the Latin Kings, West Texas Mafia and the like, and in any case, I'd spent the better part of fourteen years trying to avoid the 50 Krew, so I knew what my answer had to be.

'Nope.'

'OK, Mulgrew,' she said, ripping a piece of paper clear of her notebook, 'you're cleared for general population. Give this to Malone, on your way out.' Rather ominously, she added, 'Good luck,' as I closed the door behind me – for the first time sounding as if she meant it.

To be honest, I was less interested in this, than what she'd said about 'general population'. I thought I was going to solitary. Still handcuffed, I proffered my slip of paper to Malone.

'Wow, straight into general pop! Good luck with that,' he smiled. Another one wishing me luck. I suddenly wished I could go back in to the psychiatrist's office. Maybe I could start acting a little unhinged – or talk up my years of involvement with the deadly 50 Krew. Anything to get myself a few days' solitary. Panic was really beginning to set in as Malone pulled me again by the arm, sensing my hesitation.

'One more to go, Mulgrew, then you're out there with

the general pop–u–lation,' he said, enjoying the emphasis. I shuddered. I wasn't ready for the general population. I tried to get a grip of myself, but my heart was racing. I'd only just arrived and already I felt cheated. I wasn't ready for this. I was supposed to get time to get ready – get a single cell for a few days in a separate area – that's what I had read about on the Internet!

Numbly, I stood for the last examination, which involved me stripping naked again as an officer detailed my tattoos. This was how they could tell gang affiliations and those details of an inmate's general history that didn't feature in his prison file; the tattoos were often personal story–boards of a life lived on the edge. After being introduced by Malone once more as 'the Enron guy', the bored officer, still seated, got to work.

'Stand over there. Strip off. Point out your tats. All of them.'

I only had one tattoo, a Scottish thistle surrounded by Calum and Cara's names on the top and by the Japanese kanji 'ki-gyu' on the bottom. I had lived for four years in Japan, in what now seemed like someone else's life, so the kanji had some resonance for me. Plus it meant 'freedom' – somewhat ironic given my current circum-stances. I pointed to my right arm, at which point the officer started to photograph it from several different angles and take some notes.

'You an opium trader, Mulgrew?' the tattoo expert asked after a few minutes of staring at it through a small glass scope.

'No, he's the Enron guy,' interjected Malone, his enthu-siasm for that remark undiminished by frequent use.

The other officer squinted at me. He was probably in

his early thirties and seemed neater, tidier and better educated than the others. Unlike Malone, his uniform was pristine and ironed, he was clean–shaven and smart looking, and he wasn't chewing gum or tobacco. 'The Enron guy, huh?' he mused. 'What's an Enron guy got an interest in opium for, then?' He scooted back on his chair, for the first time looking at my face. 'Was that your bag then, Mulgrew? Is that how you and Skilling got off?' Skilling had been the CEO of Enron and, at that time, he was Public Enemy Number One. I had only ever met him once and had instantly liked him, although I can't say we lit up an opium pipe together.

'Is that what you did with the money, Mulgrew, all that money?' Money sounded more like 'muuh . . . ney' – a loving, intimate pronunciation. He was looking at me, expecting an answer.

'I don't understand,' I murmured, deferentially.

The officer raised his eyebrows and, scooting back across the floor, jabbed at my tattoo.

'The poppy,' he said.

I glanced from my green and purple tattoo to him and back again. 'It's a thistle, sir,' I exclaimed a bit too enthusiastically. His eyes narrowed. 'Because I'm from Scotland,' I added hastily.

Without another word, he examined the tattoo again, in closer detail, like a diamond dealer with a suspect stone. Eventually he spoke, pulling back in his chair, clearly satis–fied with his work. 'Thistle . . . My . . . . Ass! I'm marking that mother down as a poppy, 'cos that's what it is!'

With that he chuckled to himself, gathered his papers and his scope and disappeared. Then, before I could gather my thoughts, Malone handed me first one card, then some papers. 'That's your prison number – carry it around with you at all times and especially when you go for chow. And this here is the rules for Big Spring – it'll tell you all you need to know about survivin' in Big Spring. If you can!' he added with relish that I didn't enjoy.

For a moment I thought my legs would give way on me, but I mentally got a grip of myself, determined that Malone wouldn't see my nervousness.

They weren't seriously going to put me straight in with all these people, were they? The moment of truth had arrived and the thought simply terrified me. I wasn't ready. I needed more time. We walked down the corridor towards a door I guessed would lead to the outside and into the prison yard. As we approached it, Malone stopped then turned to me and double-checked my handcuffs.

'Now, Mulgrew?' he asked, suddenly assuming a considerate tone – which alarmed me even more. 'Probably best if you don't mention that Enron thing whilst you're in here.' Malone seemed oblivious to the irony of this piece of advice. 'Some people lost a lot of money in that thing,' he went on, earnestly, 'and they'll be pissed once they heard that you got it.'

No longer surprised by what else this day would hold, I hesitated as he reached for the door. '"My tattoo's a Scottish thistle." That's some cool shit you tried to pull there, Mulgrew. Cool shit!' Before I could reply, he had opened it, pushing me gently out into the blinding heat and sunlight.

5

INTO THE LIGHT

BLINDED BY THE INTENSITY OF THE light, I hesitated for a moment.

'Come on, Mulgrew. Ain't nothing to be afraid of,' goaded Malone, as he tugged me forward, clearly enjoying my panic. I was trying to get my eyes to adjust – to make out the Yard, the buildings, the people moving around, just the sheer scale of things – but I still couldn't see properly. Covering my eyes with my arm, I shuffled forward, trying not to give Malone any further scope for torment.

That's when I heard the first call: 'Hey Beckham! Beckham! Dav–id Beckham!' I tried to see where the shout was coming from. 'Hey look over here, man! Hey! What's up wid choo?' I saw him out of the corner of my eye. A tall, angular African–American wearing a scarf tied round his head, like a female factory worker in the forties. 'BECK–HAM!! BECK–HAM!!'

'Oh, just ignore him,' said Malone, seeming a bit more nervous than I wanted him to be and suddenly moving me along faster.

'Hey, ho, Beckham! I am talkin' to you. I'm talking to you, motherfucker.' He now moved along parallel to us, but still keeping his distance. I was shocked by his language and his seeming disregard for the fact that Malone was with me. By now I could focus and I realised we were in a tunnel–like enclosure, a funnel into the main yard, surrounded by high wire fencing in a section 150 to 200 feet long and maybe 30 feet wide. There were possibly ten to twenty inmates just hanging around here in the relentless heat, and beyond this little area was a much bigger compound, filled with what looked like hundreds, if not thousands, more inmates milling around. Although my eyes still hadn't fully adjusted to the light, I felt they were all looking at me. Either side of the crowd were two huge brown buildings – austere and plain. These were the accommodation blocks, I later learned, and christened, by some ironic poet, with the names Sunrise and Sunset.

Without realising it, I had been hesitant in my steps and had allowed Malone to get in front of me, signalling my reticence and fear. I was trying to process so much information at once, to take in the totality of what was all around me. I told myself to get a grip, and consciously tried to stand more upright and to walk slightly in front of Malone so it didn't seem as if he was leading me in there or I was cowering behind him. I tried to breathe, but I felt the panic come in waves. Still the catcalls were coming out. Something about 'having a fresh one' and 'Que haces, cabrone?' (How goes it, asshole?), and various others I couldn't properly make out, and possibly didn't want to. So many people were whistling and shouting at me. I was concentrating on how I moved and how I held myself. Still looking straight ahead, I allowed a little of the anger in me percolate to the surface. That bit was easy.

'Stand tall,' I chided myself. 'C'mon Gary, stand tall!' I remembered the advice Sergei had given me back in Houston – that everyone was afraid. Perhaps they were. Perhaps anyone doing this walk would be scared, and all I needed to do was to be strong and act with dignity. I told myself once more that I could do this.

'Will. You. Look. At. Me. Mother. Fucker?' my stalker implored, this time coming much closer to my face.

What was up with this guy? The heat was getting to me and the handcuffs were suddenly beginning to irritate my skin. We walked towards an opening where a couple of Hispanic inmates were sitting on the steps leading into a small, plain-looking building. They were eyeing me carefully, confidence oozing from them as they lazed out like cats on the steps in front of us. They were blocking the way, but seemed to have no intention of moving for either me or Malone.

'Where you come from, man?' a short one, crouched at the front, asked me very calmly, with a friendly nod.

Disarmed by his gesture, I turned slightly as we moved to the side of the steps to pass them. 'Pollok,' I answered, as if my Glasgow home would mean anything to him.

What was I thinking? Why didn't I just give him my address?

I knew this; I had read that when you enter prison the first thing they always ask you is where you came from – as in 'what prison?' not where you were born, how's your mum and what's your star sign! What a fool. Schoolboy error number one; first of the many I would be making no doubt.

'Cool,' said the guy, to general nodding from his other three *cabrones*, all of whom seemed impressed. That was a surprise. Had news of the 50 Krew scaled the prison walls of Big Spring? 'How long you done there?'

Slightly bemused by his interest, I answered, 'Fifteen years,' at which point he whistled and nodded approvingly to his buddies. This confused me even more.

'Oi Beckham, Beck-ham!' screamed the black washerwoman again, sounding more exasperated than ever and now standing just behind me to one side. 'Why'd do you talk to him and not to me, you English faggot!?'

'English!? English!? Did he say English – cheeky bastard?' I thought as I swung round and looked at him.

But before I could speak, he held his hands up with as perfect a beaming smile as you are ever likely to see and said, 'Oh, OK, OK!' much more calmly now. 'No one's hurt, no one got dead. I didn't mean nuthin' . . . you're good to go. You're good to go Mister Beck-ham.' He sashayed past me towards the main Yard. Malone continued to stand beside me, lightly holding my arm as this all unfolded.

Thinking I had entered the funny farm, I turned back around just as the Hispanic guy spoke again. 'Hey man, respect,' he said nodding his head as he lifted a clenched fist towards me from his seated position with the others nodding in unison beside him. I looked at it for a second, confused. Obviously I wasn't supposed to shake it, so I made the same shape and somewhat awkwardly, given the cuffs, 'bumped' it back, bemused as to why I was getting this type of 'respect'.

As we eased past my new Hispanic buddies, I tried to listen to what they were saying but I was unable to make out anything from their rapid dialogue in strong Mexican accents. They spoke so fast and used words I'm sure I hadn't read in any of my textbooks or covered with my Spanish teacher.

We moved up the steps and walked into a small room that reminded me of a post office, complete with four counter bays. Nothing much seemed to be happening; just a few African-Americans getting respite from the heat, a huge mountain of various khaki-coloured kit piled ceiling high behind them.

'Got a new one for you!' announced Malone with glee as he started to de-cuff me for the last time.

'Shit, Malone!' answered a thin-looking young guy suddenly leaping up and eyeing me suspiciously. 'We said to you to stop bringing no more white boys in here! We don't need no new redneck motherfucka helping a re-di-stribution of the pop-u-lace in this prison.' He started walking around me and eyeing me suspiciously, uncomfortably close.

Malone was smiling as I rubbed my wrists, glad to be free of the cuffs. 'This one's different. He's from Europe!' he announced with some pride, as if he'd brought me across the Atlantic himself.

This aroused my new tailor's attention, and he looked me up and down for a while. 'OK, I'm seeing XXL on the pants, a me-di-um on the Ts and size 12 in the shoes,' he shouted out to no one in particular.

These being roughly the dimensions of Coco the Clown's work-gear, I thought I ought to speak up. 'I'm a large in the pants, XL in the T-shirt and a size 10 shoe.' I spoke quietly and carefully, conscious not to seem rude, or to baffle anyone with my Scottish accent.

'Make that an XXXL in the pants,' my tailor immediately shouted, moving back towards the counter. 'This white boy's got an ass that could cause a partial eclipse over the whole of Europe!'

'Best not to say anything,' said Malone, leaning conspiratorially close to me. 'Just let them have their fun. You only need to wear these clothes for one day, like all the new inmates, then you get your proper khakis tomorrow.'

As I shuffled up to the first booth, a vast black man handed me one pair of khakis (XXXL); one white T-shirt (M); and a size 12 pair of blue boating shoes that had seen both better days and bigger feet. These were followed by one pair of thinned-out grey socks (had seen action) and a one pair of blue prison boxers (had seen far too much action). All of these little things I had prepared myself for, so I tried to tell myself none of it bothered me or mattered. I just wanted to get through this day and get into the relative comfort of my cell, wherever that was.

I moved over to a small alcove to get changed. Malone ambled over with me and stood right beside me inside the cubicle as I started to change into my new fatigues. I immediately felt crowded and put upon, but again I told myself it meant nothing and I had to get used to the fact that privacy was a luxury I would no longer be afforded.

Malone was explaining why for the first day only you wear different fatigues from the rest of the population, because that way if you make a mistake or stray 'somewheres you oughtnta' they won't 'necessarily shoot you'. This made him laugh and momentarily took my attention away from the track marks I saw in my boxers as

I reluctantly pulled them on. Of course this garb also advertised you to everyone in the prison as 'fresh fish' and would be like walking around with a neon sign saying, 'Hello, come and get me!' I made a mental note to spend the whole day in my cell if I could, until I could get the 'normal' clothing that would let me blend in as much as a Scotsman ever could in this place.

'Hey Mulgrew?' Malone asked, moving even closer towards me as I was pulling on my tent-like trousers. 'Why d'you tell Rodriguez you'd gone done time in Pollock?' His good eye was roaming up and down as I tried to squeeze into a medium-sized T-shirt that would barely have fitted Calum.

'Because I'm from there,' I answered, wondering what he was on about.

'From there?' Malone echoed. 'You haven't done any time there, boy. You don't have a jacket!'

'Jacket?' I echoed. Dimly, I remembered from my Internet research that a jacket was a prison record. A thin shaft of understanding began to break through. 'There's a prison . . . somewhere . . . called Pollock?' I asked warily.

'Hell, yeah!' said Malone. 'One mean-assed USP in the South. Right smack bang in the centre of Louisiana. Toughest in the South,' he continued. 'They'll all think you're a player, Mildew!'

As mistakes went, I figured it perhaps wasn't a bad one – until the truth emerged, which it surely would.

Resplendent now in my enormous ballooning khaki trousers, I rolled up the trouser legs then twisted them around at the waist before I reappeared from the alcove to be greeted by my grinning tailor. 'Perfect, I would say. Perfecto, don't you think?'

'Aye, perfect,' I responded, emotionless. My T-shirt felt spray-painted on and unconsciously I found myself puffing my chest out as I stood there, being surveyed by all. The shoes were barely staying on, but I again told myself not to bother about it. I wanted to get on with this.

The large black man who had tossed the clothes at me now spoke up.

'Hey, where in Europe you from, man?' he asked – more gently than I would have imagined.

'Scotland.'

'Scotland, Scotland? That where they got that mother-fucka Braveheart!?'

My tailor interjected with some glee. 'Man, that was some serious shit, all them big motherfuckin' swords and shit! You see shit like that there, Scotland?' I gathered Scotland had become my new name.

'Well, not so much the swords now . . .' I offered hesitantly.

'Listen to you, McKenzie!' piped up another guy emerging from a pile of disused clothing, directing his comments at my tailor. He was smaller, but very well built, and also African-American – they clearly all were in the clothing store. He was dressed in the same khaki uniform, but had a mess of Afro hair like he'd just plugged himself into a socket and got fried. He also had a large plastic comb stuck at the top of it, but despite this he had an air of authority about him, like he was the guy in charge, something which seemed to be confirmed by the way the others responded to him. 'They don't use swords and shit over there. That's just in the movies. Man, have you got shit for brains? They got Uzis and Kalashnikovs and serious shit like that. Ain't that the truth, Scotland? Ain't that the truth!?' he asked, looking right at me, and talking to me as if he knew me. 'Tell him, Scotland; tell this dumb-assed motherfucka. What you carryin' over there, Scotland? Tell him!'

They all looked at me expectantly. Even Malone. The word had always been that Finn, the leader of the 50 Krew, used to carry an open razor, but I'd never had the pleasure of seeing it. My only real involvement with weaponry was whenever I wore my kilt (reasonably often for banking functions in New York or London) on which occasions I'd have a *skean dhu* (a small ceremonial dagger) down my sock, but that was the extent of what I'd ever been 'carryin''.

'Well,' I began tentatively, conscious of my accent and its initial impact on people, as well as of Malone craning forward to listen in. 'I always liked to carry a *skean dhu* down my sock.'

'A what!?' three men asked at the same time, all craning towards me.

'A *skean dhu*,' I repeated with more emphasis, amazed at the direction the conversation had taken.

There was silence for a moment as everyone looked confused. 'A "skin do"? A "skin do"?' erupted McKenzie, my tailor, excitedly moving around again as if life was a permanent dance. 'That sounds like some serious shit! That sounds like some special shit, like you're gonna skin some motherfucka; like your gonna peel his mother-fuckin' skin off!!' By now, he was dancing around like a dervish. 'Is it like a semi-automatic or something, this skin do? Or a flame-thrower, takin' their skin straight off, or . . . or . . .?' He could scarcely get the words out for excitement.

'Shit man,' said the leader, moving forward. 'Scotland done said he carried it in his sock. How's a motherfucka gonna carry a fuckin' flame–thrower in his motherfuckin' sock!? Are you stupid or something?' McKenzie withered under the leader's rebuke and fell silent. I felt sorry for him – almost.

'Scotland,' the top man went on, all eyes turning back to me. 'What does a skin do, do?' he asked awkwardly.

'Er, well,' I began, feeling the hole beneath my feet getting deeper. 'It's a . . . a dagger,' I said, rousing some authority to my voice.

'A da–gguurrrr!!' repeated the leader, with a passable imitation of a Scottish accent. 'Now that's what I'm talkin' about,' he mused. 'A skin do is a da . . . gguurrr,' he said again, sounding like he was licking the words as he spoke. 'That is some serious shit,' he concluded appreciatively. 'Like they use to skin some motherfucka up quicker than he can use a motherfuckin' gun! Yeah!' All around me, faces were nodding and smiling in agreement and appreciation. Even Malone seemed to have joined in.

'You a'ight Scotland, you a'ight,' said the boss, looking at me closely in my Coco the Clown outfit. 'Just don't go running with those white boy motherfuckin' ABs and you be quoted, man.' With that, he started to pull out some blankets and sheets for me, rejecting some which looked too old or dirty.

The 'ABs' was the second reference I'd heard to the Aryan Brotherhood, the prevalent white supremacist gang that operated in many of the prisons in Texas,

Louisiana and Alabama. Although they were mainly driven by the demands and rewards of organised crime, the Brotherhood still had strong racial overtones and many of the Southern Whites joined them for protection, particularly when they found themselves in the minority in places like Big Spring. I hoped I'd never have anything to do with them.

Malone moved me forward to the next counter window and I picked up a laundry bag, two thin blankets (which I thought was at least one too many in this heat), two washcloths, four small thin towels (clean), four Bic razors – I was glad I'd prepared for them – one tube of tooth-paste, one small toothbrush and one bar of soap.

As an afterthought, the big guy looked at me for a minute and said, 'Here Scotland. Here's a pillow.' He pushed it through the counter to me. 'You need anything, my name's Tank. You can check me out. You need some-thing, you holler . . .' Now he pushed a second pillow my way.

Barely listening to him, I looked down. Two months of sleeping without a pillow, two months of serious neck and backache, and now they'd given me two pillows. For a moment I considered handing them back, but the stupidity of that suddenly struck me. Pulling my thoughts back together, I picked up my stuff and said, 'Sure – I'll holler.'

I had no intention of ever hollering.

I signed a number of forms to say that I had received the various items and to acknowledge that they were the property of the Federal Government and that I would look after them and would endeavour to return them in the same condition in which I had received them. I was also reminded that to steal said items was a Federal offence, punishable by up to five years in prison.

I said my goodbyes, relieved, as the store-house gang all got back to the serious business of doin' nuthin'. The sun was still blazing when we got outside, but thankfully the crowd had thinned down considerably. 'Where is everyone?' I asked Malone as he started to unlock the large wire gate leading into the main section of the Yard.

'Workin',' he replied, as we walked through the guard house between the two sections, passing under a metal detector along the way. There were a couple of officers hanging around, but they seemed completely disinterested in me or Malone. This was, after all, a typical daily scene – just another prisoner checking in. It occurred to me how few officers there seemed to be anywhere.

'A'ight Mildew,' began Malone. 'You're housed in Sunset, Bunk 003U, Range 4. Go straight over there,' he said, pointing to the furthest away of the two large buildings, 'and report at the front office and they'll figure it out from there.' Bunk? Range? 'That's a funny number for a cell,' I thought, but was focused more on the fact that Malone was leaving me. Leaving me to go out there on my own and walk through the Yard. I looked from him to the wide open space that led to my cell-block. It wasn't particularly busy, but there were still at least fifty people milling around, and I was about to walk through them with my 'kick me' clothes on, together with a set of sheets, pillows and blankets, making it obvious to anyone who needed to know that some new flesh was walking through. I hesitated. It looked so daunting, so dusty, bleak, and exposed. No shelter from the sun and no shelter now from the other inmates. I suddenly realised I'd grown accustomed to Malone during this two-hour, frenzied induction. I wanted him to come with me.

'Now before you go, Mildew, the one piece of advice I give to every inmate, but is especially true in your case because of that Enron stuff you did, is . . .' he paused here as if for emphasis, 'to do your OWN time,' he announced with a self-satisfied flourish.

I looked at him blankly. 'What the fuck does that mean?' I thought, as I surveyed the emptiness of the Yard in front of me.

'Go on, Mildew; they won't bite,' he said, grinning at my reluctance. The panic rose unchecked within me as I started out on the 250 or so metres across the Yard towards the entrance of Sunset.

I had only taken a few steps before the catcalls started and the questions flew in from everywhere.

'Hey Scotland, how long d'you do in Pollock?' (News travelled fast, I thought).

'Escosais, Escosais, did you see Rosario when you were there? Manuel Rosario, everyone call him Manny? D'you know Manny?'

'Scotland, look over here motherfucka!' And so it went on. Some came right up to me, but I resisted the temptation to cuddle my blankets or my new luxury pillows higher on my chest, instead holding them down by my side and walking as calmly as I could across the Yard.

That resolve lasted about ten steps before I started to waver. Sergei had said that everyone was scared, but there was one dude sticking his face right into mine who just didn't look all that afraid to me! Reluctantly, I found myself glancing repeatedly at him and couldn't help but notice a series of spiders tattooed from his neck in a precise journey around his chin, up his cheek and across to his left eye. No, this guy wasn't scared; he was fucking crazy.

'Ahhhhhh!!!' my mind screamed. 'Run, fucking run!' I managed not to, though.

'*Que cabrone. Cómo estás?*' Spiderman mumbled, looking me up and down, his breath stinking of eggs or fish or something horrible. '*Que cabrone?*' he kept saying over and over again as he kept up with me, maybe fifty steps in, a good two hundred to go to my destination. He didn't look like a Latino; he looked white. Small, thin, gaunt, bad teeth, unshaven and dangerous; the spider shit on his face definitely did not help the look.

I shrugged my shoulders a few times at some of the questions being hurled at me and kept walking. Halfway across the Yard, my attention was caught by a beautiful hand-carved bird house. It was brilliantly white; and stood out like a beacon against the dull brown buildings stretched out on either side of the Yard. There were birds flying in and out and busying themselves all around it. How incongruous, I thought, to see free birds living against the backdrop of barbed wire fencing and all these caged men. 'What you looking at, *cabrone?*' said the white nutcase, in English this time, again moving uncomfortably close to me.

'That,' I said, pausing briefly as I shifted the pillows and blankets to my other hand so I could point at the bird house. It appealed to my sense of irony that the birds would hang out here, in this place. Maybe they wanted to see humans caged, because we did it to them so often. This distraction seemed to work, as Spiderman had stopped in his tracks with me and was looking at the bird house like it had just miraculously appeared. Making the most of the opportunity, I strode on quickly and, as I had imagined I might do many times when I thought about this moment, I repeated some of the words from Psalm 23 over and over again in my head:

'Yea, though I walk through the valley of the shadow of death,
I will fear no evil: for thou art with me; thy rod and thy staff they comfort me.'

And comfort me it did as it carried me across the rest of that Yard into the promised land of Sunset. A few people in the Yard kept calling out to me and asking questions – mainly, to my mounting discomfort, questions about life in Pollock prison – but the shouts started to blend into each other and I didn't hear them the same way any more. Thankfully, most of the onlookers quickly lost interest and got back to doing, well, seemingly nothing. As I got closer I noticed that I'd picked up an audience at some of the windows, each member of it assessing the new guy, each wondering whether or not I'd crack, survive or end up as someone's bitch. They were probably already aware that my name was 'Scotland' or 'Escosais', as I was never known as anything else from that day forward.

6

SCOTLAND, SOUTH DAKOTA

S TEPPING INTO SUNSET FELT LIKE STEPPING into a
sports arena minutes before kick–off. There were
inmates everywhere, queuing for the phone, queuing to
use what looked like a little microwave area, and cram–
ming into a tiny room that housed a TV. Everyone seemed
to be moving about frantically as if the day was about to
end. It felt like there was some air–conditioning, but it was
stifling hot and there seemed to be little oxygen in there
as I stepped into the chaos. Ahead of me, and right across
from the entrance to Sunset, was a small office with two
officers sitting, seemingly oblivious to the bedlam outside.

I knocked on the door. They ignored me. I knocked
again, and one of them looked over then ignored me
again. I stood for a minute feeling like a dick in my
baggy clothing. Then, impatient to get into the relative
privacy of a cell, I knocked for a third time and then
just opened the door and poked my head in.

'I'm a new prisoner,' I said, instantly regretting the use
of the word 'prisoner'.

'And?' said the guard who had glanced over at me earlier. He was mid twenties maybe, fit and trim with the sort of tremendous handlebar moustache rarely seen since the days of the Village People.

'I was told to report to you,' I offered.

'And now you have,' said Village People, and turned back to his conversation with the other officer, who still hadn't even so much as turned around and looked at me. I hesitated.

'Yes?' Mr Handlebars snapped, sounding put out that I was still there.

'I was wondering where I am supposed to go.'

'What bunk number?' he asked, sighing.

'Bunk 003U, Range 4,' I replied smartly, feeling like I might have just passed some prison initiation test. Terminating the discussion, Village People just pointed over my left shoulder and went back to his discussion with the faceless officer. Picking my way carefully through the inmates, I walked out of the office, passing the small TV room – one TV with about thirty–five seats I noted – then a small kitchen in which I counted three micro-waves and a large sink. I was surprised I was allowed to walk through all the inmates unescorted, but tried to look at it positively – hopefully I would assimilate more quickly left to my own devices. It was intimidating walking through the other inmates, trying to look assured but feeling that each one looked more sinister than the last. Many of them were staring at me, or ostentatiously eyeing me from top to bottom, and a few asked me where I was from or when I'd got in, but I ignored them. I tried to concentrate on maintaining the stern expression I had practised early that same morning. I worked my way through a warren of narrow corridors, which twisted and turned with different rooms jutting out at each turn, trying to find my cell, but being unsure of the numbering system.

All last traces of hope or positive thought came crashing to the floor as I entered a smaller corridor with a large '4' painted on it (for Range 4, I assumed), walked up six short steps and turned to view my new living quarters for the foreseeable future. I stood rigidly still, too shocked to move. No cosy cell for me – I had entered an enormous noisy room about 80 feet long and 40 feet wide, crammed with nothing but cast-iron yellow bunk beds, all screwed to the floors, with small lockers squeezed in between. As I started to stumble through it in a daze, stupefied at the thought of being constantly surrounded by so many people, I could see the room could hold roughly eighty men. To the side there were two small adjoining rooms which housed the bathrooms and showers. There were maybe three or four toilets in each, no more than six or seven showers and no privacy anywhere.

I was totally crestfallen. All my coping strategies, all my preparation, all my mental cajoling, had been built on the premise that I'd be kicking back in a cell at the end of each hellish day and able to block it out for a few hours. I only had ever figured on dealing with one inmate; one cell-mate, maybe two at the most. I'd always felt I could handle one or two inmates no matter how demented or dangerous they were, but this . . . This wasn't punishment, it was an experiment: the *Big Brother* house with wall-to-wall psychos.

I realised I'd started wandering round and round in a bit of a trance, unable to properly concentrate on finding my bunk, and people were looking at me, the new fish. So I started to look again for my bunk, this time focusing more on that than on my surroundings. What looked like a native Indian guy was sitting on his lower bunk close to me, drawing something . . . Indiany – all feathers and buffalo and stuff. It looked great, even when viewed from upside down.

'You the new Scotty guy I heard about?' he asked, looking up to face me, smiling. He had the demeanour of someone who had been there a long time. 'My name is Gabriel, but you can call me Chief. Everyone else does.' He pushed a fist out to me. Shifting my blankets from my right to left hand, I bumped him right back. He looked like he was in his early thirties, a little overweight, with a weatherbeaten face. Something in his deportment and the awkward way he sat suggested an injury of some sort.

'How you doin', Chief?' I responded, trying to seem relaxed. 'Nice drawing.'

'You like it?' he viewed it himself critically. 'It's symbols from the Zuni, my tribe. I hear your tribe is from Scotland, right?'

'Er yeah, I suppose,' I responded, not really seeing Alex Salmond in the same light as Geronimo or Sitting Bull.

'Gabriel, er, Chief, do you know where bunk 003U is?' I asked.

'Right behind you in the corner there. That's a good spot, Scotty. You can keep your back to the wall and you got that little window to look out!' he said, still shading a piece of his drawing.

'How comforting,' I said, without quite meaning to. I'd read that even the simplest jokes could lead to many of your biggest problems – and the Americans weren't always the best with British–style sarcasm. I had to keep that sort of thing in check.

'Yup, I'd say that's a sought–after piece of real estate you got there,' Chief went on with a slightly different smile, like he'd fully got my joke. 'They must have got word that you came from Pollock,' he added – again suggesting by the merest trace of a grin that he knew full well which Pollock I'd come from. I liked the Chief.

My new apartment was a tiny space. There were no tables and chairs, and if you weren't lying in your bed, you'd have to be sitting on top of it or standing in the thoroughfare everyone else used to get to and from their own beds. There was a small locker, maybe two feet high by a foot wide. I opened it and looked inside – I don't quite know why; I wasn't expecting to find something in it, a welcome pack or a bowl of fruit. I guess I wanted something to do. My heart was sinking faster than a fat man on thin ice and it sank further as more inmates started to come into the room, each one having himself a good long look at the fresh meat. Trying to ignore them, I went about making up my bed – which took all of three minutes – then I decanted my worldly possessions into my locker. I felt about as low as I could ever remember, but then I congratulated myself that I had actually been lower. Getting extradited and telling Calum I was leaving him had been worse than this; way, way worse.

I climbed up onto my top bunk and looked out of my tiny window. It was just like that little window I used to look up to when I spent those cold and lonely nights in Quarriers Homes as a little boy. This one had seven bars in it, but I was as much a prisoner then as I am now, I thought. Self–conscious and uncomfortable,

I propped myself up on my bunk and began reading the Correctional Rules for New Inmates in the Big Spring Correctional Facility – surely one 'Correctional' too many – trying to ignore the fact that I was the subject of much staring and discussion as more and more inmates filtered back into the room.

Each new entrant to the *Big Brother* room looked scarier than the last. About two-thirds of my new roomies were Hispanic, with about a dozen Blacks, a few more Natives and maybe only five or six Whites – very much the minority. What they lacked in numbers, however, they made up for in sheer threat value, as most of them were the kind you wouldn't want to see on a dark night, or on a bright day either. These first few white toughs were boy scouts, though, compared to the two scrawny looking dudes with skinheads who suddenly came marching into the room. Immediately I could see they set a number of people on edge. One of the Hispanics theatrically spat on the floor then wiped it with his shoe as he turned away from them. I sat with my legs dangling from my bunk watching the skinheads as they surveyed the room. 'What are they up to?' I wondered, and then, to my dismay, I found out, as the saw me and moved directly towards me.

'Scotland? You called Scotland?' asked the slightly shorter of the two as he approached me, offering his fist in a bump. I reluctantly bumped back and thought of saying 'Who's asking?', but not feeling bold enough, I just nodded instead. They looked in their mid twenties, each with dental issues. The one who spoke looked almost wasted away, but he exuded a kind of nervous energy that was already unsettling me and seemingly everyone else around, except Chief, who kept right on drawing.

'Yeah, I'm Scotland,' I answered, quite liking my new name and enjoying the fact that I was sitting high above these two psychos on my top bunk. I started to focus on their tattoos. The short one who had spoken had a swastika tattoo on his neck and the other taller one had something tattooed on his shaven head, which I couldn't quite read at first. After shifting a little, I made out the first line as 'God Forgives . . .' which seemed quite encouraging, although they didn't strike me as Christian Fellowship types. Any lingering hopes that they might have come to hand me a Bible and invite me to a singalong were dispelled, when I saw the second line: '. . . the Brotherhood Doesn't'.

They were, I realised in that instant, a deputation from the Aryan Brotherhood. I recoiled from them both. Why were they coming to see me? I was mesmerised by the 'God Forgives; the Brotherhood Doesn't' tattoo. 'Imagine having that tattooed on your head,' I thought, wondering if it had been sore. Subconsciously, I must have started pulling at my sleeve to cover my Cara and Calum lovefest tat as I saw Tattoo Head look at it. He had the look of an enforcer, the muscle, like he was coiled ready for action.

'Scotland, South Dakota?' the shorter, scrawnier weirdo asked me.

'Eh?' I responded, confused.

'Scotland, in South Dakota?' he clarified.

'Scotland, Scotland!' I responded emphatically, feeling, not for the first time, that I had landed on a different planet.

'You're not from Scotland, South Dakota?' Tattoo Head asked, clearly unable to keep pace with this highbrow conversation.

'Naw, I'm from Scotland, Scotland!' I responded, sounding irritated – which I was. I felt emboldened sitting above them, and I just wanted these bald-headed Nazis to go.

Everyone was watching our exchange and I didn't want to be associated with people like this. I saw Chief had stopped drawing, his pencil resting on the pad, clearly tuning into every word of this exchange. I felt it was important, but I wasn't yet sure why.

'Can you come down here, Scotland?' the shorter skin-head asked, with something that could almost have been a smile, if he'd had enough teeth. 'It's kinda awkward speaking to you when you're up there,' he continued, craning his scrawny red neck for good effect.

I hesitated. 'Naw. I like it fine up here,' I replied, allowing my Scottish accent its full range as I always did when I felt threatened.

'OK,' the smaller guy mumbled, sounding irritated, before switching tack and asking, 'You did time in Pollock?' They were both so edgy. The taller one with the tattooed bonce barely ever raised his head to look at me, simply staring straight in front, seemingly at the wall, as if he wanted me to focus entirely on the message on his head – what we might have termed in manage-ment terms as his personal 'USP', or unique selling point. He kept rubbing or flexing his hands as if he was preparing them for combat, and this set me on edge even more. Both wore sleeveless vests, worn and stained, giving the shorter one the look of Rab C. Nesbitt on a crash diet. He had foregone the skull-branding option, and instead had a large tattoo right across his chest, in bold writing, which was partially obscured by his vest. I could make out that it was three words, the second one of which said HATES in some kind of elaborate gothic font, and I kept trying to catch the other two words. Sometimes it looked like the third word might be ME. HATES ME. Something or someone HATES ME. What a sentiment to have on your chest, I thought, as my discourse with the two hillbillies continued.

'You did time in Pollock, Scotland?' he asked again.

'Erm . . .' I pondered, genuinely wondering how to answer that one. 'I lived in Pollok, Scotland, but I didn't do time in Pollock, no,' I responded, instantly wondering if anyone had understood what I just said. The skinheads looked at each other as if I had just spoken in Farsi.

'I lived in a place called Pollok, in a town called Glasgow, in a country called Scotland,' I offered carefully, thinking a more detailed explanation might help. 'So yes, I come from Pollok, but I've never been to Louisiana.' Tattoo Head started scratching it, while Tattoo Chest looked as if he had just had a quick explanation of the mechanics of nuclear physics. Silence ensued. A couple of times, the shorter one positioned himself as if to speak, but each time thought better of it. The silence continued. I couldn't think of anything to add to my detailed and thorough explanation, so I didn't bother and focused instead on trying to figure out what the first word of the HATES ME tattoo was. Tattoo Head just kept staring ahead at the wall and as they seemed much more uncomfortable with the silence than I was, I let it ride. Suddenly I got it – BOB! BOB HATES ME. The tattoo was partially obscured, but that first word was clearly three letters with the 'O' fully visible in the middle and the tops of the first and third letters cut off by his vest, but they definitely looked like a couple of Bs.

BOB HATES ME! I thought, 'What the fuck does that mean?' The silence was starting to make me uncomfortable too. Who the hell was Bob? Why would you tattoo that on your chest? I could imagine a lot of people hated this guy, but what made Bob so special?

After a moment or two, Tattoo Chest nudged his taller accomplice, who grunted and suddenly proffered something up to me.

'This is sum shower shoes an' shit to git you started,' he drawled, handing me some heavy plastic flip-flops and what looked like some coffee, some biscuits and a bar of chocolate. Suddenly my mood changed, as I realised too late what was happening. These guys were recruiting for the Brotherhood. That's what all that bullshit preamble was about. Without thinking of anything but the chocolate, my hands had been on the package, but I withdrew them just as quickly.

'I don't want that shit!' I said, fast and loud. I hoped everyone heard it.

The shorter one put his hand on Tattoo Head's arm to stop him from withdrawing the offer.

'Now lookie here, Scotland. Don't go misunderstandin' nuthin'. We like to look after our own here. Ain't nun of these other fuckers,' – he looked around directly at the Blacks in the corner, before drawing closer to me – 'ain't none of these other fuckers gonna take care of nuthin' but their own. You know what ah'm sayin'? Us white boys got to stick together, you hearin' me?'

I was hearing him alright. He had taken on a much nastier demeanour and I felt the tension rise between the three of us.

'Now why don't you just take a little time to consider

what you'd like to do, Scotland?' he said, taking the
goodies away from Tattoo Head and placing them carefully on my bunk. 'You really don't want to be walkin'
alone in this Yard, and if you ain't runnin' with us, we
will see you as agin us, you know what I'm sayin',
Scotland? You feelin' me, Scotland?'

I was feeling him.

He moved back and smiled at me, a menacing, tooth-
less and graceless grin. He patted my knee.

'Take yer crap off my bunk,' I said calmly, 'and fuck
off.' Inside I was shit–scared, but I just kept focusing on
the two messenger boys in front of me. I didn't have a
strategy or a plan, even though I'd always known I would
face a recruitment drive sooner or later. I just hadn't
expected it this early and with so few corporate
benefits.

Tattoo Head was twitching uncontrollably and kept
looking from the shorter one to the floor. Itching to get
started on me, I thought.

'Scotland, I'm going cut you some slack and ask you
once again to reconsider ma offer,' the shorter one began
again, slowly. 'You really don't want to be pissin' us off
and havin' to walk that Yard on your own now, do ya?
You ain't gonna git no help from the Negros or the Paises
or the Injuns now, are ya? All you've got is your own
kind,' he went on. So this was melting–pot America, then.

He stopped talking. In the silence, I started to re–examine
my logic. I don't want to be sucked into their turf wars
and battles, and I knew that in joining them there would
always be a price to pay – probably a messy job like
beating up some poor guy that had pissed them off in
some way; maybe even doing something worse. But then

again, I couldn't 'walk that Yard alone' as the skinhead had put it, or – worse still – with the might of the Aryan Brotherhood coming after me. Surely not everyone must be affiliated to a gang? If I could just get rid of them and show I wasn't interested, maybe everyone else would leave me alone?

'Look,' I said, leaning towards them and speaking more quietly. 'I'm not from around here, and I'm not your kind. I don't want to cause any trouble with you guys and I ain't trying to be disrespectful. But I'm a Scot, from Scotland. I'm British. I play football and eat chips.' I found myself immediately regretting that these were the only examples of British credentials I could summon at that moment, but I don't suppose my interlocutors minded. 'I'm not part of your battles, and I won't be part of your Brotherhood. You know what I'm sayin?' Tattoo Head involuntarily nodded and my confidence grew.

'So why don't you take this shit . . .' I said, gradually raising my voice as I picked up the package of stuff, '. . . and ask Bob to forgive you!'

The Bob jibe seemed to have confused them somewhat as they both looked at each other in a bemused fashion. Eventually the shorter guy said, 'OK, Scotland, OK. If that's how you wanna play it. Just don't come cryin' to us when the shit hits the fan. And the shit hits the fan most every day in Big Spring,' he added with a mischie-vous grin, as if all the shit emanated from him. 'C'mon, SlumDawg,' he said, as he turned to walk away, the 'dawg' part extending to well over three syllables.

SlumDawg looked like he wanted to stay and drag me off the bed. 'SlumDawg!' Tattoo Chest said again, this time more forcefully. SlumDawg looked up at me fully for the first time with the confidence of a true enforcer and instantly my own confidence evaporated. He smirked at me and began to walk off, grinning at all the other inmates who had watched this unfold. Suddenly the shorter one turned around and walked swiftly back towards me. Not bothering to look up at me, he put out his hand and said, 'Chocolate . . .'

'Oh yeah!' I exclaimed in mock surprise. 'Here, here you go.' I handed it over, regretting the loss of that little luxury. 'Man, I'm hungry,' I thought as I lay back and wondered if I'd already cooked my own goose. For the next ten minutes my heart was racing as I replayed the scene over and over again in my mind and I tried to work out if I had played it right. I could sense everyone in the room was watching me, discussing me.

Without really realising it, I'd been ignoring the need to go to the bathroom, the playground for so many of my darkest fears. Switching to autopilot, I swung round on my bunk and leapt down in one movement, landing on my feet with a loud smack from my Coco the Clown boating shoes. Everyone around me looked up at this sudden sound. I stood rooted to the spot as if I had just executed a perfect triple axel with pike at the Texas Olympics. My feet stung from the six-foot leap, and I saw Chief wince then chuckle to himself. Pulling my trousers tightly round my waist, I hesitated about moving towards the bathroom, but my need quickly superseded my fears. With as much dignity as I could muster, I ambled along, my feet stinging and my bladder bursting. I felt like everyone was watching; that a path was clearing for me as I stepped awkwardly towards the bathroom with the gait of sixty-year-old with chronic piles – not the cool confident persona I had imagined myself conveying.

The toilet room had four urinals on the right followed by three stalls, with the sinks lined up on the wall opposite. Each of the stalls had a door, but no lock, and these doors only covered about two feet of the middle section, so you could easily see the inhabitant's head and feet. There were two Hispanics in there already, seated, and casually talking to each other like they were sitting side by side at a football match. They stopped talking when I shuffled in, and stared at me, adding further to my sense of unease. At the farthest end of the bathroom were some shower stalls. The shower stalls afforded at least a degree of privacy, with separate stalls and shower curtains covering the fronts. Most of the action would take place in there, I figured.

Standing by a middle urinal, I fumbled around for my zipper, before realising it was pointless as I could just pull my trousers straight down. As I did this, two Hispanics appeared either side of me, their skin briefly touching my skin as I froze and stood staring rigidly ahead. They were talking jovially but I didn't initially even glance at them, just kept staring ahead, panic enveloping me.

I couldn't pee.

I looked down at my willie then involuntarily to my left where my new roomie was smiling at me.

'Hola,' he said.

'Hola, hola, fucking hola!!' my mind screamed, convinced he'd got me at 'hola'. I thought of simply pulling my trousers back up and leaving, but I realised that would look even worse, so I willed myself to pee once more. I looked to the other side of me, keeping my eyes firmly at head height, only for the second Hispanic man to smile, then, without a hint of embarrassment, to stare directly down at my willie. This was all getting too much and I swivelled around to the left again to see that the first Hispanic was now eyeing my backside which I had inadvertently exposed by lowering my clown pants halfway down my bottom. One hour in and I was already parading my big white arse – at this rate I was in danger of becoming known as 'Scotland the slut'.

Fortunately this momentary distraction seemed to have eased the mind–bladder deadlock, and the relief I felt as I faced straight ahead again was magical. Confidence restored, I felt like I was reasserting my masculinity and I smiled and gasped, 'Aaaahhhhhhh!!' – ridiculously proud of the strong flow I was producing. My two comrades seemed happy as well, so we all stood there smiling, me still looking straight ahead. Yanking my trousers back up to cover my bottom, I turned away from both the Hispanics and began to wash my hands. There were no hand towels or soap, so I quickly rinsed one hand and rubbed it on my trousers instead.

The relief I'd felt after finally relieving myself was dissipating now, and I was getting anxious of making a mistake again, any kind of mistake, so I shuffled out of the bathroom as quickly as I could, ignoring some mumbled entreaties from the two Hispanics to join an altogether different kind of gang. A gang with more bang, I guessed, as I shuffled back to my bunk, relieved at least that I had survived my first visit to the toilets.

7

POLLOK, SCOTLAND

I F ANY INMATES WERE STILL STARING at me, I barely noticed. I felt tired and drained as I pulled myself awkwardly back up onto my bunk and started looking out of my little window.

Beyond the bars, I could see the Yard and then the bird house. I watched the birds flying in and out for a while, feeling a little bit less hopeless. The two, bleak slabs of building, Sunrise and Sunset, reminded me of the rows of tenements I'd grown up around in Dormanside Road in Pollok. Dormanside stretched for nearly two miles top to bottom, only occasionally interrupted by side streets. This was where my best friend Joe and I, and my brothers Mark and Michael, would hang out come rain or shine, playing football, or a game called 'kerby' which involved throwing the ball against the opposite kerb and trying to catch it on the rebound. The parallels with the landscapes of my childhood made this feel like a designer-made nightmare, full of subtle comparisons and metaphors that even in those first few moments perturbed me.

Some days after we had left the Home and Mum was bringing us up in Dormanside Road, I would hear her crying. She was always so strong for us boys; always giving us a strong moral grounding, making sure we all sat down for a family meal together every evening, no matter how sparse. She worked two jobs and I could see how exhausted she often was, but still she encouraged us and loved us. We had so little money, but what we had she spent on us. She seldom went out on her own and seldom had adult company other than her brothers, my Uncle Martin and Uncle John. Everything was dedicated to keeping us out of trouble and to teaching us to be 'good boys'. Somewhat ironically, she used to worry that if she didn't keep a tight rein on us, we would end up in prison like so many others from Dormanside Road. I guess she never envisaged I would take such an exotic route, however.

Mum was a strict disciplinarian and we had a daily rota on the wall to cover all the housework when we came home from school. She would usually be back by 6 p.m., but two or three nights a week she would go straight back out to her 'second job', singing at a few clubs in Glasgow. She had a wonderful voice – but she can't have wanted to head out to perform after a hard day's work, leaving the warmth of the home to go back into the city.

On those few occasions I found her crying alone in her bedroom, she would quickly gather herself together and say it was nothing. There was no unburdening herself on her youngest son, no attempt to help herself – just a continuation of her role as the 'strong one', the glue that kept the family together.

Despite being the brightest of three children, Mum had left school at fifteen to look after her terminally ill mother and to take care of the household. My grandmother had passed away from tuberculosis – a big killer in the smog-filled Glasgow of the late fifties – when my mum was only seventeen. By twenty-one, my mother had already met my father, married, and had her third son. By twenty-two she was separated, and ostracised by a strict Catholic family who believed she should stay with my father no matter how obvious his indiscretions. Only her brothers took her side. Even the local priest tried to advise her that my dad was just being 'a young man, stretching his wings'. But he had wrapped his wings round one too many birds for my mum's liking, and when I was just three months old he was gone. I didn't meet him again until I was a teenager.

We moved to Spain for a few years, then came back to Glasgow when my father's bankruptcy stopped any maintenance payments. With my Uncle Martin serving in the Navy and Uncle John having moved to London, my Mum began to really struggle with three boys under the age of six. In the early 1960s, particularly in Glasgow, being a single mother was a shameful thing for working-class Catholics. My mother's parents turned their backs not only on her, but on her children as well.

After staying in a friend's spare bedroom – an impossible set-up for one adult and three kids – we were initially separated and placed into foster care. I have a vague memory of that, though I was only three years old. I do remember a taxi ride, my mum anxious and Mark and I crying; Michael (the eldest) was resolute as always. I remember going into an office, then my mum saying goodbye and crying, then a blur of people trying to be kind to me – an older couple with a big gas fire that they let me sit in front of. They kept offering me food, but I had it fixed in my head that if I took it, even though I was hungry, I wouldn't see Mark and Michael or my mum again. I didn't take it.

I also didn't speak, just wrapped my arms round my legs and rocked myself back and forward in front of the fire. Michael was at another house trying to achieve the same result, but by a different method. He had smashed a glass and a plate and thrown his food against the wall. When the man of the house had tried to calm him down, he'd bitten him and tried to punch him, then he told his wife to 'fuck off'. Meanwhile, unconfirmed reports had Mark at a house nearby tucking into egg and chips with his feet up on the couch and watching *Joe 90* on the telly. Mark was always the most pragmatic of the three of us.

With two out of three of us not settling, the decision was made to move us three Catholic boys into the all-Protestant children's Quarriers Homes – an orphanage ten miles outside of Glasgow, which was a significant decision in a still very sectarian city. The Home had been founded in the 1850s by William Quarrier 'for the abandoned or orphaned children of Glasgow and beyond' and even in the 1960s it was enjoying a roaring trade. We were labelled as short-termers, but ended up spending over two years there. I hated it. All my first concrete memories came from that Home, and the enduring recollection was of counting the days until we could get out. But at least it kept the three of us together. Michael continuously ran away – on two occasions he was found only a few miles outside Glasgow – and he would often be in trouble for fighting. I was quiet and insular, talking only to Mark and Michael or Donald, my best friend then, and the only 'coloured' boy in a home of 1,500. Mark loved it.

Mum was allowed to visit us once a month, on a Saturday, and would walk the three miles from Bridge of Weir to Quarriers in all weathers just to see us for an hour or so. She would write to us every week, always including three sixpences Sellotaped into the letter. The Cottage Mother – reasonably enough – would take the sixpences for the 'kitty' for all the children, most of whom had no parents. Mum's letters always spoke of when we would be home, a dream we all three held on to. But the weeks became months, and months became years, and we stayed in Quarriers Homes, never even leaving the grounds of the Home. My life consisting of either being in our cottage, number 21, with thirty other children, or walking the short distance to school each day. Still, the letters and visits from my mother and the fact I had my brothers with me made me feel lucky – I was, after all, surrounded by orphans.

I was quite bright at school and by six years old I'd figured out it was exactly 157 steps to walk to school, although I could make it as much as 212, and once as few as 124. Counting the steps was an enduring memory for me. On Sundays we would march down holding hands in twos in our second-hand Sunday 'best' to the church for Sunday Service (between 265 and 322 steps, depending upon who was my partner), then all the way back again to the cottage where I would spend the rest of the day either in the garden or in the house. We were set chores for each day, and with only one Cottage Mother for each cottage, the discipline was severe – the lady in charge of our house preferring to lock you in the garage for an unspecified period if you'd done something to offend her. There were hundreds of kids, but it was a lonely existence. We had no visitors other than Mum, and sometimes long periods would pass without seeing anyone from the outside world at all.

In those days a single mother would be near the bottom of a council list, not the top. So Mum worked and saved, worked and saved, and eventually we got a flat in Dormanside Road in Pollok. A row of tenements that stretched for as far as I could imagine, Dormanside Road was pretty bad, even by Glasgow standards. Gangs, muggings, stabbings, 'chibbings' (permanently marking someone's face with a razor, knife or screwdriver) were commonplace. But I was overjoyed when we left Quarriers and moved there. There were no real gardens so we played on the street all day. There were no shops, so you would get your 'messages' (shopping) from a double-decker bus that parked halfway down the road. The guy that ran it was friendly, a large ginger fellow called Alex, with two front teeth missing. He sold the usual staples of working–class life then – lard by the ton, potatoes by the hundredweight, sugar, bread, tea, sausages, eggs and, when you were feeling exotic, fish fingers or long spaghetti. Mark used to joke that he was eighteen before he discovered that spaghetti bolognaise had meat in it. To us this 'exotic' meal was served with a knob of butter and lashings of tomato ketchup.

Usually I played football with Mark and Michael and up to ten other kids from the street, including my best

GARY MULGREW

friend Joe. Joe was a great player then, a standout, and went on to play for Clydebank in the old Scottish First Division, but chucked it in at twenty-three to concentrate on plumbing, where he could make much more money with overtime. Changed days indeed. Joe and I had a number of part-time jobs together, including selling bread rolls through the 'closes' (the entrance to the tene-ments), selling football coupons and a paper run. Like me, Joe had to earn money for the household, so we always worked. His mum would make us 'pieces and jam' to eat as we worked our way through our round, which would usually take about an hour and a half and stretched the length of Dormanside. Other than Fridays, when we collected the money, we would do alternate nights for the paper run, but quickly got that mixed up so people were getting two papers one night and none the next. This didn't bode well for our future careers together.

Our biggest challenge was collecting the cash and keeping it, which always made Fridays our toughest night. Joe was always strong and well built – I was tall, scrawny and geeky looking. We would cut through the back gardens collecting the money, one 'keeping the edgy' at the front of the close in case someone tried to take our weekly takings, while the other, usually Joe, tried to charm his way to a decent tip. It was noticeable that Joe always got more tips than me and although this had remained unspoken between us, I eventually broached the subject with him.

'Why do you think you get all the tips?' I asked him tentatively.

'Huv ye seen yerself recently?' Joe responded, laughing.

I instinctively touched my bushy, curly hair. I had lots of hair. I thought I looked like Starsky out of *Starsky and Hutch*. I even had the big cardigan.

'You look like a big, skinny drip,' Joe went on. I was regretting asking. 'Your heid's huge, wi' that big mop on top and you're pasty white as a sheet and skinny as a pole. You stand in front of them saying nuthin' and lookin' like a big struck match, wi' that huge heid of hair of yours. They don't know whether to pay you or feed you.' With that he jumped over the fence, on to the next customer.

The main danger for us was avoiding Finn. He was the 'leader-off' of the 50 Krew, and he was a nutter, pure and simple. A grown man when Joe and I were twelve, he was a flaming ginger with a big ginger beard, which often contained remnants of the latest live pig or chicken he had just devoured (or at least that's what I always thought). A truly fearsome character, he had been 'chibbed' a couple of times, with the larger scar running from his right eye to somewhere in the nether reaches of that big, hairy, ginger beard. Rumour had it that Finn had killed three people, including the two who had been foolish enough to chib him. I had nightmares about him.

Unfortunately, those nightmares were about to have added resonance as I stood keeping guard at the front of the tenement while Joe charmed his way to a bigger tip upstairs. I think I shrieked like a girl when a hand was placed on my shoulder. I know I screamed when I turned round and, even though it was dark, the moonlight illuminated the ginger beard and the hair. Finn towered above me.

'Where's the money, ya prick?' Never one for introductions was Finn.

'I . . . I . . . er,' I stammered. By now he had a firm hold of my shoulder, his hands twisting my clothes around.

'Why you wearing a cardigan, by the way?' he asked, throwing me completely. It didn't seem a good time to point out my uncanny resemblance to the curly haired Detective Starsky, so I did what I normally did – I said nothing.

'Where's the money, ya prick?' Finn repeated, his voice more sinister this time. I could smell alcohol, or perhaps boot polish, on his breath. 'Do you want chibbed?' he asked menacingly, moving close enough that I could feel his ginger bristle against my face. I definitely did not want chibbed and would have gladly given him the money, except I didn't have it. Joe did.

'You gonna answer me? Geez the money or get chibbed!' he said emphatically as he produced something sharp from his pocket – probably not a *skean dhu*, but I wasn't looking closely.

'Oi, you . . . Let him go!' It was Joe, confident as always, standing about ten feet back in the garden. Finn turned away from me, momentarily releasing me, the blade still in his hand. 'There's the money, there,' shouted Joe, throwing something across the close floor into the corner. It was hard to see in the dark. Finn turned away from me and started moving towards the package.

'Run!' shouted Joe, and off I went one way, Joe darting the other. Now, while I was rubbish at football, one thing I could do was run. Powered by fear, I streaked down Dormanside Road like Pollok's answer to Forrest Gump, my cardigan billowing in the air behind me. Through the close entrances, I could see Joe, the complete athlete, leaping over fences, while in the background I could hear Finn shouting, 'You're deid! You're chibbed, ya big skinny prick,' but by this time I was running on pure terror, and he wouldn't have caught me if he'd been in Starsky and Hutch's own car.

'What did you give him?' I asked as we met up behind the middens (bins) at Joe's tenement.

'The pieces of jam ma maw made us.' How I wished Joe was here now to watch my back, but got the feeling I need more than him and some pieces of jam to protect me in Big Spring.

8

CHOKER

'HEY ESCOSAIS! WAKE UP MAN, WE need to talk.'
I realised I must have dozed off. The reality of
Big Spring was back upon me in an instant.

I looked down from my bunk and saw a short, bare–
chested and heavily tattooed, Hispanic guy already
walking away from me towards another inmate who,
from his clothing, had obviously also just shown up that
day. Even the back of the man who had called to me
was completely covered in tattoos. He looked like one of
the guys you'd catch on cable late at night on *Inside
America's Nastiest Prisons*. To the other new inmate he spoke
just as brusquely, only in Spanish. I jumped more gingerly
down from my bunk and stood and nodded to the other
new guy, not quite sure yet what the greeting etiquette
was. I felt an idiot, holding onto the rope of my pants
and twisting it round to stop them falling down. I had
thought of taking off my top and showing my finely
honed body and my cool 'poppy' tattoo, but having seen
how muscular this Hispanic guy was and how scary some

of his tattoos were, I thought better of it. I could see he had the names of people on his chest and arms, with a load of dates – I doubted this was to remind him of their birthdays. I also caught sight of a tattoo which I knew from the Internet signified the Surenos gang: a picture of a decapitated King of Spain with bright red blood dripping from his severed head. Somehow my little green and purple thistle with Cara and Calum's names above it suddenly didn't quite seem so menacing.

The Surenos, meaning 'Southerners', were mainly based out of Southern California, and originated as a splinter group from the powerful Mexican Mafia. Often second-generation Mexicans, the rumour was that to join you had to have committed at least one murder or at least stabbed someone and caused significant bleeding. They mainly worked the narcotic trade inside and out of prisons, and also derived a considerable amount of their income from extortion. No one ever left the Surenos – or indeed any of the other gangs – unless it was in a body bag.

The Range was still almost completely empty – everyone had gone back to work, other than half a dozen guys, all Hispanic, playing cards, chatting away in Spanish or just lazing around on their bunks. I also realised there were no cops in the room, nor indeed was there anywhere for them to be positioned. There didn't seem to be any CCTV cameras. Surely we weren't left entirely on our own in here?

It was hot and claustrophobic. Chief was still sitting alone on his bunk drawing away, calm and relaxed. To all the world he looked like he was totally oblivious to what was going on, although I had an idea he was taking everything in.

'*Habla español?*' the heavily tattooed guy asked me.

'Er, no,' I responded quickly.

'OK, my name is Choker,' he said in heavily accented English.

Choker, I thought, gulping. Nice name.

'This ees how it's gonna bee,' he began.

The Sureno Choker guy gonna tell me how it's gonna be, I thought, or else, or else, I'll probably be for the big choke. That's probably how he did his 'hit' to join the Surenos – with his bare hands. My mind was racing ahead and I tried to concentrate on what he was saying.

'. . . respect for each other, respect for your bunkie,' he was saying as I tuned in again. 'When you use the bathroom, leave it clean. Don't leave your hair and shit in the plughole, you clean it out. Lights go out at ten o'clock; some guys have to work kitchen shift so you have to respect them and keep the noise down to a minimum. No music or loud talking tolerated after 10 p.m. That ees a rool. Keep your bunk and your shit tidy. We get inspected once a week and that decides which Range gets to go the chow hall first . . .'

He continued with this bizarre lecture, but by this time I had caught sight of his hands. He had huge hands. I swallowed hard again. He could choke me with just one of them, I thought. 'You cool with what I'm saying, Escosais?' asked Choker, looking right at me.

'Yup, er, yeah. Cool.'

'Cool, Adam?' he said, just as aggressively to the other new guy, who nodded in agreement. He was also Hispanic, medium built, maybe twenty–two or twenty–three. He seemed very edgy and had a decidedly dodgy Errol–Flynn–like pencil moustache that did nothing for him. Choker walked off, induction talk over. His back was just a wall of tattoos. He had only one or two on his arms, so from a distance it looked like he was wearing a dark tank top. He was a lot cooler than Adam.

'You just got in today, Scotland?' piped up Adam, eyeing me. Before I had time to answer, Choker turned around again and came purposefully back towards me.

'Hey, Escosais,' he began, 'you not runnin' with the Whites?'

I wondered why everyone was so interested in who I was runnin' with and I noticed now Chief had stopped drawing and started to watch. I shrugged my shoulders like it was no big deal, and waited nervously to see if this would launch Choker and his giant paws into action.

'Who'd you run with in Pollock?' he asked, clearly not about to let it go. I didn't feel I could be flippant with Choker the way I had been with the ABs, so I tried a different tack this time.

'Oh you're thinking Pollock spelt "ock",' I began slowly. 'I come from the Pollok spelt "o . . . k." OK?' The second OK felt superfluous the minute I'd said it.

'O . . . k . . .' Choker echoed, hesitantly narrowing his eyes, although I couldn't tell if it was a question, a statement, or a spelling.

'Oh . . . kay. Not oh . . . cee . . . kay . . .' I reiterated, scouring him intently for a sign that he'd got my drift.

He shifted his weight awkwardly from one leg to another as he pondered this, looking intently at me the whole time.

'You hung with the Whites in Pollock, though, right?' he continued. This was a minefield but I still didn't feel I could come clean about this mess of my own making.

'Erm, well, everybody is white there . . .' I began to lose the will to live. I could also see Chief chuckling to himself on his bunk, keeping his head down.

Fortunately my evasiveness seemed to be boring Choker and he started looking around, then cut me short by saying, 'Well, just make your mind up soon who you're runnin' with. I don't want to have to be cleaning up after you.' I nodded in agreement, despite having no idea what I might have agreed to.

'*Adam, nosotros te venira ver hasta.*' We will come and see you later. He said this in a very business-like manner, which seemed to please Adam no end. Then he turned and marched off back towards his bunk halfway down the room.

I returned to my bunk and lay down for a while, conscious that there were no seats for me or anyone else. Chief was still drawing, seemingly oblivious to the noise and chatter around him. The room was getting about half full, but many of the bunks around me in my corner, including the one below me, were empty. I wasn't sure whether that made me feel better or worse. At any rate, I'd seen no prison staff for a long time – everything, from the basic induction into the rules, to the handing out of the welcome packs, seemed to be in the hands of the cons. Or more accurately, the gangs.

I suddenly felt very tired again, drained. I was also very hungry. Was it only fourteen hours since I had awakened in my apartment in Houston? I replayed parts of the day in my mind: saying goodbye to Reid, being processed by Malone, getting my Coco the Clown outfit, then the tragic loss of the chocolate bar. I involuntarily shivered when I thought of how much more I could be losing as a result of the bravado I had foolishly displayed. I knew I needed to strike a balance between being tough enough to cope with the aggressiveness of the inmates, while not going far enough to provoke a response. I had to be sure they didn't see me as a soft touch, but I didn't want to have to fight anyone to prove it.

Realising that people were coming in and out of the Range freely, I decided to jump down, more gingerly this time, and have a quick look around the rooms I had briefly seen on my way in. Holding onto my baggy pants, I walked the ten paces or so to the door, but before I could leave Chief called over to me.

'Hey, Scotty,' he said, still not looking up. I turned to face him.

'Fixin' to go out, are ye?' he asked, this time looking up from his drawing.

'I was.'

'OK then. Just don't go too far. Count is in fifteen minutes,' he added, returning to his drawing.

'Count?' No one from the prison had actually explained how anything worked – I was just thrown into the big room in my clown clothes and left to swim or flounder.

'Man,' he beamed a smile. 'You really didn't do much time in Pollock, did you?'

'I guess, I guess people misunderstood me.'

'Oh they misunderstood alright, Scotty,' Chief replied with a chuckle. 'Everyone in the Yard thinks you did fifteen straight in Pollock – that makes you a player, dude; a serious player. That and all that Enron shit. That's why they so interested in who you gonna be runnin' with.'

The 'runnin' with' thing again. The thought of more confrontations like the last one – with other, possibly even meaner gang recruiters – filled me with dread. 'You enjoy your chat with those white boys?' Chief asked, the mischievous grin still playing on his lips.

'Not really,' I said moving closer to him. 'They're not that popular here, right?'

'Some people cause happiness wherever they go. Other people whenever they go,' responded Chief looking up directly at me, his smile gone. 'A count, by the way,' he continued after a brief pause, 'is when the officer done come round and see if your sorry ass is still here where it's supposed to be!'

I motioned to ask if I could sit down on the bunk across from him.

'Sure, that's Kola's bunk, but he's cool. He's one of the Natives.'

'Natives?' I sat uncomfortably on the bottom bunk across from Chief, my head bent forward and neck craning away from the steel frame of the top bunk. 'Who's Kola?'

'I'm Kola.' A man materialised at the foot of the bunk. He had the thickest neck I'd ever seen in my life and a squat body to match, as if he'd just stepped out of a compactor. He wore heavy black glasses – standard prison issue, I found out later – with thick lenses that magnified his eyes to an alarming degree.

'Who the fuck's sitting on my bed?' he asked, the glasses adding weight to the question, as if he might not actually be able to see who was sitting on his bed. I imagine the question had a similar impact on me as Daddy Bear's must have had on Goldilocks.

Before I could leap out of my skin and scarper off his bed, Chief had responded, 'Ni-ya-hey, Kola! This here's Scotty Boy, I told him it was cool for him to sit there. He's new.'

'What's up, Scotty Boy?' said Kola with a smile I couldn't have imagined him carrying just a few seconds earlier. 'You come to hang out with the Injuns in our own mini reservation?'

'Scotty's tribe are from Pollok. In Scotland,' said Chief, clearly enjoying the irony of it.

That got Kola's attention. 'They have a shithole called Pollok in your land too?' he mused, as if he'd found a franchise to rival McDonald's.

'Well, sort of. Not quite the same thing,' I responded, regretting that I had ever uttered the word Pollok in the first place. The lack of space disturbed me and even in changing his clothes, Kola bumped into me two or three times. They were obviously used to it because Chief never batted an eyelid, even on the numerous occasions when Kola's arse came perilously close to his face. I couldn't imagine what it would be like when other inmates came to use the top bunks and there were four people crammed into this tiny area. It began to dawn on me that I was going to lose all sense of privacy or solitude. There was simply no space in this room at all – and it had been arranged that way deliberately, to punish the people in it.

'How come all the beds aren't occupied?' I asked, trying to suppress my rising fears.

'Oh Range Four has only just re-opened since the riot,' answered Chief in a relaxed tone.

'Riot!?'

'All those fucking chomos!' responded Kola, looking and sounding like Daddy Bear again. I resisted the temptation to ask what a chomo was, but I sensed it was bad.

'All the gangs got together for that one, although the Natives would have no part. Even though they are paedophiles and molesters, and I hate every fuckin' one of those sick freaks, we Natives don't take sides and we don't judge unless it's one of our own.'

'So there are child . . . chomos . . . in here? Along with everyone else?'

'Some of those dudes got fucked up real bad,' Chief replied. 'In there.' He motioned with a slight nod of his head towards the shower and toilet room. The proximity to such violence was disconcerting, but not surprising – in the few hours I had already spent in this room, I'd felt the steady undercurrent of aggression and violence. Was this how it always was, or had I just stumbled in on a bad day?

'Are there any, er, chomos in here now?' I asked, anxiously switching my view from one side to another as if they would be easy to spot.

'Hell yeah,' said Chief. 'They done shipped out half the population who instigated the beatings, everyone else got forty-two days lockdown, and then they just invited those motherfucka chomos right back in here.' Kola shook his head in disgust, and I realised that even within this band of thieves, dealers and killers, there was a hierarchy. Everyone knew their place in it, too. Except me.

'COUNT! COUNT TIME!' shouted one of the two officers who suddenly entered the room. 'Stand by your bunks!' One of them had already started off in an anticlockwise direction, the other going clockwise, as inmates scrambled towards their beds. I got there double-quick, only to notice that a number of others, such as the large-handed Choker, just ambled along back to theirs, still chatting, seemingly impervious to the authority of the officers.

The room smoothly descended into silence as all radios and chatting ceased and everyone stood quietly by their bunks. It made me aware of just how noisy it had been before – so many men crammed into one room will do that. For some reason I felt nervous, my heart racing again as I waited to be counted, firstly by the anticlockwise officer (squat, partially bald, round faced and slow moving) and the clockwise guy (the handlebar-moustached man I recognised from before, almost jogging round). Both were white, I noted, as nearly all the officers seemed to be, except for a couple of Hispanic ones I had passed on my way in earlier. I hadn't seen one black officer and I wondered if there was any significance in that in an environment where race seemed to be the single most important social signifier, next to being a 'chomo'.

The count finished quickly, but not before I heard the short squat guard confirm to Village People that there were thirty-seven inmates – less than half full. Given how noisy and claustrophobic it already seemed, I wondered how I'd cope when we got up to the full complement. Having exchanged notes on the number, the two officers departed just as quickly, ostentatiously slamming the door to the room shut behind them. Everyone started moving around again and the radios and chatter resumed as I climbed back up onto my bunk. The radios were predominantly playing Hispanic music – bland, continuous, the sort of thing you might hear if you were trapped in an elevator in a Mexican department store. I familiarised myself with my rock–like pillow and tried to imagine what the rest of this excruciating day would hold.

Staring at the ceiling for a while, I shut my eyes and tried to concentrate on some of the positives. In the last few years I had developed a habit of saying thank you for ten things each night before I fell asleep. Despite all my difficulties, I'd always managed to find at least ten and wondered if even today I might still have a shot at it. I had a nice corner location, had met a couple of nice native Indians and survived my initial skirmish with the Aryan Brotherhood. No one had tried to stab me or beat me and Choker had resisted the temptation to check out my collar size – on the whole a pretty positive start. I knew that the first few days and weeks would probably determine how things went for my whole sentence here in Big Spring. Make a good start, and I'd have a reason-able chance of surviving the rest. And that was the plan. Survive. Get home. Find Cara. Love Calum. Everyone needed a plan.

Some of my roomies had already started queuing at the front of the locked door to our room, in expectation of being fed. Many had their own plates and cutlery, although I noticed there were no knives. Mind you, I reflected, a fork could be just as dangerous in the wrong hands, and many of the hands here seemed pretty wrong. There was an excited chatter as I heard the assortment of tattooed gang–bangers discussing what was likely to be on the menu that day. Others stood with a wide array of ingredients, I guessed for use in the small kitchen area.

The chow hall just represented another challenge. I had thought of maybe not going while I was wearing the neon outfit, but having been tantalised by a Nazi's bar of chocolate – white chocolate, no doubt – I was hungry now, and I realised I'd best face this sooner rather than later. But in all my nightmares of prison, the dining hall was where a lot of it kicked off – the gladiatorial arena. In those nightmares, if it wasn't going off in the shower, then it was going on in the dining room. Even if there was no outright violence involved, I imagined myself pathetically meandering from table to table, unable to sit anywhere, until everyone started pointing and laughing at me. Maybe I would just stay on my bunk, at least until I had normal prison clothes and could blend in with the other inmates.

Kola had come over to my bunk and was stepping up on the bed below to get a look out of the window.

'Any movement out there, Scotty?' he asked, craning his neck to see. Other than a few birds flying in and out, the no-man's-land between Sunset and Sunrise was completely deserted. 'They call the diabetics and other sickies first,' he said, still peering out of the window. 'Then they call it in order of the cleanest Range. They inspect us once a week,' he added smiling at me, 'so make sure your bed is always made and all your shit is put away. You don't want to cause us to be last out down to chow hall. 'Cause then your roomies would have a problem with you.'

'You mean Choker would come and visit me?' I said, in a lame attempt at humour.

'Who's Choker?' asked Kola bemused. I nudged over my head in the direction of a smiling Choker, currently chatting away happily to some of his compadres in the corner. Kola looked across and then smiled.

'Oh, you mean Joker? Yeah, he's a funny guy.' He shook his head. 'I thought you said Choker!' he laughed.

Too embarrassed to admit my mistake, I just smiled back. 'Guess it's my Scottish accent,' I said sheepishly.

At that moment, I heard the door to our Range being unlocked and a shout of 'Diabetics and meds!' echoing through the room. Looking back out of the window, I saw them start to emerge. Wheelchairs, crutches, crooked and broken bodies, shuffling and sliding as they funnelled out from the main central exit, fanning out into the dusty space between the buildings and then starting to head down towards the left, where I assumed the food hall must be located.

'Would you look at those poor fuckers?' mused Kola quietly. It seemed to me even the birds around my bird house had stopped their activities and were watching this awful spectacle as the sick inmates shuffled torturously towards their food. I saw two guys who only had one leg apiece, and a few others missing an arm, in each case with no prosthetics, maybe in case they used them as a weapon. Without wanting to, my mind's eye conjured up an image of some crazy white supremacist guy suddenly unscrewing his false arm and beating my head open after I had upset him in the dining room by asking for the salt. I had to try to stop thinking things like that. And still the 'meds' came out, each one slower than the last, their steps painfully crooked, misshaped and full of misery. Was every sick or disabled person in Texas in this jail?

Without thinking, I mumbled to Kola, 'It looks like the opening scene to Michael Jackson's "Thriller" video.'

'Shit!' exclaimed Kola, turning round to Chief. 'You hear what Scotty dog just done said?'

'Nope.'

'Said those poor fuckers out there look like the start of that Michael Jackson video.'

Chief stared at me. I wasn't sure if he was upset, bewildered or just furious. 'The "Thriller" video,' I added lamely.

There was another dreadful pause, and then the Chief erupted in gales of laughter, joined, to a lesser extent, by Kola. I had no choice but to smile along with them, realising as I did so that this was the second time I'd been smiling on this, the most awful of days.

'Come on, Scotty dog,' said Kola as he got down from the bunk and slapped me on the foot. 'Come and have chow with the Natives.' I knew I had to be careful about trusting people in this place, and I knew that one of my weaknesses (in this environment, at any rate) was that I tended to trust everyone. But I couldn't help liking Chief and Kola. I'd always liked the Indians more than the cowboys whenever I used to watch those Saturday afternoon Westerns on BBC2 with my mum when I was a little boy. I would sit at her legs in front of the fire, and she would sometimes aimlessly play with my curls, rolling them between her fingers – one of my fondest memories from childhood. My brothers, Mark and Michael, used to like the cowboys, who invariably won, but my Mum and I supported the Injuns!

Kola and Chief seemed like a couple of decent Injuns to me, I thought, wondering for the first time what they were in for. Wondering, too, why they hadn't asked me why I was there. How did they know I wasn't a chomo? 'What's the prison etiquette about asking this stuff?' I wondered, as I started putting away my Correctional Rules for the Big Spring Correctional Facility in my locker.

'You don't want to read all that shit,' said Chief, shuffling up beside me. 'What you need to know to survive in here isn't written down anywhere!' he added, with a smile. Kola nodded enthusiastically. I felt how close they were both standing to me and realised they were oblivious to the fact that in the outside world this level of intimacy would be considered odd, but I tried not to let my discomfort show as we stood there, all three of us compressed between the lockers and bunks.

'Let's go before chow's finished,' said Chief as he slapped me on the back.

Once we left our Range and got into the corridor we were soon moving at snail's pace, as inmates were streaming down from every direction towards the only exit from the Sunset building. There were hundreds of people, and it felt like slowly moving through a football crowd. I was anxious not to make eye contact with anyone, but I noticed quite a few people checking me out – I wasn't difficult to spot with my day one attire on. Chief told me later that he thought it wasn't the outfit so much as that I just looked 'different'. 'You look all European or somethin',' – that was his verdict.

Chief was right beside me as we slowly filed along. 'OK, Scotland. First thing you need to know is we have controlled movement here. That means five to and five past the hour are the only times you can move around

the prison, except weekends when there is free movement until 5 p.m. If you miss the move, you stay in
whatever section of the facility you are in until five to
the hour again.'

The heat and the crush of bodies was bothering me,
but I tried to put it out of my mind. So many of the
characters around me looked intimidating. For a moment,
I wished I was shorter and not so visible. I thought about
crouching a little, but reminded myself to try and stand
tall and not look fazed. I desperately wanted to get out
into the evening air and breathe, but when we finally
did reach the exit, the heat offered little respite.

'There are three counts a day,' Chief continued, oblivious to my discomfort. 'One at 6.45 a.m., one at 1.30 p.m.
after lunch, or 5 p.m. on a weekend, and an evening
roll-call at 9 p.m. Don't miss the count and stand still
by your bunk or else it's serious shit.'

'Burritos tonight!' interjected Kola, with considerable
relish.

'Ah, I hate Mexican food,' I said, to no one in
particular.

Both Kola and Chief stared at me. 'Shiiit!! You are
gonna starve then, man!' Chief exclaimed. 'That's all they
serve here. Burritos, tortillas an' all that shit. The kitchen's
overrun with Mexicans.'

This was another blow. I hate spicy food, and I had
avoided Mexican fare like the plague in the twenty-two
months I had lived in Houston – which had not been
an easy thing to do. What with the heat and the Mexican
food, this place was a Scotsman's Hell.

'Next thing you need to learn is how to queue,' said
Kola, as we crept towards the hall itself.

'Fortunately, one thing we all got plenty of is time,' Chief quipped. There was an awkward pause for a minute or two as the queue continued to creep slowly forward. 'How much time d'you get Scotland?' he added, clearly having decided it was time to ask a key question. Both he and Kola were looking at me expectantly.

'Just over three years,' I said quietly, looking straight at them for a reaction.

'Shit, that ain't nuthin',' said Kola disparagingly, as Chief looked right at me, his smile gone and his head shaking. Kola had turned his back on me – not overly dramatically, but I felt there was some message in it. It was as if I had seemed alright, then let them down.

'That's short, Scotland. Short. You're short already. Three years ain't nuthin',' Chief confirmed. 'Most guys here got at least ten or fifteen. Shit, Kola here got twenty.' There was silence for a moment or two as the shortness of my sentence (which seemed a lifetime to me) was digested further. Chief turned around to me again.

'Why'd they bring you all the way out here to Big Spring if you only got three?' he asked, looking at me closely.

'I don't know why I'm here,' I answered honestly. 'No one told me, no one explained. My co–ds (co–defendants) both got nicer prisons on the coast – I guess I just got unlucky,' I said, feeling very, very unlucky at that moment.

'What your co–ds get?' said Kola, suddenly spinning round quickly to face me again. The atmosphere had changed, and I could tell that this conversation was taking on some new significance and that it held dangers for me. A few others around us seemed to have tuned in and stopped their own conversations, seemingly waiting for my response. It was suddenly very quiet, and I felt under threat. The heat only added to my confusion. I wanted to tell them to fuck off, to walk away and eat on my own, but realised that wasn't an option.

'They got thirty-seven months like me,' I answered slowly and precisely, watching for a response and resenting the implication behind the question. It wasn't my fault I had such a short sentence. It seemed long enough to me. And what was everyone staring at?

'What?' I said to Kola, deciding to confront the situation. 'Do you want to ask me something?' Still nothing was said. So I said it for them.

'Bank robbery,' I said, breaking the tension. 'I'm supposed to have robbed a bank.' I figured that saying I breached my employment contract would sound ridiculous. I saw Chief raise his eyebrows a little and nod his head lightly, as if in approval.

The queue began to move again and that seemed to ease the tension further. Kola had his back to me again and we continued to slowly edge forward towards the burritos. Chief put his arm on my shoulder after a minute or two and told me not to mind his brother, Kola. He had just had his sentence reviewed and had failed to get it reduced, so was very sore at the moment. It was nothing personal.

'He was worried you might be a rat. That you got a light sentence because you testified against your co-ds, that's all.'

The truth was that the Department of Justice (DoJ) had approached the three of us repeatedly to see if we would 'rat out' on each other, every deal offered slightly better than the last one, and always with the promise of a thirty-five-year sentence for the ones left fighting.

'First one to plead out gets the best deal,' the US prosecutor had gleefully told the three of us, as we arrived in court in Houston the day after my introduction to Marshal Dave. It was, in fact, the only words someone from the DoJ would ever speak to me – before then or since. Of course, at that stage we were all sure we would win and had privately mocked him later. 'Twat,' I had called him. 'And a cocky twat, at that.'

Of course he had the right to be cocky; in a Federal prosecution the US Government hold all the cards. After eighteen months in Houston and four trial delays our resolve had weakened; a lack of access to witnesses – few of whom were willing to expose themselves to the glare of the world's press or be associated with anything connected to Enron – had just about finished us off. Around that point the DoJ approached Giles with an offer that he could go home immediately if he pleaded guilty.

'If you don't plead, we'll go to Bermingham next (David), then Mulgrew. One of you will be home for Christmas,' the cocky twat had added. Reid was worried Giles would plead out, and Dan Cogdell, David's lawyer, even more so. But I wasn't worried. Giles and I had been great friends for over twenty years, since I had first moved to London and started working with him. Giles was godfather to Cara Katrina, and I to Lucy, his third-born. And besides, we weren't guilty of what they had accused us of.

'Have you seen your buddy in the last few days?'

Cogdell asked me one day, when I rolled up, late as usual, for our bi-weekly meeting in his downtown Houston office. Jimmy, David's other lawyer, was watching me expectantly. I was always a lot closer to Giles than David, and for much of our time in Houston we had hung out together when we could find a lawyer to be there, the judge having ordered that we couldn't be alone together without the presence of an attorney. He hadn't specified what kind of attorney though, so we had co-opted Troy, a local lawyer more used to dealing with traffic offences or minor drug infractions, enticing him with beer and tacos. He'd even joined a five-a-side 'soccer' team with us, playing in a weekly league. And it worked well – except when he was late for a match, when I'd tell Giles I wasn't allowed to pass to him, judge's orders.

'I haven't seen Giles for a couple of days,' I admitted, sitting down and wondering for the first time if there was any significance in that.

'So no one has seen him since the DoJ contacted him to do a deal?' Dan sighed, leaning forward. 'Schwartzy? Did you get that?' he asked, speaking loudly into the speaker-phone. I hadn't realised David Schwartz, a key leg of my legal team, was on the speaker-phone from his Washington office.

'Yup, I heard it,' said David in an I-told-you-so tone. David did most of the day-to-day work with me on the case. Like Reid and Kevin, he had become a good friend and had a tremendously inquisitive mind.

'Hi David,' I said, trying to sound positive.

'Hi Gary,' a much more morose-sounding David responded. The atmosphere became leaden. Jimmy stood up and looked out of the window.

'Come on guys, Giles wouldn't talk to them,' I said, looking at their unconvinced faces. Even my own voice sounded like it had lost the edge of certainty.

The room was oppressively still and Dan was just gathering himself up to say something else when the door opened and in bounded Giles, meatball sandwich in hand, full of energy and smiling happily.

'Hey. How's it going?' he said, seating himself in the middle of the room. He unwrapped his sandwich and leaned forward and took a bite. Wiping his lips with a napkin, he became suddenly aware of the silence. He looked quickly from face to face, staring a little longer at mine.

'What? What?' he asked all of us, still taking mouthfuls of his sandwich.

Dan leaned forward across the table, just opposite Giles. 'Hi Giles. Nice to see you. I was wondering if you'd spoken to your buddy Leo, the prosecutor?' asked Dan, getting straight to the point. Giles stopped chewing. He looked again from one of us to the next, again resting his eyes longer on me – no doubt the focus of his disappointment. He carefully placed his sandwich down, his appetite seemingly lost.

'Oh, I get it. I get it,' he began, addressing the table initially. 'You want to know if I've ratted out on you to get myself home?' he asked, raising his head to face us. I couldn't look at him. How could I have doubted my good friend for even a second?

'Well Giles,' said Dan in a very precise, calm, lawyerly fashion, 'it must be a big temptation for you.' I liked Dan. When we had first arrived in Houston and the judge had released us on tag, Dan had stepped up to the plate and said we could stay at his house – all three of us – until we could find somewhere to live. Although those first two weeks staying in his daughter's bedroom had been difficult, I'd never forgotten his kindness. He was also a great guy to socialise with, very charismatic and funny. But this wasn't the side we were seeing now.

'Do you think this is about me? Do you think any of this is about me!?' Giles began. He looked disgusted with us, and I averted my eyes as he suddenly pointed at me.

'It's about him!' he continued, the emotion bubbling up in his voice. 'It's about his daughter, Cara Katrina. My goddaughter! It's about his son waiting at home for him to come back. It's about David's children and his wife Emma; my girls, my family, my friends; the thousands of people who supported us on Friends Extradited; all the people who marched in London.' By now all of our heads were hanging.

'Do you think I would even contemplate it for a second? Do you think I would put you two in jail, while I went home and lived my life knowing I'd ratted you out to save my own skin? Do you think I could get up each day and ever look at myself in the mirror again . . .?' He left the last question hanging indignantly in the air. Thankfully Dan spoke, still calm and assured.

'Sorry Giles, we needed to ask. It must be a temptation . . .' he said quietly.

'Needed to ask? Needed to ask?' Giles almost shrieked, the strain clear in his voice. 'Don't you know how desperately I want to see my girls!? Do you have any concept of how much I miss them, of how much I miss my fucking life?' He was standing up now, leaning directly over the table. I felt ashamed. I raised my hand to him to calm him down, but he just flicked it away. His heavy breathing dominated the room. David was looking at the table while Dan still looked calmly at Giles, compassion in his eyes. Giles's breathing seemed to ease as he began to speak again, more quietly this time.

'No matter how much I'd give to go home,' he began, slowly and deliberately, 'I would never, ever, even contemplate doing it at someone else's expense.' I had a surge of pride in him and wanted to stand up, hug him and say 'I told you so' to the others – and to myself. Unfortunately, David got in before me.

'Giles,' he began softly enough. 'Dan was only checking because he's got to ask.'

That was pretty diplomatic for David, but barely waiting for him to finish, Giles picked up the rest of his tomato and meatball sandwich and hurled it across the room, shouting, 'Fuck you! Fuck the lot of you. Why don't YOU go do a deal, fuckers?' as he stormed out of the room.

David and Jimmy gazed on in shock as Giles hurled the sandwich at them, and in a scene reminiscent of the movie *Pulp Fiction*, they looked firstly at their pristine shirts, both miraculously untouched, and then to the wall behind them, which was festooned with dripping meatballs and tomato sauce, sliding slowly down to the floor. They both grinned foolishly as they realised they hadn't been hit.

'What just happened?' a disembodied David Schwartz asked from the safety of the speaker-phone.

'Giles just launched a meatball sandwich at Bermingham and Jimmy,' a chirpy Cogdell responded.

'He missed,' Dan added.

'Shame,' said David, his meaning not entirely clear.

*   *   *

By the time I had entered the chow hall, Kola had relaxed and was explaining a little more about how the prison operates. The dining hall was swarming with inmates and filled with the smell of burritos. We queued along the left-hand wall and collected our trays just near the far end of the hall. There had to be at least five hundred inmates eating at any one time – a third of the total population – and I guessed the slowly moving queue was partly necessary to regulate the flow of inmates. At the top of the hall was a series of aluminium counter-tops where kitchen staff served the inmates – cups of water, bread rolls, then the dreaded burritos and the fillings. Many inmates had their own plates and cutlery, otherwise you used the plastic plates, and the combined fork and spoon called a 'spork' on offer beside the trays.

The dining room was split in two by a rather incongruous salad bar in the centre and another water fountain. But the main split was on racial lines. The Blacks occupied about half of the space on the far side of the hall. The Hispanics filled in the rest of that side and almost half as much space again in the near side of the hall. Then there was a small gathering of Natives, where I guessed we would head, and then an enclave of no more than forty or fifty Whites just beside the Indians. I tried not to look at them, but I could sense they were looking over and I quickly picked out SlumDawg and Tattoo Chest. They were looking right at me and pointing me out to a particularly nasty-looking skinhead, who appeared to have been sculpted, badly, out of white putty. I was too far away to make out his tattoos, but I guessed they were the usual array of artistic delights. Kola was talking to me, but I was barely listening. I was concentrating on not making an idiot of myself as each inmate served me, and also trying not to get too distracted by the continuous assault on my senses from every direction. At the end of the food queue there was a drink fountain offering some strange coloured juices and then to the right of them a section occupied largely by white men sitting either alone or occasionally with one other.

'Chomos and psychos,' whispered Kola as he caught the direction of my gaze. I saw Spiderman sitting there alone, and recalled his rancid breath and the spittle on my face as I crossed the Yard.

'Total fucking psycho,' Kola said emphatically, following my gaze. 'You stay as far away from that motherfucka as you can!' he elaborated, as he lifted his tray and led the way over to what I hoped was the relative security of the Natives' enclave.

The burritos were every bit as bad as I imagined, and I picked at my food until Kola asked for it and quickly devoured it. The chat was mainly about the mundanities of prison life, but it was all useful information for me and I listened without saying anything. The enormity of this day and the reality of the life ahead of me in Big Spring were hitting me both at once. When we had finished, we returned the trays to the side of the kitchen area and walked past the two cops checking people periodically for food theft from the kitchen. It occurred to me again how few guards or cops there were around and how much we were left to our own devices throughout the prison.

'That's how they like it,' Chief told me. 'The prison is really policed by the gangs.'

'How do I find out about them?' I asked.

'They'll find out about you. They'll know already you ain't running with the ABs. They'll come to you soon enough,' he continued, this time without a smile.

By now I'd reached information overload. Kola was going for a walk at the top of the Yard but I was drained and wanted just to head back to the Range and to try and sleep. That felt like the safest option. Chief came back with me and returned to his drawing. I envied the solitude he seemed able to find, as I lay silently on my bunk and thought as little about Big Spring and as much about home as I could. Chief had confirmed to me that it would take at least three or four weeks before I'd be able to make a telephone call as all my numbers had to be submitted on a set form each Tuesday (today was Wednesday), then pre-approved before I could dial them. I had already told Calum I didn't want him to come and see his father in this place and I was glad now I had made that choice. Letters and phone calls would prob- ably be my only contact with the outside world. The pre-approval process involved the prison calling the number to ask the householder if they wanted to accept a call from you. Chief told me that was often the moment a new inmate would find out his relationship was over, or that friendships you thought would endure had not. 'Shit, that's the day some dudes find out even their own mothers don't want nuthin' to do with them no more,' he told me whilst shaking his head.

In the same way, it would be a few weeks before my 'account' would be open, allowing me to use the prison shop on my one allotted time per week (also a Tuesday) and obtain vital supplies like paper and pens, stamps, tea, coffee, toiletries and shower shoes. I thought again of SlumDawg and more wistfully of the chocolate and other goodies they'd offered me. It seemed strange that the prison authorities would ensure that you had absolutely nothing and were so isolated for the first few weeks on entering prison just when you were most vulnerable to extortion – a situation that played right into the hands of the gangs and must bolster their power. Surely they must realise that this was how things worked? But then I was already beginning to sense an uneasy truce between the guards and the gangs – almost a 'live and let live' approach.

Too intimidated to try the TV room, and with nowhere else to sit, I lay back down on my bunk. My bed was narrow and rock hard, and I wondered if I would roll off the top bunk during the night and fall the six feet to the concrete floor below. I needed the bathroom again, but couldn't face making that trip and having to deal with the next nutcase or psycho. I may have started drifting off to sleep, when I felt a nudge and saw two grinning Indians looking up at my bunk.

'Here Scotland,' they said, 'it's not much,' before offering me a coffee and a few broken biscuits, some writing paper and a pen. 'And before you ask,' added Kola smiling, 'no, you can't join the Natives' gang!' Before I could thank them, they had turned and headed back to their bunks. I wondered, as I drank the coffee and demolished the biscuits, if I'd ever been given a more beautiful gift. With that thought, though, came a sense of unease. I wanted prison to be black and white for me, full of bad guys that I could keep my distance from, convinced in my mind that I wasn't like them. That would make it so much easier to get through my time here. Acts of compassion or generosity just complicated things. I was starting to like these guys already, which was the last thing I wanted.

The nine o'clock count came and went and no one else approached me. No one noticed me as I lay there wondering how life could take such twists and turns and lead you to a moment such as this. I tried to block out the incessant noise and wondered again how I'd cope as the Range filled up. At ten o'clock exactly, the lights went dim, but they did not go out, and an uncanny quiet descended upon the room. I sat up on my bunk and looked around and watched the overhead lights flickering weakly. So the lights never went out in Big Spring. I smiled to myself as I thought how that was one fear I didn't have to face. There would always be at least a little light, a little hope – a simile for my life here, perhaps. Maybe one day I'd get my life back, get back to my children. It was surprisingly chilly at night as the air-conditioning seemed to finally kick in, and that was a welcome respite. I pulled both my thin blankets around my shoulder and repositioned my pillows. I turned to face the wall and started to count ten good things from this most traumatic of days. And I found them, more easily than I found sleep.

9

TOILET CLEANING

'**M**ULGREW!'

'Yo!' I shouted, quite impressed with my response.

An officer with a clipboard was standing near the centre of the room as I leapt down from my bunk. After a restless and difficult night, I'd been awake for a few hours watching the other inmates get dressed and head off to work.

'I'm Mulgrew,' I said moving towards him while hanging onto my huge pants. He barely looked at me, instead just offering up a bucket with a couple of tired-looking brushes in it.

'Latrine duty!' he said matter-of-factly, as I took the limited cleaning equipment off him.

'Oh, right,' I said trying not to sound too crestfallen.

'$7 a month pay, until further notice. Sign here for the equipment and remember to return it when you're done,' he said brusquely.

I signed an official form stating that I acknowledged

that the loo brushes and detergent were Federal Government property and that I faced at least another 140 years' imprisonment if I dared pinch any of it. With that, the officer was gone and my on-the-job training was over. Most of my other 'roomies' had already departed and I was alone, other than a few waifs and strays, and a small group of Hispanics down near the end of the room who never seemed to actually work. Among them was the fearsome Joker, who I could see was rubbing his big hands together, laughing and joking again.

I tied up my balloon pants as tight as I could, rolled up the legs and headed over to one of the two toilet rooms. It seemed the air-con was ineffective during the day, so the heat was oppressive. I wasn't wearing my ridiculously tight T-shirt, having already decided I had to go bare-chested if I was going to survive the heat for even one day in this room. That made me feel more vulnerable, but many others in the room were bare-chested and it was just too sticky to put my tight T-shirt back on.

My cleaning equipment consisted of a bucket, a scrubbing brush that you would typically use to wash dishes, and a heavy, hard brush for scrubbing those particularly tricky spots. In addition, there were about ten small packets of some kind of powder – maybe ammonia or bleach or some combination of the two. With that I was good to go. I stood there for a moment trying to figure out where to start, when a Hispanic guy I had noticed the night before came up and spoke to me.

'Hey Escosais. You want to clean this one or the other one?'

'Are they any different?' I asked, to which he smiled and said, 'I think the other one sees more action from *el gordo hombres.*' The fat guys.

I smiled back. 'I'll do this one then.'

'*Tu habla español?*'

'A little, *un poco*,' I answered, annoyed at myself for letting that slip.

'OK, I will start in the other one. Don't fuck around with me, Escosais,' he added, his smile suddenly gone. 'If you don't clean good, I have to clean after you. *Comprende?*'

I nodded, nervously. He was maybe around thirty, well built, with a handsome face and a decent bushy moustache. Like me, he wore no top, but he had shorts on and some decent shower shoes. He had a couple of tattoos on his muscular forearms but I couldn't see them properly without staring.

'Should take no more than two hours then we done for the day, but don't ask for the mop until later so the cops don't know we're done. OK, Escosais?'

'OK, I got it,' I said relaxing a little. This was getting easier. I could do 'cool', I was Escosais, Scotland, the new cool kid on the block. 'Hey man, what's your name?' I asked trying to move a step forward, wondering if I should have used the word 'man'.

He smiled. 'They call me Gateau,' he said raising his fist into bump mode.

'Oh, like the cake!' I said, way too quickly, thinking French, not Spanish.

'Erm . . . no. *Gato*, like the Spanish word for a cat,' he said, giving me a dubious look, and turning his fists around to show a huge cat tattoo on each forearm.

'God, you're a diddy,' I thought as I mechanically bumped his fist. So much for trying to act cool. Who the hell would call themselves 'the Cake' in prison, unless perhaps the Pillsbury Doughman got banged up? The two huge tattoos of cats on his forearms, I learned later, were the mark of a renowned burglar. No building or bank was too difficult for the man I'd called 'the Cake' to enter. I shuddered to think what kind of tattoo I deserved.

I'd had loads of different jobs in my life. I started selling rolls in Dormanside Road with Joe at the age of nine, before we graduated to the newspaper run together. After I had been indicted by the Americans in 2002, Joe and I – still the closest of friends – bought a building company in Lewes called Allen & Joy, giving it a legal name of 'Dormanside Rd Limited'. Ironically, NatWest ended up lending me more capital to set up my new business ventures than I was ever supposed to have stolen from them in the first place. All this in spite of my indictment being plastered all over the Internet and attracting so much publicity. That's what I call a loyal bank.

Throughout my life, whenever I did any job, I tried to do it well, no matter how horrible or boring it was. I took the same attitude with the latrines. I had always worked. I'd even spent a whole summer shovelling shit, so cleaning the bogs for eighty inmates wasn't going to faze me. It was, of course, quite a contrast from my time spent working in the City, then New York and Tokyo. I'd worked throughout Asia, Europe and Latin America, at one point becoming NatWest's youngest Managing Director, with a few hundred people reporting to me. I'd made it to the so-called top from a very low starting point, but now here I was, cleaning toilets in a Texas penitentiary. 'So be it,' I thought, because deep down I felt in some ways I deserved it. It was six years since they had indicted me, and although I didn't believe what I was supposed to have done constituted a crime, in time I had considered that in some ways it was a moot point. There was a greater wrong there; a wider offence against society. Despite my humble upbringing, somewhere along the road to success I had taken a wrong turn. The one benefit of a poor childhood should have been a heightened sense of responsibility towards the less fortunate. Instead, by the peak of my career, I ran a group whose one purpose was to take the accounting or tax rules and find ways to 'mitigate' (or avoid) them for the benefit of our clients.

New rules would come into play, designed to ensure that big corporations paid the appropriate levels of tax. The assembled geniuses in my group, managed and cajoled by me, would then spend all their time figuring out how to get around those rules while still staying on the right side of the law. At some point someone in Enron decided to go a step further but that was just the step into illegality – the step into immorality had been taken by all of us, myself included, some time before.

The more tax or accounting benefits we gleaned for our clients, the more we were paid. The more we bent the rules, the harder people would try to straighten them, until we found kinks in them again. We were producing nothing, making a negative contribution to society, just making ourselves and our already rich clients even more wealthy, and deluding ourselves that we were of value. Hardly any of us ever thought through the consequences or gave consideration to the morality of these actions – in the world of banking, such an approach would have been thought suspect. You had to be in that industry to win – otherwise someone else would quickly take your place.

But I did think about it. And I should have known better. I was from a different background – I understood that when one group gets ridiculously rich, another gets catastrophically poor – yet because I was on the right side of the line this time, I played along. The truth of it was that when I got paid the big bucks I enjoyed it – not so much for the money itself, but for the validation it gave a working–class boy from a children's home in Glasgow. It felt like I had beaten the system, managed to stand up for myself and achieve something in a world where people like me didn't belong.

But now at the end of it all, I stood in a Texas prison, looking at the urinals with my bucket and brushes in my hand, with an overpowering sense that I'd been found out, and placed where I really belonged. Maybe I deserved this prison after all; maybe I deserved a lot worse. I had climbed the ladder of success only to realise I'd perched my ladder against the wrong wall. One thing I didn't feel – didn't allow myself to feel – was sorry for myself. The sad thing was I was boxed in. I knew if I lived my life a hundred times over, I would still have needed that success, that validation, that sense of achieve-ment and belonging. I would have done the same thing over and over again. All the roads led me here.

I walked over to the urinals and got down on my hands and knees and started to scrub, with an intense sense of starting all over again. This was the beginning of the way back, the nadir, the low point. I gave them a pretty decent scrubbing using the magic powder supplied in each of the packets. They weren't too bad, other than an initial scuttling of cockroaches as I disturbed them, and I was grinding along thinking I would be easily finished within an hour. That changed a bit when I got into the first cubicle. Getting down on my hands and knees again I started scrubbing hard. Then I looked under the rim and saw that it was total carnage.

'Man, this hasn't had a good scrub in a long time,' I thought as I started applying a little elbow grease to my work, part of me perversely amused by how eagerly some journalists would have leapt on this final fall from grace. I could imagine the headlines and that amused me further. To keep my mind off how disgusting the job was, I challenged myself to come up with some other positives about my new position while I kept scrubbing. I thought of my commute first of all. I had a good – no actually, change that – an outstanding commute. I used to travel up to an hour and forty-five minutes to get in and out of the City, now I only had to walk about forty-five steps to the urinals. Instead of having responsibility for a few hundred employees and the good name of the bank, I now only had to be sure not to piss off 'Gato the Cat'.

I was thinking about what other positives there might be, and getting up quite a sweat as I continued to dislodge some serious human debris from under the rim, when I noticed two bare-chested Hispanics standing outside the cubicle watching me and chatting. Tuning into their conversation, I picked up a couple of words here and there. *'Gringo, vea, bueno, rodillos, limpian,'* which I guessed basically meant 'good to see a white boy on his knees cleaning.'

Ignoring them, I just kept on belting into the Great Rim Challenge, periodically adjusting my position to glance over at them both still standing there, arms folded, fascinated, it seemed, by Scottish cleaning techniques. Eventually I stood up, accepting of the fact that I was a sinner, a flawed man, sweating heavily both from my body and forehead. It was so hot that even the simplest exertion resulted in you being bathed in sweat. I was significantly taller and bigger than the Hispanic guys, but they both looked muscular and unfazed by the size differential. The front one's entire torso was covered in tattoos – testimony to a long and distinguished career in some Latino gang, no doubt. He also wore a bandana, which I had to admit made him much cooler looking than me with my baggy pants and Coco the Clown shoes.

The second guy was also covered in gang memorabilia and looked just as intimidating. As I looked at him I noticed a nasty facial scar, which gave him an even more fearsome look. Both sported moustaches, which pigeon-holed them as 'two wee Mexicans' in the complex filing system my mind had set up to figure out who was who in the Big Room. I was quickly realising, however, that the category of 'a wee Mexican with a moustache' covered about 60% of the room, and I was going to have to work on my descriptive techniques.

'I haven't cleaned those two toilets in there if you need to go,' I said slowly and in English, turning and pointing to the two other stalls next to me and hoping that might make them go away.

'No. We use this one!' said the leading Mexican emphatically with a big grin that revealed a couple of whopping big gold teeth, as his buddy nodded in agreement. Thrown by his gaudy gnashers and by his strong lavatorial preferences I hesitated for a moment, wondering what was so special about this particular little palace. I looked around for a moment, sighed, thought disappointingly about my half-finished rim job, placed my brushes and powders back into my bucket, and started to head out.

'No, *cabrone*!' said my friendly little Mexican gangbanger, this time looking not nearly so friendly. His hand was out in front of him in the universally known 'stop' sign, so I duly obeyed 'You clean. I shit. Then you clean again!' He smiled once more to re-emphasis the expensive nature of his dental work. This stumped me. I never faced this type of situation at NatWest.

'Yeez,' added his number two in much more heavily accented English, 'then I sheet. You clin and I sheet again.'

His English wasn't great, but I got the general picture.

'What do you do now, smartarse?' I asked myself, staring at the two grinning *hombres*. Of course, in the movies, this would be the bit where I stuck the bucket over their heads, nutted one of them, kicked the other one in the balls, stuck one of their heads down the toilet and flushed it. But these guys looked tough and were probably well versed in dealing with the whole 'gringos in the toilet' sketch. One thing for sure, though, I wasn't about to get on my hands and knees and start scrubbing again, let them shit, and then start cleaning again. Fuck that. I was sure that would go round the room in about two seconds and next thing I would be hand-wiping anyone's backside who wanted it. I felt my heart start to race – I had a decision to make.

It seemed too early in the morning for someone to be beating up another inmate; I always thought that kind of stuff would happen after the watershed at 10 p.m. Hoping I was right, I smiled, picked up my little brush and theatrically threw it into my bucket. Then I picked up the bucket and slowly walked out past the two of them, trying to emphasise, as best I could, my height advantage over them. I didn't look long at them – just the briefest eye contact in case they went for me (at which point my plan was to hit one of them as hard as I could, Sergei-style). Instead I just brushed past them, skin briefly touching skin (much to my discomfort) as I moved out of the bathroom across the room and hauled myself up onto my bunk in a ceremonial huff. I lay back and looked straight at the ceiling above, waiting for the fallout to come, my heart racing, my breathing heavy as I wondered if my penance was about to deepen.

They never came.

Half an hour or so later, I was back in cleaning the stalls, having given up on stall #1 as I couldn't bring myself to re-enter, it having so recently seen action. Gato had come over and was helping me out with the sinks. 'Those two guys like to play around with all the new cleaners?' I asked the Cat, as we scrubbed two adjacent sinks.

'No *cabrone*,' he began seriously. 'You are an easy target. You stand out; you're not a gringo and you're not one of us. You can't afford to take too long to decide who you eez runnin' with, or else you are isolated. That is a bad thing here. Why did you say no to the two guys last night?'

'Those two white men?' I asked rhetorically, worried by his tone. 'They are racists right? Aryan Brotherhood. I have zero in common with them; nothing. I can't join up with a gang like them.' I tailed off, wondering how isolated I might become.

'*Oye cabrone,*' he said. 'Very brave, but maybe very foolish. People may think that you find trouble, then it becomes very dangerous for you in Big Spring.' With that, Gato walked off to his bunk.

In the afternoon I was called out to change into my regular prison attire, my first-day suit having served its purpose. McKenzie seemed pleased to see me and actually made an effort to give me clothes that fit this time: five everyday khaki shirts; two pairs of khaki trousers; six white T-shirts; seven pairs of underpants; eight pairs of socks; and one pair of industrial-strength black reinforced boots. There was probably some logic in the quantities, but it escaped me. In addition, I received one set of 'visit clothes' – basically the same khaki shirts and trousers and undershirt, but in slightly better nick.

'Not new, Scotland; just newer!' McKenzie surveyed me approvingly in my new prison fatigues. 'Now you almost look like you belong,' he added, obviously pleased with his work. Tank and the others looked on, disinterested and sluggish in the heat.

10

THE RAT & THE COWARD

IN PRISON, TIME PERFORMS THAT STRANGE trick of seeming to pass slowly and swiftly at once. A couple of weeks went by, suddenly and yet tediously, taken up with a simple routine of scrubbing the toilets with Gato in the morning, writing a few letters and studying Spanish in the afternoon, then heading to the chow hall in the evening with Chief and Kola. During that time I was keeping a low profile, and hadn't explored any further around the prison. A glitch – or perhaps just the enduring sluggishness of the system – ensured that I still had no money, so no phone calls and no training shoes, which you needed to be allowed to go up into the gym and the Yard. I felt a million miles from home. I'd already decided that even when I did get money, I wouldn't spend it all on the usual luxuries of coffee, biscuits and chocolate and the like. Phone calls were $1 a minute to call the UK, buying me all of 7 minutes a month on my toilet pay so I guessed I would need all my money for that and stamps for my letters. Anyway, I wanted the discipline of the spartan lifestyle. I thought it would be better for me never to get too comfortable in my surroundings.

The Range was filling up rapidly, with five or six more people arriving every week or so – all transfers from other prisons. Focusing on the positives, I'd received two sets of legal papers: those for Cara Katrina and those from my case. The former were to refer to in case anything happened with or to Cara while I was inside; the latter my case papers so I could confirm with my Case Manager the deal the Department of Justice had made with me.

There was another reason everyone needed their case papers; so their roommates could confirm they were in there for the reasons they'd stated. One of the reasons Kola had been suspicious with me at the start, I later found out, was that the despised chomos would often claim to have 'robbed a bank' rather than admitting their true crimes.

The Range's checking-in process was every bit as detailed as the one performed by the prison officers – twice as deadly if you slipped up, too. Every day, in between writing letters or reading my book, I'd watch the new inmates arriving as our room continued to fill up. Within a short while of dumping his stuff, the new fish would be approached by the members of his own ethnic group as had happened with me with the AB's. He would be told to remove his top and trousers and a careful inspection of his tattoos would take place – not dissimilar to the inspection the cops would have completed as the inmates were booked in. This would be accompanied by a close grilling about where the newbie had been transferred in from, which august members of America's burgeoning prison population he'd served time with, and what gang he'd run with, if any. There being no glitches in his story, then and only then would the new arrival be furnished with his shower shoes, toiletries and other essentials.

Towards the end of my second month, as I was kicking back in my bunk one afternoon, an older inmate walked in. I noticed him straight away, because he walked faster than people normally did when they first entered the room. Usually they walked in quite slowly; looking for people they knew or might have heard of. This man looked scared straight away. Mid fifties, I guessed, with a full head of grey hair and a grey beard. Betraying your fear wasn't that unusual, but he was Hispanic, and I noticed that none of the other Hispanics came near him as he found his bunk about ten beds away from mine – no more than thirty feet away. I'd never seen that before; even to my untrained eye, it didn't look right. My corner bunk position afforded me a perfect view of the room but I didn't want to be caught staring, so I positioned myself so it looked like I was still reading. Chief had lent me his headphones and his radio and I turned the volume down when I heard Joker bark out some instructions to a couple of his minions, who then ran quickly from the room. It was clearly something to do with the new arrival, and Joker stared unapologetically in the man's direction before turning his back on him and continuing his card game. The tension in the room was palpable.

What happened next unfolded so quickly I barely had time to process it. Four men entered the room, moving at speed. They were completely silent and bare-chested, with their heads and faces covered by assorted scarves and shirts. They each took a separate path through the maze of beds in the Big Room, each heading directly towards the new arrival. I don't know if he saw them coming, they were upon him so fast. I noticed that two were carrying a 'lock in a sock': the weapon of choice in Big Spring when a good old shank wasn't available. With Joker and the rest of my roomies all turning their backs on what was about to unfold, and calmly going on with their business as if nothing was happening, the first protagonist came from behind his victim, grabbed his arm and his hair and quickly rammed his face straight into the cast-iron frame of the bunk. No introductions, no conversations, just swift and brutal justice, Big Spring style. The sound – a cross between a cracking noise and a more general thunk – would have made me wince, had it not been followed up so rapidly by a number of other connections; each one swiftly executed and each one seemingly worse than the last.

My view was partially obscured as the victim fell to the floor and it was only the sounds I was reacting to. The clinical nature in which the attackers laid into their quarry, and the fact that everyone else continued to behave as if nothing was happening, added to the surreal, almost eerie feel of the moment. I had expected violence in Big Spring and had steeled myself for it, but this just didn't seem real. The older man was so limp he now needed two of his attackers to support him, as they held him up then rammed him once more straight into the iron frame. There was a sickening crack and then he was dropped again to the floor. The other two attackers stepped in and delivered the *coup de grâce*: the 'lock in the sock' raining down on the now motionless figure. Still no one spoke. The music continued to play away – the Mexican department store Top Twenty elevator hits interspersed by the vigorous whack of sock–encased padlocks thumping down on the prostrate body. Through all this, I kept sneaking glances at Joker and the others around him. All of them kept their backs to the action, although a few seemed compelled to steal a nervous glance or two. Joker never once turned around. His card game over, he was now folding some of his laundry, his back to the fight, although his posture suggested he was listening to each sickening blow.

It had all happened so fast. After thirty or forty seconds only, the four attackers moved swiftly back out of the room, each taking a separate path. They only started to remove their head coverings as they approached the door. There was a brief silence before the usual chatter of the Big Room resumed. No one went near the victim. I realised that I'd blown my reading cover and that I had been staring for the last minute or so. Joker looked over at me without a flicker of emotion and held my gaze for a second, as he kept folding his laundry precisely and meticulously with his unfeasibly large hands. I swallowed hard as I looked away – I guess he'd always be Choker to me.

Still no one had moved to see how the new arrival was. I could only see his foot, which twitched violently a couple of times. Any pretence that my life in Big Spring might be easy or that I would avoid all the violence had just been blown away, replaced by a new, harsher reality. I saw Chief continue to draw, Kola sitting cross–legged on his bunk playing cards on his own, despite being no more than five feet away from a man who'd been beaten unconscious.

'The best thing you can do, Scotland, is to see nothin',' he told me later. 'And it's a lot easier to see nuthin' when you don't see nuthin'. You got me?' I got him, but by then it was too late – I had seen somethin'. I tried to go back to the book my step–mum Audrey had sent me, but I couldn't begin to concentrate. All I could think about was a man bleeding in the middle of our room. I was increasingly distracted, frustrated. Although only minutes had passed, they felt like an eternity. Still no one moved towards the prone figure; clearly no one cared whether he lived or died.

'What's wrong with these people?' I thought, the inhumanity of the situation suddenly hitting me. I had already jumped down from my bunk and taken about four steps towards the man before I was intercepted by Chief in a move that belied his overall physical condition.

'No, Scotland!' he said, putting his hands firmly on my chest and pushing me with a conviction that surprised me. Startled, I looked at him, and then beyond him. My new position afforded me a better view of the beaten man.

'I just want to see if the guy is alright.' It was more lament than anything as I raised my arm out towards the prone figure, who was still not moving. By this time Kola had jumped down from his bunk and was on me as well, blocking my view and my way forward.

'Bad idea, Scotland. Bad idea,' he was saying over and over again, as I tried to move away from them and get a better view of the man. They kept pushing me back and repeating their warnings, even as the man at last struggled to his feet. With astonishing dignity, he started first stemming the blood loss from his face and head and then, having gathered himself, started remaking his bed. It seemed like a determined statement of his intent to stay put.

Just then, Kola whispered in my ear: 'Trust me, Scotland, get back up on your bunk, turn your back and read your book. Trust me,' he said for a second time, looking searchingly into my eyes. I looked between him and Chief, suddenly wondering if I really knew them at all. But something in Chief's look – compassion maybe; or was it just fatigue? – caused me to stop. I pulled my arms away from them both and without saying another word, climbed back up into my bunk. All the while Joker had been watching me, only briefly turning to watch the new arrival remake his blood-spattered bed. I saw him make another hand gesture to his minions. Like before, they flew out of the room without a word. Everyone knew how this sketch played out – everyone that is, except me.

A moment or two after I had climbed back up on my bunk, three men appeared – different, I think, from the first four – again bare-chested with their faces and heads covered. The second beating was equally brutal and swift, and again the victim offered no resistance and no words were spoken. People continued to play cards and to fold laundry; I continued to pretend to read, shocked and appalled by what I was witnessing, but too cowardly to do anything about it.

Again the victim lay prone on the floor. This time I could see his blood trickling down on the hard concrete surface of the Range floor. Although everyone was continuing to ignore him, the tension in the room was reaching breaking point. I was going through huge personal turmoil. Why wasn't I doing something? What was happening to me in this place? Was I going to become like these people: folding pants while some poor guy was getting his head kicked in a few feet away? How could these people live like this? How could the cops allow this place to function in this manner? The longer he lay prone there, the more desperate I became. I contemplated going to help again, but I could feel Kola and Chief watching my every move. Just as I thought I could bear it no longer, the victim once more hauled himself to his feet. This time he staggered into the bathroom and washed off his bloodied face. It occurred to me I'd have to clean that up in the morning. Again I saw the slight nod of Joker's head as another minion darted off on a violent errand.

This time three more men appeared, yet again bare-chested with their heads covered and definitely different from the previous group. How many of these thugs were there? The established pattern was followed through once more with sickening speed and cruelty. This is the price you pay for being recruited with shower shoes and chocolate – you become a foot soldier for whatever gang had enlisted you. This time, halfway through the beating, another man entered the room, without any covering or mask, and headed straight towards the already unconscious victim. He was shouting, screaming almost, as he entered the room, and the others simply stepped aside as he paused over the unmoving figure before aiming a kick deep into the prone man's midriff. The abuse in Spanish continued as he assailed the punch-bag below him. He spat repeatedly on his victim, punched and kicked him some more, running gradually out of steam. This attack was different from the others – it was personal.

I had given up all pretence of not watching and sat on my bunk, my legs folded up in front of me, with my back to the wall, wondering where the hell I was. I hated all these people. I hated myself for watching it. I hated the people who had sent me here. Is this what those cunts in the DoJ wanted to teach me? Was this how anyone was supposed to be 'corrected'? I wanted to scream, to tear the walls down, to attack them all, but I just sat there like I was watching a movie, trying to ignore a memory brought back by the beating – a memory I thought I had buried.

I was around fourteen or fifteen years old, and I was walking back home one night with my two brothers, Mark and Michael, best pal Joe and a few other school friends, Billy Lee, Jim Mullan and Raymie Weir. There were also a couple of girls with us. We were approaching the walking bridge between Penilee and Pollok, always a hazardous journey as there were never any functioning lights and often a number of the 50 Krew, including Finn and his chief enforcer, DumbDumb, would be lying in wait for any unsuspecting victim. Normally, as the 'Mulgrews fae Dormanside', my brothers and I were OK, but on this occasion – perhaps still smarting from being cheated out of our paper-run money and probably fuelled by glue – Finn, his sidekick DumbDumb and about five others lay chase to us straightaway.

I managed to hide in a storm door with a couple of

the girls, but as I hid there I heard DumbDumb catch up with my brother Mark and start to kick and punch him. From the crack in the door, I could see Mark wrap himself around DumbDumb's legs tightly, much to DumbDumb's irritation, as he couldn't get a clear shot at him. But I did nothing. The girls were squealing; I just hid in the storm doors with them. Then I saw Michael appear out of the blue. Although much younger and smaller than DumbDumb, who was a fully grown man, Michael launched himself at him and Finn with a vicious-ness that belied his size. His intervention turned the tide, and with Billy and Joe joining in now, Finn and DumbDumb ran off. Re-emerging from behind the storm doors, frightened and ashamed, I couldn't look at Mark or Michael or Joe. No one ever mentioned it, but they knew. And I knew.

That memory, that shame, had stayed with me. Over the years I had realised that none of us are necessarily cowards, nor are we courageous all the time. You have to try to choose what you will be as the circumstances present themselves and sometimes shit just happens to you. I had tried to learn to be more courageous after that incident. I'd thought perhaps I *had* become more courageous, and might one day have a chance to atone for letting my brothers down, but here I was in Big Spring, Texas, a coward again.

Joker barked some new orders to a couple of the men around him, who jumped up and steered away the attacker from his quarry. Still the insults continued, but I couldn't make out any except the word '*rata*', said again and again, with increasing venom. So he was a rat, and this was the retribution. The attacker spat on his victim once more and then was ushered from the room still ranting and shouting abuse. Everyone was looking at the attacker with genuine concern, it seemed, while the victim lay ignored and bleeding on the floor. 'The parallel world of Big Spring,' I thought, my head spinning.

I tried to return to my book, feeling sick to my stomach. The victim, I noticed with dread, had pulled himself back onto his bunk for a third time. But this time, he started to pack up his things. The Joker was motionless; this scene had clearly played out. I never saw a cop the whole time, and I realised then that in Big Spring I probably never would. They policed the edges of the place – the inmates were in charge of the rest.

Once he had gathered up his belongings, the victim made a slow and painful exit from the Range – less than twenty minutes after walking in. This time some other Hispanics lined up either side of him as they watched him go, spitting on him and kicking or punching him, often to the floor, his humiliation complete as he dragged himself back to his feet, picked up his load and stumbled forward again. As I watched this, I had a deeply uncomfortable memory of Sunday school classes and scripture lessons. This scene could have been taken from Palestine, two thousand years earlier, but back then some had been brave enough to step forward and help. I stayed on my bunk.

The savage beating had immediate consequences. Almost as soon as the old man had staggered out of the Range, the sirens went off and we went into lockdown: TV rooms closed off, phones disconnected, microwaves off, everything terminated. Even as the man was making his way out, some inmates had started jostling for the water fountains, realising that lockdown was imminent and that they needed to stock up on water. Some of the lockdowns in the past had lasted for days, the infamous 'chomo beatings lockdown' for six weeks.

This one was over in three hours. Having closed our Range, the guards ordered us all off our bunks and told us to strip down to our underpants. There then followed a limp inspection of every person in the Range, the guards 'scrutinising' our hands and fingers for any signs of damage caused by punching someone, or any bloodstains anywhere else. Of course there were none, and the lack of enthusiasm of the officers showed they neither expected to find anything, nor cared too much either way. Incidents like this were an all too regular occurrence.

By the time the door to the Range had been unlocked and the inmates started to file out for chow, everything seemed to have returned to normal, other than my mood. I felt very low, wondering how I'd ever survive in this level of inhumanity.

Kola tried to cheer me up telling me that, 'This makes life in Big Spring interesting,' and reminding me that I couldn't solve every battle, or right every perceived wrong.

I listened in silence to Chief as we walked down to the food hall, my cowardice still taunting me. 'Shit like that happens every week in Big Spring. Only people from other Ranges ever come to our Range to beat up some dude and vice versa. They cover their faces for obvious reasons and they're bare–chested so no blood splatters onto their clothes for the cops to see later. And the deal is everyone else looks away. No one sees it; so no one can tell the cops about it. It's gang business.'

'But what kind of business ends like that?' I asked loudly. Chief and Kola winced, so I lowered my voice. 'With a man nearly being beaten to death with padlocks?'

Chief shrugged. 'That old dude had a twenty-five-year sentence, which was suddenly commuted to five. Word got out he was transferred in from Alabama, and they kept him in solitary for a while until the cops were ready to place him quietly in the Range, in the hope he'd skip under the radar and miss out on the retribution. See, he got the reduction because he ratted out on some other gang members – someone in the Aztecas. The surprise is that they didn't kill him. The shot-callers must have made that decision, otherwise he would just have been left alone initially then shanked during the night.' Chief said all of this so matter-of-factly; his dispassionate tone sunk my mood further. I wanted more from him; I wanted him to care.

'That's how they treat a rat,' Chief continued as we joined the dinner queue. 'They will beat him until he drags himself from the room and checks himself back into solitary. And that will be the pattern for the rest of his stay in prison. The gangs will keep tabs on him and follow his whereabouts and each time he leaves solitary, they will beat him until he checks himself back in, completes the walk of shame from the Range. The Feds will always try and 'lose' him somewhere in the system, but this time they screwed up. Usually the guards are thick enough with the gangs that they will tip them off about who's coming onto the Yard. 'Cos even the guards hate rats. And the dude that walked down without a mask on and was screaming an' shit? He was the brother of one of the men he ratted on. His brother got fifty-two years.'

'Why don't they just kill him?' I asked, sickened by the whole episode.

'Oh they will, Scotty,' said a tired-sounding Chief, 'but five years in the Hole is five years of pure hell. They'll wait till he thinks he's almost home, before the Aztecas will make sure he'll get his.'

'Hey, tacos tonight!' exclaimed Kola, right on cue, as the serving counters came into view.

'Cool,' responded Chief, as they eagerly grabbed a tray each and continued to move down the food queue.

After chow – most of my tacos went to Chief and Kola – I climbed up onto my bunk and, ignoring the books and letters I'd received, I just turned my face to the wall and tried to block out some of the chaos and noise around me. Sometimes it felt like living on a building site or in a busy shopping centre – just less comfortable. I hadn't managed to eat or sleep very well since my arrival and thought about maybe dozing off and trying to block the last few hours out of my mind. I tried to read again, but the events of the day kept rattling through my mind. The moral dilemmas I was facing were draining me, and I found them deeply unsettling and confusing. I closed my eyes and tried to take my mind home to a place in Scotland, a quiet valley near Glencoe where I could walk untroubled through sights and sounds that reminded me of home. I had to hold onto them tightly, lest they would fade and leave me abandoned here.

11

PLEADING

I HAD A FEELING THERE WOULD be consequences for my near-intervention in the beating – my breaking of the rules by interfering in 'gang business' – and it didn't take long before I had a visitor.

'Escosais?' I recognised Joker's voice before I turned round. I'd wondered when he'd come calling. Beside him was another guy, taller, medium build, with a far more pleasant countenance. He had a goatee and jet–black hair, pulled back tightly from his face. He looked Hispanic, but probably second generation, and this was confirmed by his American accent. They've probably come to choke me, I thought, feeling so tired and drained I didn't actually care.

'Hi Scotland, how you doin'?' the second guy asked, as he offered me a fist bump. Bumping back, I sat upright on my bunk wondering what was coming next.

'People call me Angel,' my new friend said chirpily. 'Can you come down, Scotland? We need to talk.' With that he turned to the non–smiling Joker and, putting his hand on his shoulder, said, '*Gracias amigo.*'

Joker had a quick glance at me – not in an aggressive way, I thought, more as if I was an irritant. Angel, meanwhile, walked off to a quiet corner of the Range. I could see instantly, from the way people seemed anxious to either acknowledge him or avoid him, that this man commanded significant respect. He also had the most outrageous swagger I had seen in a long time. In Scotland, we would have said he was 'pure *galas*' – he positively bounced along, exuding complete confidence.

I jumped down from my bunk as competently as I could, and followed him across the room, passing Chief as I did so. He was silently nodding to me, affirming something I didn't really understand.

Angel sat down in quiet section of the Range where there were still four unused bunks. Seemingly without instruction, I noticed a few guys in the adjoining bunks stopped whatever they were doing and moved off so we would not be in earshot of anyone. Angel motioned for me to sit opposite him and immediately dispensed with the pleasantries.

'I understand you wanted to get involved in what happened here the other day?'

'Erm,' I began, then I stopped. Angel smiled slightly and waited patiently for me to continue. Unlike nearly all of the other inmates, he had a real sparkle in his eyes and seemed almost clean–cut, not bedraggled and worn out. It was as if he belonged and prospered here. 'I guess I wanted to see if the guy was OK,' I managed.

'You knew the guy was a rat, right?' Angel responded instantly, still retaining a slight quizzical smile.

'I know now. I didn't know at the time,' I answered, deciding that honesty was the best policy. There was nothing immediately threatening in Angel's manner, although I sensed the whole conversation oozed danger for me. One wrong answer and he could sashay out of the room and order in the sock–and–lock crew. This guy wouldn't waste time with me or get his hands dirty. He was the real deal, a serious player in the prison trade.

'I'm still learning the ropes here, and don't understand a lot of what goes on,' I continued, trying to sound as calm as possible. Angel struck me as an intelligent guy and it seemed I could talk straight with him.

'Do you have your papers with you?' he asked, after chewing over my last response for a second or two.

'Yeah,' I looked over to my locker.

'I'll need to see those. You say you defrauded a bank, right?' He was all business now and clearly well informed.

'Erm . . .' I began uncertainly. 'It's kind of bank fraud, I guess.'

'You guess?' he queried. I realised I had to be more assured.

'I heard you ripped off Enron,' he continued, still confident. 'Why'd you tell people you robbed a bank? Which one was it, Scotland – you rob a bank or ripped off Enron?'

Frustrated as I always was by this misunderstanding, and beginning to feel very much on the back foot, my response betrayed the irritation I felt.

'It's complicated. Really complicated,' I growled.

Angel paused then leaned closer towards me, staring intently as he spoke.

'Listen, Scotland, and listen good. I'm not a cop, and I'm sure as hell not a genius, but I'm not fucking stupid either. Why don't you just take your time and explain to me what it is you did to get yourself in here? And save yourself any trouble bullshitting; just keep it straight and explain it to me in simple terms. Then we'll see where that takes us.'

As he said this, Angel held my gaze and placed his hand heavily on my shoulder. The physical proximity and his gaze were disconcerting, and there was a clear inference that if I tripped up here I would have to face the consequences. Strangely enough, since I had first self-reported my investment to the Financial Services Authority (FSA) all those years ago, I had craved the chance to put forward my account of events to the Americans, to anyone, but it had never happened. Despite having gone forward to the authorities of my own volition, I had subsequently been indicted, appeared in court numerous times on both sides of the Atlantic and now been imprisoned, still without ever having the opportunity to respond to my accusers. Not one word, not one question; not one chance. No one ever took me into a side room and shone lights into my eyes and asked me 'Did you do it?' like you always saw in the movies.

How ironic now that the first person seemingly interested in getting to the truth, was a convicted felon.

The thought relaxed me and I decided to tell him as plainly as I could.

'I made an investment in a company based in the Cayman Islands, which was offered to me by Andy Fastow, one of the top guys at Enron,' I began. 'He was a good client of mine when I worked at NatWest, a British bank based in London. I had previously been in charge of the group that sold a deal to Fastow and he re-structured it into this investment. The investment made a lot of money very quickly,' I continued, eyeing Angel closely to see if he was following me. He was.

'I trusted Fastow and there were plenty of other people, other bankers, in the investment, and since it was connected to an Internet stock and it was early 2000, the big return was feasible, if unusual.' Angel, uncommitted, nodded for me to continue.

'The problem was Fastow had ripped off Enron to make the money; he hadn't made it legitimately,' I concluded.

'So you conned Enron?' asked Angel making that logical conclusion.

'No,' I responded. 'Fastow made it clear to the authorities that he acted alone, and that neither I nor any of the other investors were aware of his actions. The other investors, including me, had been invited in unknowingly to hide his own return in the deal.' I paused again as Angel digested this. He moved awkwardly on the bunk.

'I don't understand. What did you do then?' he asked.

'Well, this is where it starts to get complicated. In retrospect, I shouldn't have invested in a deal I had already sold for NatWest, but I was leaving them and had sought their specific permission through my lawyer. Still, it probably lacked a bit of integrity, and I often wonder why I didn't think that way at the time.' I'd gone slightly off track as my mind started thinking more about my actions, but it didn't seem to have dampened Angel's interest.

'When Enron started to go tits up, I went into the authorities in the UK, called the FSA, with my two buddies.' I paused watching him intently. 'That's the Financial Services Authority . . .'

'I know who the FSA are; like the SEC here,' he inter-jected, seemingly irritated. I hesitated, slightly disconcerted, as I continued to try to figure out which level to pitch this at. The surprises never end in here, I thought.

'So,' I faltered trying to get back on track. 'The FSA thanked us for coming forward. A few months later, Enron went bankrupt and a criminal investigation was launched.'

'Bush's Task Force,' Angel added, with a certain disdain.

'Yes. Well, the FSA asked if it could send our informa-tion to the Task Force and we agreed,' I said, tailing off slightly. The stupidity of this action seemed greater than ever as I sat among the luxuries of Big Spring. Angel said nothing, but I caught that flickering moment when his face betrayed the feeling that he was sitting opposite a buffoon, a novice, a dickhead.

Sighing slightly, I continued.

'We never heard shit from the US for six months until I turned on the TV one day and found out I was indicted. Given they couldn't say we defrauded Enron, the indict-ment claimed I had defrauded my own employer, NatWest, by breaching my employment contract. In essence, I stole the opportunity to make the investment from NatWest, as Fastow was their client, and thus the opportunity belonged to them.'

'The opportunity to invest in a fraud?' asked Angel, without missing a beat.

'I guess,' I responded, feeling that it all sounded stupid. It always did.

Angel was quiet for a minute or two, and I found my nerves starting to fray again.

'It's all in my papers,' I said eventually, hoping this

would help to sway things my way. Angel nodded thoughtfully before speaking.

'So Scotland, this is still kind of confusing, and I still don't get the bottom line. I still don't get why you are here.'

'I don't understand . . . what do you mean?'

'Why did they want you? Why did they go through all that trouble to extradite you when they could have dealt with you in England?'

I remained silent for a moment as Angel continued to stare at me intently. I wanted to be truthful but worried about how he would react to what I was about to tell him. 'The thing is . . .' I began slowly,' we did actually try to get ourselves investigated or charged in the UK . . . we created legal history by taking the Serious Fraud Office – our FBI – to court to try to force them to investigate us . . . or charge us' I tailed off awaiting his reaction. He seemed bemused.

'I don't get it?' he responded.

'I know, it barely makes sense to me. In the end they wouldn't even investigate us because they said there was no evidence of a crime and the Judges backed them. The US didn't need evidence to extradite us so they stepped into the void and the Judges backed them too.'

'Wait a minute. Are you saying you actually tried to get yourself indicted?' Angel asked looking more confused by the second.

'Well not exactly' I responded sheepishly, wondering how anyone could ever explain something so illogical. Angel was looking at me as if I was mad – I guess from his point of view it would seem a bit crazy, but we had felt that if we could have persuaded the SFO to begin an investigation then we would quickly have been exonerated. The problem was, with no evidence and no complaint from NatWest, the SFO had nothing to investigate.

Angel seemed pensive and this unnerved me further.

'But I still don't understand what was the point of dragging you all the way over here and sticking you in this shithole?' he asked, more softly this time, as he moved closer to me again.

I looked directly at him. What the hell *am* I doing here? I would probably never know.

'Politics,' I eventually responded. 'Politics, I guess. At the time of Enron and then WorldCom going bankrupt, the US was anxious to show that the system wasn't corrupt, but that just a few "bad guys" had got greedy and that the system would punish them. The "bad guys" would go to jail, then everyone could get on with making money without any troublesome regulatory or system changes.'

The fact was that Bush had made a speech using roughly those words just two weeks before I was indicted, so I felt strongly that what I was saying was the most likely reason.

'Someone had to go to jail to make everyone feel better – I guess the details were largely irrelevant . . .' I tailed off as my mind raced forward. The collapse of Enron and WorldCom were to me the antecedents of the mortgage collapse a few years later – again caused in the main by over-leverage and an unregulated market. The chance to avoid that collapse, and all the catastrophic ramifications ironically for companies like NatWest and its parent company RBS, had been missed as people sought to blame individuals rather than a system that was clearly already out of control when Enron went down.

'Someone had to go to jail,' I repeated more wistfully, 'and my own country didn't seem to have a problem nominating us for the job.' I was thinking of Blair's obsequious relationship with President Bush.

'Mmmmmm.' Angel paused for a moment before adding, 'Sounds more to me like you volunteered for it, Scotland.'

I nodded my head, thinking how stupid I'd been to believe we would be welcomed as whistle-blowers and protected by the FSA.

Angel smiled, before going straight for the jugular again. 'What sentence did you get?'

'Three years, one month.'

Angel noticeably shifted in his seat, unsettled. 'Not very long.'

'Long enough,' I responded.

'How much did you steal?'

'Nothing. I didn't steal it.'

'OK, that's a novel answer in here,' he smiled. His mood and demeanour had suddenly changed once more and it felt like we were sparring again.

'How much do they say you stoled?' he asked.

'$7.3 million.'

Angel whistled. '$7.3 million, yet only three years? That doesn't stack up,' he said, matter-of-factly, and still with the smile. 'There are guys in here who took a fraction of that and their doing ten or fifteen.' He had a point. If we had really stolen $7.3 million, it would have been a ridiculously short sentence.

'Three years and one month,' I pointed out, as if the additional month mattered. I guessed it would to me eventually.

Angel's mood had darkened further and he barely acknowledged my correction. 'Yeah,' he said, seemingly deep in thought now. 'You co-operate with the Government, Scotland?' he asked, looking straight at me.

After the meatball incident, true to their word, the US Government had gone straight to David Bermingham and offered him the same deal as they had offered Giles – home for Christmas, limited or no jail time and no need to testify against the others. To most people on the outside, after the length of time we had been stuck in Houston, that would seem a very tempting offer and DoJ no doubt expected a deal to be done. Although David had a very different personality to Giles, and our friendship had never been as deep or as long (I had only met him a few years earlier when he came to work in my group), I was sure he would never cop a plea. He had served as a captain in the British Army and had done time in Northern Ireland, and to him these issues were uncomplicated and easy. He declined a deal.

That left me. I was amazed that the DoJ had come to me last. Giles had told me that was because they saw me as the ringleader; the architect and the brains behind the fraud – which was further proof, if I needed it, of how little they had either investigated this 'offence' or understood it. Reid called me the day David turned the DoJ down. He had Schwartzy and Kevin on the phone with him – great guys and a great team, but whenever the three of them were on the line, it spelt trouble. The call was awkward and at times unpleasant and it left me with a decision to make.

I decided to write it all down. The positive part of the deal was that I would serve minimal – if any – time in a US prison, with a good chance I could be home by Christmas. That was quite a thought in itself. The alternative was to go to trial with all the pressure that entails. I worried whether we could mount a proper defence in any trial in Houston, particularly without the key witnesses we needed from London. If we lost – which I understood was a real possibility – we could face up to fifteen years in prison, maybe longer given how seriously Judge Werlein seemed to view these Enron cases. Even if we won, the DoJ had already indicated they would seek to continue to hold us in Houston for another two years or so if necessary for a retrial. None of this was encouraging, and although I had been aware of all of this for a while, I sighed as I wondered again if I'd ever get home – if there was any way out of this.

If that wasn't enough, the DoJ had laced their 'offer' with some new 'personal' enticements to encourage me to plead guilty.

The first one was that they would countenance an immediate short-term trip home for me to meet my London lawyer and my lawyer in Tunisia so we could make some progress in tracking down Cara. They had completely resisted my entreaties on these matters before, but either had found a sudden new spring of compassion or, more likely, were cynically targeting my soft spots.

After eighteen months of complete silence on Cara, the thought of actually meeting face-to-face with the two lawyers I had found to help me through the legal process of getting her back was sorely tempting. The best we had ever managed were telephone calls from the US to London or Tunis – hardly the ideal way to make progress in locating Cara. I had made some headway through the UK courts, who now properly recognised Cara's case as a parental abduction, but I was always hampered by the simple fact that I was not there. I was the father trying to get his daughter back from Tunisia to England while he was confined in Houston, Texas. Ironically, even being in prison in the UK would have given me a better chance of getting her back than being 'free' in Houston. Incarceration can come in many guises.

I sat back in my seat to think about this and to contemplate the even greater bombshell the DoJ had dropped on me: that Laura my ex-wife had been in Washington a couple of times talking to them, with the first meeting having taken place shortly after I had arrived in Houston. All that time, all that effort, all the frustration and all the hurt in trying to find her and they knew; they knew all along where my daughter was. I was stunned. I never realised the game was played this way. I never realised these people worked like this. I thought that even to them, the safety of my daughter transcended the mere rights and wrongs of the stupid investment we made – that everyone could see, could understand, how much more important a little girl's welfare was. More important than this shit.

The *coup de grâce* came with the clarification that if I didn't accept a deal, then the DoJ as well as seeking the maximum sentence they could, would never agree to a transfer home to a UK prison. As no one could be transferred back to a UK prison unless the DoJ first of all agreed to allow it to happen, I would serve the entire sentence here in the US with all the implications that had for me in terms of Calum and Cara, and the rest of my family. I would be finished as a father, my life over. I had often used carrot-and-stick techniques in negotiating business deals in the banking world, but this was a whole new dimension of brutality.

I wondered about the prosecutor sitting in his Washington office, interviewing Laura, knowing she had broken the law in England and disappeared with my daughter, and was still sought by the UK police for being in contravention of a specific High Court order to return Cara to her home and family in England. I wondered how he did that; how he got comfortable with that both legally and morally. I wondered if he had children – children he went home to and played with at night – and if so, whether he ever contemplated the horror of losing one, and not knowing where she was.

I sighed again and rubbed my temples as I tried to take this all in.

The way the plea–bargaining system worked provided its own twist to the pressure to 'rat out' on the others around you. Once the judge had ordered our separation when we arrived in Houston we weren't allowed to communicate or be in the same room without a lawyer present. Each client had to have individual and separate legal advice and it didn't take long before the lawyers would start to suggest that one or both of the others may be guilty – or if not guilty, perhaps too weak to resist a deal to go home. I understood that the only person who I could actually be sure was 'not guilty' was me. I couldn't know for certain if Giles or David were guilty of a crime, just as they couldn't know for certain about me or indeed each other. The DoJ had assumed that all three of our actions were interchangeable and that we were reasonably aware of what each other said or did, or emailed or indeed intended throughout. But we knew that wasn't actually true. Any one of the three of us could have been aware of what was going on from Fastow's perspective, or hidden a key piece of evidence or information, or decided not to say or do anything that would have led the others to abandon the deal. There were thousands of permutations, maybe all unlikely, but all I knew with certainty concerned my own actions and thoughts, not those of Giles or David.

I must admit I had had my moments of doubt and I'm sure the other two must have had them about me as well. There were loads of inconsistencies, of failed recollections or misunderstood events. With lawyers constantly around, I had lost the ability to talk freely to David and Giles and the doubts about them and how they were viewing me began to increase. David had already told me on more than one occasion that he was told, 'Mulgrew's missing daughter makes him a shoo-in to do a deal.' Clearly the DoJ thought so too.

But I tried to dispel such thoughts from my mind. Inconsistencies were part and parcel of human recollection – one man remembers a green room while another saw blue. When we finally gained access to the emails that had contained so much of the inflammatory materials used to extradite us, it had been four years since we had been indicted and six years since we'd written or received them. I can struggle to remember what I meant in an email sent last Tuesday, yet still the lawyers would spend hours re-examining potential nuances in every email. It was pointless. All I knew was I hadn't set out to defraud anyone. I never would.

In an attempt to sweeten things, the DoJ had also stated

that if I accepted a deal, I wouldn't have to testify against my two friends, although they stressed that they might reduce my sentence further if I did. But I knew even if I didn't testify against them, just the act of pleading guilty would almost certainly lead to their conviction. The inference a jury would draw from my guilty plea and the fact that Giles and David couldn't count on my testimony would be enough to sink them, guilty or not guilty.

That is the problem with so-called 'conspiracy' cases: during the plea-bargaining process, at some point you can become the de facto judge. Now, if I changed my plea to guilty, I was effectively sentencing David and Giles to years in prison; judging them based on nothing more than a few lawyer-induced random doubts or feeble inconsistencies, just as surely as if I stood there and admonished them myself. Sure we all had doubts, and in the hard times we had endured in Houston any paranoia was easily fed. But Giles and David had both gone through the same doubts about me and about each other, goaded no doubt by lawyers required to do the best for their client. Maybe one of them was guilty, maybe they both were guilty of something – I'd never know – but my sense and experience of them suggested otherwise. And anyway, who was I to judge?

I looked down at the paper again and consider once more the nature of this 'deal' and the people who were offering it to me. I felt cheated, angry, insulted and amazed by the squalid nature of their approach. I paused for a second before I ripped the piece of paper up and threw it across the table.

Reid had told me once that he'd seen brothers plead against brothers, fathers against sons, and having tasted the pressure exerted first hand, I could understand why. I began the journey thinking I had lost my country. But even for a man who tended to think of himself principally as a Scot, there was something very British and dignified about the way we three individuals independently determined not to assume the role of judge or executioner of the other two. Maybe I was getting my sense of country back; maybe one day I would get it all back. Anyway, I wouldn't be pleading guilty.

'I don't need to waste time thinking about this anymore,' I thought, my anger and determination growing as I reached for the phone to call Reid. I wanted to tell him to go back to them today – to go back to them now, this morning, immediately after my call – and tell them, in words as stark as his lawyerly professionalism would allow, 'to go and fuck themselves'.

The memory of that morning re-ignited the anger in me. Angel was still sat on the bunk, patiently waiting for my answer. 'I don't think there is anyone,' I began with a passion that probably surprised him, 'that hates those fuckers more than me. I wouldn't help them if my life depended on it. Read my fucking papers and see for yourself. I wouldn't rat on anyone.' I stood to get up, as Angel's hand locked onto my wrist.

But I was way beyond being frightened of Angel or anyone else at that moment, and he seemed to sense that, quickly letting go of me with a nod and a smile. 'OK, Scotland, OK. That's cool. I'll take your papers and get it all checked out, then get back to you. I hope for your sake they stack up, I really do. You understand we need to check through these things.'

I didn't say anything, I just nodded. I was still thinking of the Department of Justice, that institutional misnomer. I hated those people. Loved America, loved its people, hated its justice system. To me, the DoJ were no better than Angel, no better than the people who had perpetrated the beating in the Range the previous day, or the people who had looked away.

'Can I go?' I said to Angel, my face set in stone.

'Sure Scotland,' he responded offering me a fist bump. 'I pissed you off?' he added, intrigued.

'No, no,' I responded, reminding myself a little of the delicacy of my position. 'You just started off a lot of bad memories. Let me get you those papers.'

Back then, Reid tried to get me to take longer to consider my decision, but I knew I would never change my mind, and he eventually delivered my message to the DoJ, although I doubt it was with the gusto or the wording I would have preferred. He was too professional for that. It looked like we were all set for a trial a few months later in October, but then in a move that surprised us all, the DoJ offered a deal to all three of us to plead guilty. In what Reid saw as a coincidence and I saw as an orchestrated move, the judge ordered a further delay in the trial 'to at least January, but possibly the Spring' on the same day the DoJ approached us with this new, collective deal. The official explanation was that a state murder trial was to take precedence over our case, even though Reid and Dan told me they had never known any state trial to trump a Federal prosecution.

The deal was this: a straight thirty-seven months for the three of us, with a significant twist. Provided we agreed to waive all rights to any future appeal, the DoJ would agree to transfer us home 'in an expedited manner'. That was our shabby deal. 'Expedited' was as far as they would go, despite our best attempts at some stronger assurance. The price of waiving our right to an appeal was inviolate; the DoJ recognising without doubt that the nonsense to which we were pleading guilty was quite likely to be overturned in time.

Transfers normally took anywhere between eighteen months to three years to arrange; so Reid's guess was we were looking at around a year if we got lucky. Having geared ourselves up for trial and having resolutely refused an individual deal, it was amazing how quickly the cracks in our resolve now appeared. We could be home late the following year – almost four years since we had left. We were tired, drained and had all been away from home for too long. People had died, life had moved on. Life was in danger of leaving us behind.

And so we all agreed to plead guilty. Bizarrely all that remained with the sentence already agreed was what we were pleading guilty to. To be honest, I was past caring, but in the end we worked out what was known as a Statement of Facts. I understood that as long as every-thing in it was true, or at least I had no knowledge to suggest it was untrue, then I could sign it. It didn't matter if there were material omissions.

In the end, when I read it, I was still unclear of the crime I was supposed to have committed: a breach of my employment contract with NatWest because I had apparently failed to ever mention the investment oppor-tunity to them. It was rubbish and in a court in England, where I could have compelled witnesses to appear (we couldn't compel them to come to Texas), it would have been thrown out in a day with testimony from NatWest alone, but by that stage, I'd have pleaded guilty to being Osama bin Laden if they'd asked me. I just wanted to get home.

I handed my papers containing this nonsense to Angel. 'You're welcome to that,' I said, sitting on the bunk below mine as Angel started flicking through the papers. After a while he looked up, briskly, all business again.

'OK. Once we've checked these out, we need to talk about who you're running with.'

'Why does it matter so much?' I asked, wearily.

'Because it does,' he answered quickly, before pausing slightly then changing his tone. 'Look, Scotland . . . it's like this. Each gang runs a certain part of the "business" of the prison.' He leant forward on the bunk, hand gestures patiently mirroring his words, like a teacher. 'Each gang has a shot-caller; the guy who calls the shots. Everything goes through him, and he determines what actions, what punishments or retributions take place. If we sort things out ourselves, in the quiet of the Ranges, then the cops never need get involved, and they are happy and we're happy,' he explained. 'This way it's good for business, good for everyone.'

I doubted that. Chief had already told me that the gangs operated an uneasy truce, dividing the various 'business lines' between themselves from prison to prison. In Big Spring, those lines were gambling, steroid usage, smoking, drugs, alcohol and male prostitution. On top of these main streams, there was more of a free-for-all in the extortion market, with each gang free to find their own 'marks' to extort. Sometimes one gang would encroach into another's territory and a mini war would ensue. The war would never determine who was right, said Chief, just who was left. Then the cops would step in to restore order and allow the one gang or other to prevail. And there was big money in each of these rackets. In Federal prisons there was a complete smoking ban (unlike UK prisons, which still allow smoking) and a full packet of cigarettes retailed at a staggering $450 in Big Spring. With many of the cops on around $22,000 per year, it wasn't a stretch to imagine where a lot of the gangs got their supplies from.

'So, are you a shot-caller?' I asked. Angel smiled easily. He had a gold tooth with a diamond encrusted in it, just left of centre on the top row.

'Sure. I run the Kings. We are based out of LA. On the out I used to be responsible for two prisons,' he offered matter-of-factly as he took off his top and showed me a tattoo of a crown covering his entire back. 'That'll never come off,' he said, with some pride.

'What do you mean you ran two prisons on the out?'

'Man, you really don't know shit about shit, do you?' he said with a smile. Then he mused, more to himself than to me, 'You really did come from another kind of Pollok.' He had so much energy and enthusiasm when he spoke. He was constantly moving around; such a stark contrast from the usual sluggish inhabitants of Big Spring. 'I ran the prisons for the Kings,' he explained. 'Everything you get on the inside needs to get paid for on the outside. No one in here can pay hundreds of bucks for a packet of cigs – someone on the outside has to pay it for them. So I used to make sure the money

hits the right accounts, and then gets used properly –
most of the guys on the inside have families, kids and
shit, and we need to make sure they are looked after.
We look after our own. It also helps fund our businesses
on the outside. Once you join the Kings, you're always
a King. You never leave the Kings, unless it's in a body
bag. You know what I'm saying?'

I nodded. I knew what he was saying and I mentally
crossed the Kings off my list of potential gangs to join.
'Each prison should make about $2 million a year,' Angel
said. 'Although I think I can make much more from them
now I've had a chance to spend some time on the inside.'

I refrained from making any quips about Angel recon-
necting with his customer base. I just wanted to know
what it had to do with me. 'Not everyone runs in one
gang or another, Scotland, but for the smooth running
of operations here, we prefer that people who are high-
profile or who interfere have at least some allegiance.
And that's why we need to figure out what to do about
you. Problem is you are already high-profile: you're
European, you're seen as part of all that Enron shit irre-
spective of the facts of it, so you're too high-profile to
walk alone. And as for that shit you tried to pull the
other day, well, that just compounds matters. We can't
allow that.'

Thinking again about the beating, I nodded slightly.
'Look, I'm not from here and all this stuff is new to me,
but I'm a quick learner. You said not everyone runs with
someone. Can't I be one of those guys?' I asked
hopefully.

'No, Scotland. Shit happens around you, shit happens
to you. That's how you rock, that's how you play. You'll

be too dangerous outside a gang and it will be too dangerous for you too. You're gonna have to run with someone. Let me read through your papers and check that everything's cool there, then we'll talk some more. In the meantime, try to stay out of everyone's shit and do your own time. You know what I'm saying?'

I finally got what Malone had meant all that time ago about 'doing your own time'.

Angel stood up to leave. 'And by the way, if that lieutenant hauls your ass in about that beating, you didn't see shit!'

'I didn't see shit,' I echoed, as if it were true. We fist-bumped and he went on his way, my papers and immediate fate in his hands.

12

DON'T PANIC

I LASTED IN THE CLEANING JOB for six weeks, during which time I availed myself of every opportunity to find alternative work. I had initially hoped to continue my partnership with Gato, as I felt we made a good team and I hadn't been hassled by anyone else wanting to use the toilet while I had my head halfway down it. Gato talked to me constantly, often about the many buildings and banks he had robbed, and how he had managed to get into them and escape without a trace. I say without a trace although that isn't strictly true as he was eventually caught because of his insistence on leaving the 'paw mark' of a cat in each conquest. I asked him if he thought of leaving a fairy cake instead, but he didn't see the funny side of that. Like many others I had talked to, Gato had a barely disguised pride in his work and I doubt he was actually interested in what he stole – it was the challenge he liked. He seemed constantly frustrated that it was a drug bust that finally got him Federal time; like he was cheapened by it, since his real artistry was in breaking and entering. Sadly, however, my education was curtailed. One day Gato approached me and told me that another Sureno brother was coming to Big Spring and that he would be taking my job in the toilets, thus making me redundant. It seemed the gangs really did control every aspect of the prison – even the least glamorous ones.

This was a pity as I'd got into a tolerable routine by then. Everyone would head off to work by 7.30 a.m. and I would continue reading to around 8 a.m. I got into the habit of reading while facing the wall at that time in the morning, so I didn't have to see who specifically had just been into the latrines, or speculate as to what they might have left there. That helped me. It was pretty gruesome work, but I was usually finished in an hour and a half, by which point there would be a queue of people waiting to undo all my hard labour. I didn't mind. No one came to check my handiwork, and I would be finished and back to my bunk well before lunchtime.

That gave me time to try and find new work. Big Spring offered a number of interesting positions for the misplaced Bank Executive on a range of salary levels, peaking at $200 a month in the 'factory' assembly line, producing fine garments for other prison establishments. Unfortunately that career path required a six-month initial stint in the kitchen, unattractive to me on grounds of the sharp knives and the Tex-Mex menu. I had also heard that there was much fun and merriment to be had from placing various concoctions and organisms into certain inmates' food, and since I had to eat this stuff every day, I really didn't want to know what was in it. Fortunately, some career advice came to me from my favourite source.

'You can read and write, right?' Chief asked me one typically airless afternoon.

'Of course.'

'Cool,' he responded, 'I'll speak to the Head Librarian, Miss Reed, for you.' He went back to his drawing then, when I didn't go away, looked up again. 'Can I do anything else for you, Scotty?'

'Erm, well, this Miss er . . . librarian. Won't she want some more information from me? Or a CV – you know, résumé – or something?'

Chief chuckled. 'You just done give me your "CV" when you said you could read and write, Scotland.'

Miss Reed seemed to feel the same way. Our interview, which took place the next day, was brief, focused and involved minimal eye contact. I went off to the library wearing my best khakis, having paid another inmate – El Turko, aka Turk the Knife, who apparently was as gifted with the knife as he was with an iron – one stamp to iron them for me the night before. Stamps were the currency everyone used in Big Spring – all trading between inmates was calculated by the number of stamps needed, and fortunately Chief had given me a few to get me going until I could get some funds into my prison account. I had also shaved with a brand new Bic razor and washed my hair, placing a handwritten CV (colour–coded, no less) in my shirt pocket. Chief found all of this preparation very amusing and kept telling me it was going to be unnecessary. And he was, of course, right.

'Mulgrew!' Miss Reed shouted from behind her desk after I had been waiting nervously outside her office for ten minutes or so. I walked in, and waited to be told to sit at the chair on the other side of her desk. Her head was down writing something, her office in total chaos. Another decaying US government office and another person not looking at me. There were books everywhere, some new, some battered, some badly defaced. Book rage seemed to be an issue in Big Spring. Miss Reed looked around the mid-forties mark, although it was difficult to tell, as she hadn't raised her head yet. She had curly dark hair, partially dyed, and from what small portions of her I could see, seemed a bit overweight and caked in make-up. I hadn't seen any women so far in Big Spring, other than the psych, and I knew from Chief that the library employed 'civilians', so I was really unsure what to call her or what the overall etiquette was. So I stood in front of her desk awkwardly, waiting to be told to take a seat.

'Sit, Mulgrew,' she barked, waving her pen and still not looking at me. This began to irk me.

'I'm a man, a human being,' I thought, 'not a dog,' but just as quickly I rebuked myself. I was a fool to be looking for normal human interaction – I was here to be punished, and every engagement with officialdom was a reminder. I was a bad person, a crook, a criminal, a transgressor. I had failed society and society deemed I had to be taken out and 'corrected'. I sighed.

Miss Reed nodded her head lightly at some of the books strewn across her desk in front of me. 'Can you read from one of them, Mulgrew?' she asked, still studiously avoiding looking up.

'Fucking look at me,' I thought. This was beginning to get to me. I looked down at the books – quite an assortment, and some of them surprised me. Paulo Coelho and a number of self-help books, lots of Grisham and Patterson, and even my fellow 'crim' Lord Jeffrey Archer graced her desk. I reached for a battered Penguin copy of Charles Dickens' *A Tale of Two Cities*.

'It was the best of times, it was the worst of times . . .' I checked to see if Miss Reed was listening. She continued to write. I went on. '. . . it was the age of wisdom, it was the epoch of belief, it was the incredulity, it was the season of Light, it was the season of Darkness, it was the spring of hope, it was the winter of despair . . .' The words held resonance for me, but little, apparently, for Miss Reed. She was still writing.

Injecting more feeling into the prose and slightly increasing the volume to accentuate the negatives, I continued, '. . . we had everything before us, we had nothing before us, we were all going direct to heaven, we were all going direct the other way – in short . . .' but before I could continue, Miss Reed looked up at me. I stopped.

I was right, I thought, about mid forties and showing signs of Big Spring wear and tear. Her face wasn't as covered in make-up as I had thought and I imagined she probably had a nice countenance in the free world. But in here she was stern and unflinching. She looked back down at her work.

'You Irish, Mulgrew?' she asked as she picked her pen back up.

'Scottish,' I said, happy there was some sort of dialogue.

'Where do you work now?' she asked, back to addressing her questions to the papers in front of her.

'I clean the toilets in the Range; I've only just arrived.' I said those words, but six weeks already felt like a lifetime.

'Oh,' she said, sounding disappointed in this

information, without offering a reason why. She was silent for a while longer. 'Well,' she eventually said, 'there's a position available in a week or two working with AJ. Do you know AJ?'

'No, ma'am.' I wondered if 'knowing AJ' was significant.

'Well, anyway,' she continued, 'there's a position for you if you want it. It pays $14 a month and your hours are 7.30 a.m. to 12.05. Let me know by next week; assuming, of course, you can manage to get yourself out of working in the kitchens. Do you think you are resourceful enough to figure that out, Mulgrew?' she asked, glancing back at me briefly.

'I'll try, ma'am,' I responded, taking my cue that the 'interview' was over. She didn't speak or look up again as I exited the room, my colour-coded CV still tucked away in my shirt pocket.

I wanted that library job because I was desperate for some respite from the noise and constant chaos of the Big Room. Our Range kept filling up by the day, with new arrivals making the space feel ever more constrained. The bunk below me was still unoccupied and a few of the bunks around me as well. But I dreaded the moment, the moment I knew must come, when inmates moved into that last tiny island of space.

The most intimidating arrival of all had been a large black man (known as 'Big City') who, much to my horror, lumbered around looking for his bunk number before heading my way and occupying the bottom bed immediately next to my bunk. He was around 6ft 10, and about 350lbs, a giant of a man. He had a shaved head and a New Orleans Saints tattoo on his cheek which I recognised from all the coverage that team had received after Hurricane Katrina. Since we often called Cara by her middle name Katrina, I used to joke with her that she had a hurricane named after her, which given her feisty little character and sweep of curly hair, seemed rather appropriate.

This giant of a man was festooned with other tattoos, but as prison tattoos were mainly in black ink, they were harder to discern on black men, and you didn't want to be caught staring too closely trying to figure them out. Big City towered over everyone and I could tell I wasn't the only one intimidated. His arrival had been talked about for a couple of days before – word was he had a fifteen-year stretch for drug–dealing and had been moved to Big Spring because of some problems he'd caused in a prison in Alabama. He looked like the kind of guy who'd cause problems in a prison in Alabama. Or anywhere.

'What the fuck are you lookin at?' he fired at me, dispensing with the usual pleasantries. I was curled up reading a book, trying desperately *not* to stare at him. He looked the stuff of nightmares.

Big City's opening gambit had exposed a set of pure gold teeth, favoured by many of the African–Americans in Big Spring. He moved directly towards me, his head and shoulders comfortably clearing my top bunk. This guy could have played the part of a black Jaws in a James Bond movie, although he would have been quickly typecast.

'You from New Orleans?' I asked, unsure which part of my brain was still functioning well enough to let me speak. I guess I must have appeared relaxed lying on the bunk, book in hand, but inside I was on full terror alert. My brain cells were on hyper-alert, preparing various exit strategies. But I knew I couldn't seem afraid.

I'd heard a few new guys whimper at night during my first few weeks there. It was a haunting sound; the saddest and most desperate sound you could ever imagine. It was also the most dangerous: a clarion call to the wolves, the hyenas, the scavengers. By the morning the whimperer would be finished – the pattern of his life in Big Spring established. Part of an extortion ring maybe, someone's bitch if they were attractive enough, or someone's fun fuck even if they weren't.

The worst whimperers were the middle-aged men; the Whites, invariably. Perhaps because they had led too comfortable a life before, perhaps because there was less of a structure in the white gangs, less of that bond that seemed to tie the Indians, the Hispanics and Blacks to their individual gangs or communities. I would lie awake listening to them – hoping they would stop, wanting to help, but knowing after my Angel conversation I couldn't. It was the sound of complete despair, of defeat, of abject surrender. But then if you are in your mid forties or fifties and you enter the Big Room for your first night of a fifteen to twenty-year stretch – knowing your kids will be grown up and will quite possibly hate you, your wife or partner gone and almost certainly hating you, your career finished, your prospects nothing more than this room for years or decades to come – then maybe you would whimper too. Ironically, such things made me feel I was lucky.

For the first few months, perhaps for the first few years, most prisoners would focus on the life they had lost, rather than the life they now had. There was always a key moment, according to Chief, when the inmate would realise that his life was Big Spring; that his 'other life', his life in the free world, was over. That's when you saw the biggest change in them, and the quicker a prisoner could make that transition the better. But I was lucky. I was fortunate. My life in the free world was still there for me. I had a son to get home to. I had a job as a father to do. I had a daughter to find; to love and be with. I had cuddles to receive and love to give. I wasn't ready for whimpering.

Big City loomed ever larger. I was struck by how big his face was.

'You like the Saints?' he asked as he came right up to me, smiling and flashing me the set of gold gnashers.

'Naw,' I replied, trying to act as calm as I could. 'I don't like American football.'

This wasn't received so well, but then Big City changed tack. 'What you reading?' he asked, nodding towards the book in my hand.

'Oh, *Shogun*. James Clavell.' I'd picked it up at the library when I'd seen Miss Reed.

I wondered if I should ask Big City if he'd read it but, remembering Chief's allusion to literacy levels, I decided it was better not to. Maybe he'd think I was 'dissing' him, and highlighting his lack of education, or maybe not. I didn't know – Big Spring was still a complete powder keg for me.

'It's based in Japan,' I said airily, fumbling for some direction, any direction, to take the conversation in – hopefully one that would avoid Jaws testing his gold teeth on my throat.

'I know that, motherfucka!' Big City exploded, although

bizarrely still with a big grin on his face. I could see one of his gold teeth had a diamond in it. 'I was going to ask you if you'd read *Taipan*, motherfucka, and if you felt that had more depth as a story?'

'Erm . . .'

Before I could answer, Big City cut in quietly, 'What, you never thought some really ugly big nigger could be readin' your white honkey books?'

I looked away from him to the book, ashamed. 'Well?' he asked in a tone that left me uncertain if he was playing with me or about to whack me. 'What you thinking about, white boy?'

I hesitated. 'I, eh . . . I was thinking you're not that ugly,' I said. Big City's face lit up, gold and diamond teeth gleaming, New Orleans tattoo creased by his smile. Maybe not ugly, I gulped, but not a beauty either. 'A face fit for radio,' as my old friend Joe would have said.

'OK, OK. That works. That's OK,' Big City said, still smiling, as he offered his catcher's mitt of a hand for a fist bump. 'We could be a'ight,' he continued. 'A'ight indeed. You're from Scotland, right?' he asked, surprising me again.

'Yeah, Glasgow.' I stopped myself from saying Pollok.

'Is all that *Braveheart* shit true, then?' Big City asked, as he started unpacking his things into his locker and onto his unfeasibly small bed. Once again I was grateful to Mel Gibson for the fact that for so many Americans, and for so many of the inmates in Big Spring, their reference point for Scotland was positive. Before *Braveheart* came out it would have been *Brigadoon* and I would already be a dead Scotsman.

'No, a load of rubbish really,' I said. He stopped and looked at me.

'Shame,' he said. 'Best film Mel Gibson done, in my view.'

Another bunk filled, I mused, trying to get on with my book, and this time by someone not half as frightening as he seemed. But how long could my luck hold out? And what species of prison life would end up occupying the bed immediately below mine?

Your relationship with your bunkie, Chief told me, was closer and more intense than your relationship with your wife; the lack of space making even the most marginal infraction the cause of severe disharmony. I had a fashion parade of prospective 'bunkies': every person who had entered the room looked first at the number on their hand then scanned around for their new bunk. I didn't want a whimperer, as that would attract the hyenas to my corner, and I certainly didn't want a chomo either, as I just didn't trust my natural predilection for befriending everyone and anyone, sometimes in spite of my better judgement. That left all the usual nutcases, gang-bangers and psychos – I wasn't really choosing from a good gene pool.

All of these stresses made it all the more important for me to escape to the peace of the library. Not only would I have some calmness around me, but there'd be fewer people – therefore, less chance of me putting my foot in it with someone. If that took care of the mornings, then in the afternoons I could come back to the Range when most others were working, again minimising my chances of getting myself into trouble. That would just leave the evenings to navigate; no mean feat, but possible. It was clear to me already that in such an environment with so many men – so many dangerous angry men, confined in such cramped uncomfortable conditions for so long – and with the guards basically invisible, that 'stuff' was always going to happen. I had to stay away from that 'stuff' as much as possible.

'I've been locked up in a badassed USP high–security prison and a medium as well – both were far better and safer than Big Spring,' Chief told me one day as I hung out with him and Kola.

'I don't understand,' I said, looking nervously around me. 'I thought Big Spring was a low–security prison?'

'Sure it is, Scotty. But all that means is that there are fewer cops around. In the USP it can be one guard to five inmates; here it's more like one to a hundred,' explained Kola.

'What you have to remember, Scotty,' continued Chief seamlessly, 'is that if you put eighty normal dudes into a room in the desert and leave them to it for years it would be pretty bad. When you add in all us psychos and nutcases and gang–bangers, you're left with serious shit.'

'Serious shit,' echoed Kola, clearly enjoying the theme. 'You also got to remember that while most of them aren't in here for murder and the like, these nutcases have got more than a couple of notches on their belt – they are career criminals, if you know what I mean. What they are in for is often the least bad thing they ever did!' he added, with unsuitable relish.

Chief nodded. 'What they're in for is nuthin' to what they done.' I'm sure I caught him glancing at Joker as he said this. 'Things really began to change about six or seven years ago, when they just kept jamming more and more dudes into these rooms, and we seemed to have fewer and fewer cops. And now they pay more at McDonald's than they do a guard, so you can imagine the kind of guy that comes and works here now. Whooheee!' exclaimed Chief, as he contorted his face to look like some imbecile.

'Yeah, some of those motherfuckers are dumber than us!' said Kola, without a hint of irony. 'Shit, Scotty, you'll probably be earning more than those jackasses if you work in the library.'

Not quite. $14 a month was a good deal short of a guard's pay or the $200 on offer at the factory. But in the end it was really just a question of perspective. $14 meant I would have doubled my salary from cleaning the latrines in a little under a few months and potentially doubling my telephone minutes to 14 a month also. I'd never doubled my salary before, so I was definitely on the up. At 157 steps from the Range to the library door, I still had an outstanding commute. What more could a man ask for? The only obstacle was getting out of kitchen duty.

Fortunately, the opportunity came to me when I was sent for my work medical. In spite of the months that had passed since our last meeting, the young Colombian doctor seemed to recognise me. I was, after all, the guy with the foreskin.

'*Hola Mulgrew, cómo estás?*'

'Fine, Doctor. How are you?'

'*Muy bien*. Now let's have a look at you.'

This medical was much less intrusive than our previous encounter, and consisted mainly of answering questions about medical history and checking heart rate, pulse and blood pressure. I was in fine health and ready to be passed fully fit for work when I started scratching my hand aggressively.

'Doctor,' I began diffidently. 'The only medical problem I ever have is sometimes I get terrible eczema, dried skin on my hands.'

He looked quickly at my hands. 'I don't see any sign of that,' he responded, turning back away from me.

'It comes up when my hands get wet or are in water for any length of time. It gets pretty bad,' I continued a bit more hesitantly. All rubbish of course, but this guy didn't need help in joining the dots.

'So . . . working in the kitchen would be difficult for you?' he asked, glancing again at my hands as if some dry skin might suddenly appear.

'*Si, señor,*' I responded with a slightly embarrassed smile. Nodding his head, he looked at me for a second then turned around to finish off his paperwork. Ripping off a piece of paper, he turned back to me.

'Hand this in at the Range office. You are medically fit to continue working, Mulgrew . . .' He paused for effect, then added, without a smile, '. . . *para la cocina.*' (Except for the kitchen.)

Knowing he had just granted me a huge favour, I thought about smiling, but decided against it. '*Gracias, tu es un hombre amable,*' I said, with all the sincerity I felt. He nodded slightly and kept his back turned to me.

It occurred to me as I left his office how much my life had changed in such a short time and how, even in terrible circumstances, you can feel emotions of great gratitude, even joy, over the simplest of things. My expectations of prison were so low that the slightest kindness, the most marginal piece of luck, elicited such simple pleasure, and that thought in itself encouraged me. Maybe I really could survive this; maybe I could get home intact to find Cara Katrina, to be a good father to Calum. I'd just secured a job working in a run–down library in a Texas desert with a monosyllabic boss at $14 a month, and I positively skipped back to the Range. The thought of even a tiny victory over the system encouraged me greatly, but my elation was short–lived.

'You've got your new bunkie,' motioned Chief with a nod of his head towards my bunk. I saw a few Hispanics milling around one guy who was sat on the bunk under-neath mine, his personal effects strewn around him. I couldn't get clear sight of him, but I was already knocked off stride again. I felt anxiety clutch at my throat.

'What do we know about him?' I asked Chief, turning sideways away from my new roommate.

'Listen to you!' Chief laughed. 'What are you, suddenly the old–timer? Man, Scotland, you're somethin' else. We' don't know nuthin' about him – why don't you go over and introduce yourself?'

'Right, right,' I apologised. 'I'll go over then.' I started to walk towards my betrothed. He was wearing what looked like a dark vest, until I realised he had a full skin of tattoos, save his arms, which were largely clear, other than a few isolated, random tattoos. It was clear from the people already coming past me to greet him, all Hispanic, that he was 'quoted' as Chief would say – a name, a serious player, someone to be reckoned with. Not wanting to look too afraid, I walked forward towards our bunks and nodded towards my new neighbour.

He was young looking, fresh faced and handsome; a bit of the Orlando Bloom about him, with his pencil moustache, little goatee and hair tightly pulled back in a ponytail. Despite the tattoos, he looked very clean, very pristine and precise, and I noticed how well folded his clothes were as they lay on the bed. I also noticed that one or two other Hispanics were unpacking his things.

'Hey, *cómo estás, Escosais?*' he said jovially, as if he knew me, and pushed his fist out for the obligatory bump. I bumped back and nodded to him.

'*Bienvenu a Escotia,*' I responded ('Welcome to Scotland'), at which point his smile seemed to grow larger. He seemed very happy to be in Big Spring, almost as happy as his compatriots seemed to see him. I found out many weeks later that his euphoria was because he'd just been sentenced that day for his part leading a drug cartel, shipping in cocaine from Mexico to the United States. He had originally operated right under the Americans' noses, smuggling in the drugs from Juárez, the notorious Mexican town right on the border, four hours from Big Spring, using one or two 'bent' US border control personnel, but when one of them had started to get greedy he'd had to be disposed of (I didn't ask how). He switched the operation to the sea, and that worked well for a while. One day, at his wife's behest, he took a quick shopping trip to Miami – on the boat. Unfortunately he picked the very day the US Coast Guard did a random spot check of his boat and found over two tonnes of coke in the hold.

The celebration was because he had just arrived after negotiating a plea bargain and sentence of just ten years – more in keeping with a functionary than the son of the boss of the cartel and heir apparent to the whole operation. He'd expected fifty years and had hoped for thirty – ten was party time. He expected to be shipped back to Mexico within five, at which point, he said, he would barely serve one day more. Five, he said, he could do standing on his head, and could only help his credibility within the cartel.

He seemed busy so I made to climb up onto my bunk, conscious now that I had to be careful where I put my foot in the act of climbing. Chief had shown me exactly where to put my foot, so that my shoes made no contact with the lower bunkie's bedding – and it was a serious lesson. People got knifed for far less.

'*Tu habla español, Escosais?*' my new bunkie shouted up to me.

'*Un poco solomente,*' I responded, as I started to nervously organise myself on top of my bunk, conscious that what little space I had had, had just been halved.

'I am Ramon,' said my new flatmate in a way that suggested he spoke little of our language. He had stood up by now, but his head barely appeared above the bed. The rest of his flunkies just watched me, but it was already clear to me that they held Ramon in some esteem and expected me to do likewise. It wouldn't be a good idea to upset my bunkie at any stage, I thought.

'I speak the little English, but I good bunkie!' he said with a zest that was both charming and a little irritating. It seemed unreasonable to be that happy, but this guy was full of the joys of Spring. I had a choice to make between English and Spanish, but I was tired, numbed by the constant stress and changes of life in the Big Room; of life in Big Spring.

'That's cool Ramon. *Bueno, muy bien.* The whole

neighbourhood's on the up and up,' I said, unable to stop sarcasm emerging from under my general fatigue.

'*Que?*' he asked still smiling.

'*Nada*, nothing. *Estoy un bueno bunkie tambien.*' (I am also a good bunkie.)

While Ramon was apparently enjoying one of the best days of his life, I lay back on my bunk and closed my eyes. Beyond the light shuffling of Ramon sorting out his things below me, the din of the room began to seep back into my consciousness. The noise was incessant – so many different voices, different languages, different music. Sudden shouts, peals of laughter, cries of excitement, of anger, rising disputes, all condensed in this room with seemingly more and more people cramming into it each day. The constant traffic of other inmates coming in and out, each one looking more dangerous than the last. Big City snoring loudly at the base of my bed – how the hell could he manage to sleep in all this racket? The sounds sometimes merged together, were sometimes individually discernible, as if they were lining up to take their turn to assault my senses.

I tried to stop translating the Spanish, because the mixture of Mexicans, Colombians, Hondurans, El Salvadorians and other accents was making it almost impossible to understand the language I had taken so long to study. They all spoke so fast! I had convinced myself that if I could tune in I would pick up when I was in danger, but the constant attempts to translate made my mind feel jumbled and tired, so tired. I would construct scenarios from a word here, a word there – but the truth was I didn't know what the hell was going on. I felt like I was going crazy.

I closed my eyes and rubbed them. I felt so tired but had still been struggling to sleep. I was hungry but couldn't face another taco. I started to feel overwhelmed. I felt my heart racing, but I wasn't in any immediate danger. Or was I? It raced even more. I suddenly felt frightened, nervous, defeated. Was I having a heart attack? I couldn't breathe. I was panicking. What the hell was wrong with me? I felt a cold sweat on my brow and my mind screaming at me: 'Get out! Get out now!' I turned to face the wall, worried someone might see me. 'I can't let them see me like this,' I thought, 'or else I am finished.' Ramon's friends were all underneath me now, invading my space even more. Fuck, they were almost on top of me. Was I breaking down? Was I losing it!? What the fuck was happening? I felt so completely afraid. Still my heart raced ever faster. Fuck, I am having a heart attack, I thought. And I'm going to die here alone in this room with all these people. My family won't even know. Calum will be alone. Each new thought added to my panic and seemed to speed my heart up even more. I wasn't simply touching despair, it was absorbing me, sucking me in ever deeper. I had the urge to roll up in a foetal position and pulled my knees up closer to my chest. I'd never felt so alone; never felt such a sudden onset of despair; never felt such deep-lying fear.

Had anyone noticed? Were they looking at me now? What the fuck was wrong with me? I had to get a grip. I just wanted to go home. I was breaking down; I was starting to disintegrate. This was all too hard, too difficult. Ridiculous. These people are going to kill me. I'm never going to get home. I'll never survive this. Writhing around and putting my hand on my heart to confirm it was pumping madly away – it was – I felt myself slipping; losing control. Someone was bound to notice soon. What was I doing in this desert in Texas? 'I don't belong here, I shouldn't be here,' my mind screamed, my breathing heavy.

I'd only been inside a few months so far, but the amalgam of all those moments flashed through my head: the Aryan Brotherhood, Big City, cleaning toilets, the beating, Choker, terrifying inmates, spider tattoos. Visions of all of it came screaming down on top of me at the same time. My breathing seemed to shorten, my heart speeding up further. Then I recognised it. Within the chaos of my mind, as if standing quietly in the corner, a calm voice was talking to me. 'You are having a panic attack,' it said. I'd read about this once somewhere long ago. I could just see a form in my mind through the panic. It took the shape of a man; as he emerged, he was wearing a grey suit. For a moment, while all the chaotic thoughts continued to batter around my mind, their dominance began to fade and I could see a picture of this calm faceless soul telling me to breathe, to hold on, that it was a panic attack, that it was OK for me to be scared, that I was doing OK, and that this moment would pass. I tried to direct my mind towards him, towards that form, to listen intently to those calming words, to hold onto something and to block out all the other images of the last months in Big Spring.

As if the fizz began to go out of my fears, I momentarily started to breathe more easily, a bit heavily, as if I was sobbing. I wasn't sure if I had managed to suppress the sound. I couldn't let anyone see me like this. It was just a panic attack. It was normal, to be almost expected in the circumstances, I told myself, mirroring the comments of the grey-suited apparition. I was re-asserting control. But this was just the calm before a greater storm. My breathing had eased, but, just as suddenly I felt gripped by a new fear, a second wave, a deep unrecognisable form. An overwhelming, overpowering fear of something just lurking in the deepest shadows of my mind, something unspeakable, too painful to face, too impossible to contemplate, but something I could feel was coming, was coming to the surface, approaching me, stalking me, ready to blow my world apart. All sorts of thoughts were flying through my mind now, too swiftly for me to trap and countenance, random and dangerous, but beneath all of them there still rumbled something much more sinister. I knew it was coming and my panic deepened. It was moving from my subconscious mind to my conscious mind and I couldn't stop it.

What if he's touching her? What if they're hitting her? 'NO!!!' I shouted, not caring who would have heard.

I sat up and clenched my fists tightly then rolled back around to the wall again and opened my eyes to stare at the peeling brickwork. I was hyperventilating. I expelled a huge quantity of air as if my despair was sucking the life force out of me.

I forced my hands through my short hair, trying to grab my head as if it might be coming off, as those painful thoughts came around again. 'Shut the fuck up,' I said quickly in a whisper, my breath short, desperate, ugly. 'Shut up, shut up, shut up.' I thought I was going to cry then realised tears were already covering my face, as I tried to turn further into the wall. I'm breaking down; I'm losing it. Don't let them see me like this. Don't let them see me like this. 'Fuck them,' I thought just as quickly.

Then she came to me, as clear as day; she was alone and crying, she was alone, crying for her daddy. She was frightened and alone and I needed to get to her. I needed to get out of here, I had to get home. Didn't anyone understand I had to get home? I wiped the tears off my face. Stop crying, you idiot. I have to help her. I had to find my baby, I had to save her. She stayed with me, her pain apparent. She was sitting on a trunk. Her bare feet so small and delicate and tiny. She was cold, I could see she was cold. She was asking me where I was through her tears, she was asking why I didn't come and get her, as she looked up to a small window at the top of a cold and soulless room. I felt the pain splitting me in two, I wanted to scream, to rage, to fight, to punch, to kick, to kill. What a catastrophic failure as a father I was. I'd locked my girl in my own original nightmare; I'd placed her in my hell. I needed to jump down from this bunk and go home right now. Just start walking and bulldoze through any fucker that tried to stop me.

That's what I had to do, that's what I was going to do. I was going home. I was going to get out of here. I had faced the unspeakable thoughts; I had seen my darkest fear. My breathing was still laboured, my heart racing, but the edge had come off. 'OK,' I said to myself, 'I have to stop.' I don't need to keep thinking of this, but I know it's out there. I know that anything can be happening with Cara. I know that I have to get home to her, I have to find her. So I have to get a grip on myself. I have to calm down, to start all over again, to build the steps to get me home as quickly as possible.

I will see my Case Manager next week and I will start the ball rolling to get my transfer under way. They owe me that; they promised me that. I'll have to get in the zone for that meeting and do my best to get through to her how much I need to see my baby girl.

A few times the panic felt as if it might return, but it ebbed and flowed and at last began to drift away. My heart slowed down and I felt tired, deeply tired. I strayed between a state of sleep and consciousness, aware I was drifting off but aware, too, that I was still in the Big Room, still in Big Spring. I vaguely recognised that the lights had switched off, so it must have been past 10 p.m. I couldn't remember the count, as I thought about how little I'd slept since I'd arrived. I was in a semi-dream state and it seemed to be giving me profound comfort.

I was remembering a time with Calum, on one of his many visits to me in Houston. Even though the dream was jumbled, I felt so close to him, as if he was right there with me, helping me. We were standing in the foyer of a cinema in Galveston. In those days, aged ten or eleven, Calum would still hold my hand when we were together, and I was visualising that feeling of warmth and comfort I had, holding his little hand in mine, as we stood queuing for our tickets. We were queuing to see *Shrek 2*, or maybe a Harry Potter film, I can't remember which.

'One adult and two children please.'

We always bought an extra ticket for Cara. That way, I thought, she would know in the future that she was always missed; always with us.

'How old are the children?' the older lady in the booth asked from behind her reading glasses. Originally that answer had been nine and five, but it had moved to ten and six, and now, painfully, by this stage it was eleven and seven. What was the seven-year-old Cara like? Time was moving on; she was slipping further away. 'Where's the other child?' the lady in the booth asked. I said nothing.

'She's not here,' said Calum in a simple uncomplicated tone. The lady paused for a moment, looking at this bizarre father and son in front of her, then shrugged and handed us three tickets. Calum, so careless and reckless with most things, took Cara's ticket and placed it in the top breast pocket of his jacket with tender care. He clipped the pocket shut, and lightly touched it again as if to reassure himself the ticket was safe. I stood and watched him do this. There was an unspoken understanding between us and I felt a mixture of pain and love and pride inside. When we would get home, he would take the ticket out and place it carefully with the other things we kept in 'Cara's box': multitudes of tickets for the cinema, water parks, amusement rides and other fun days we would, and should, have all shared. Birthday cards, Christmas cards and presents that I had encouraged my family to keep sending; drawings from Calum and letters from me, all my sad attempts to keep a history for her.

That image of Calum and I standing silently in front of that ticket booth – waiting patiently for our three tickets, holding hands, each lost in his own world – lingered, and eventually, mercifully, carried me off to a fitful sleep.

13

THE LIBRARY GANG

I STARTED WORK IN THE LIBRARY the following Monday, roughly ten weeks after entering Big Spring. I'd had a few more of those meltdown moments over the inter-vening time, but if any of my roommates had witnessed any part of them, no one said. In a way, though, the silence – the fact that I couldn't talk about them – made them loom larger in my mind. I kept telling myself over and over that they were just panic attacks, but I had never experienced anything like them before, even through the extradition fight and those dark days in Houston. I suspected that Chief had noticed some or perhaps all of them, but he never said anything to me and I didn't ask. I felt ashamed; weakened by it. I knew I couldn't afford to have any more episodes like that, and tried to throw myself into creating some structure to my long, slow days in Big Spring.

When it came, the library job helped enormously with that, and so did having a few people around me, like Chief, whom I could talk to and trust. The Range Officer had frowned at my exclusion from kitchen work and Chief seemed mightily impressed that I had managed to dodge that one. He seemed less impressed by the fact that I took the effort to get clean-shaven and have my clothes ironed for my first day at work.

'You're wasting your time, Scotty dog,' he offered. 'No one's gonna take a damn bit of notice of you in that place.' He lay back on his bunk, hands casually behind his head.

'Shit Chief,' Kola added, 'I think Scotland's got the hots for Miss Reed. He done been in too long already!' They both laughed and leaned over and high-fived. One of the benefits, I suppose, of having the Range so tightly packed with felons was that you could 'high-five' a neighbour without even getting out of your bunk.

The joking and the bonding ended swiftly as one of our new bunkmates passed by. His name was John, and he was tall and pale, white, with a long grey beard and he had moved into the same section as Chief and Kola, just ten feet away from me. All the chomos were white, I soon found out – not a racist observation, just a reality. They also invariably had beards, large, shaggy ones – possibly out of some subconscious attempt to hide their shame. In Big Spring, there were very clear 'rules' on how to treat them – they basically were not to be spoken to, and not to be helped in any way. No sharing of items, no favours done, no support in any way. Chief had already told me in some detail about the events of last December and how bad some of the beatings had been. Now more were being re-introduced into the very Range that had seen a few of them murdered and scores beaten beyond recognition.

The atmosphere around John was instantly hostile. But the inmates were aware that any visible aggression towards John or his ilk would not be tolerated by the prison officers and would lead to an immediate transfer out of Big Spring into another medium- or high-security establishment. So there was lip-service to some kind of protection for them, but essentially it was worthless. The chomos were a protected species while the guards were around – which meant that most of the worst abuse simply took place after the watershed. During the day, the abuse was more gentle and seemed to be divided up, like so much of prison life, on racial lines. The Hispanics spat near the chomos, or on their belongings, with the greatest ceremony, with real meaning and aplomb, while the Whites seemed to spend more time focusing on spit volume, summoning up a greater mixture from the depths of their bowels before violently exploding it onto their target. The Blacks seemed more intent on real damage and would throw anything around that John had left on his pristinely made bed.

Initially, no one hit him though. That will come later, Chief had told me morosely. At the moment everyone seemed required to show their outrage at his presence, but to me it looked like it was all posturing, just part of the façade that the inmates maintained. Kola and Chief held themselves apart from it too. Without ever being open or friendly as they had been with me, they were nevertheless respectful of John's space, and basically cour-teous. Chief had told me he had learned many moons ago – he always spoke like that – that he was in no position to judge anyone. I liked that personal rule, and it was something I was trying to adhere to as well.

Everything about life in prison felt more intense – you got to know certain aspects of your fellow felons very well. But others were off-limits. Unless you were a shot-caller, for example, you never asked why someone was in prison. You could ask how many years they got, how many served and how many to go, but not why they were there – you waited until they told you, if they ever did. Anyway it was a mistake to define them by the crime they had been imprisoned for – nearly all of them had a much more developed criminal CV. What they had been caught doing was usually the tip of a very big iceberg. In darker moments, I would wonder what some of my roommates – the very ones I nodded to and joked and fist-bumped with – might have been up to on the outside, but in a strange way, with the exception of the hated chomos, that mattered a lot less than I'd imagined.

What mattered was what you saw every day on the inside, and there could be a lot more dignity and pride and care there than I'd seen in many other walks of life. The man who'd ironed my shirt and khakis this time for my first day in the library, for example, did all sorts of laundry tasks for a few stamps. When he had collected enough of them, he'd send them back to his family in Central America, where the meagre amount of dollars they fetched could make a real difference to their lives. I admired him for that – whatever he'd done in the past.

On my first day on the new job, I counted the steps from the Range to the library door and, thoroughly satisfied with my new commute, entered the small prefab-ricated building carrying some writing paper and a Spanish grammar book. There was no sign of Miss Reed or anyone else 'official' for that matter, so I went to the desk where I'd seen AJ sitting on the day of my interview and pulled up another chair beside what I assumed was his. The library already had five or six inmates milling around, three of whom I assessed as likely chomos, being white and middle-aged with beards. I didn't care though; all I could think about was how blissfully, magically quiet it was in this place. It was extraordinary, a revelation; a real oasis of respite, soothing my senses after months of the constant din of the Big Room. I methodically placed my writing paper and pen down in front of me and then my Spanish grammar book, revelling in the space and silence. I'd never felt happier beginning a new job in my life before. This scene was swiftly brought to an end, however.

'Awww, this is bullshit!' These were the first words AJ ever uttered to me, followed by, 'I told Miss Reed I ain't working with no white boy. No sir, no way,' he complained, to no one in particular, looking around him as if one of the child molesters might suddenly come to his aid and remove me from my chair.

'I don't think she's in today,' I replied, keeping my expression bland. I didn't care if he didn't want to work with me; I wasn't budging from this little piece of heaven for anyone. 'You must be AJ. I'm Scotland,' I added, offering a fist bump. He looked at it then looked back at me and let it hang there.

'Uh huh . . .'

My fist stayed out a few seconds longer before I withdrew it, unbumped.

AJ was a diminutive African-American with closely cropped dark hair, a pencil-thin moustache, and a

pencil-thin regard for everyone. Following our introduction, he asserted his 'space' by pushing my chair further
into the corner as he took the lion's share of our joint
working desk, all the time mumbling profanities about
Miss Reed and white boys under his breath. I smiled
weakly at him, feeling like an interloper, and awkwardly
big beside him given he was so short. After a few seconds,
he sighed loudly and looked at me again. 'What d'you
say your name was?'

'Scotland. Scotland,' I said, twice, thinking it might not
have registered.

'I got you, I got you,' he snapped. 'You don't have to
repeat yourself. I'm not stupid.'

Although the conversation was starting badly, there
was something instantly likeable about AJ, if I could just
get beyond the prickliness. 'Erm, Chief said to say hello,'
I threw in. Chief had told me more than that, actually.
AJ, he'd explained, was a real character. A crack cocaine
dealer from the age of fourteen, he'd lived all his life in
Washington and had received a ten-year stretch for
possession aged only twenty-five. He'd never been a user
himself ('He's way too smart for that!') but his mouth
had got him into trouble in an East Coast prison and
hence the dreaded transfer 2,000 miles away from home
to sunny Big Spring. AJ had been pissed off ever since
– 'A small guy with a big attitude,' quipped Chief – and
he reserved most of that attitude for people with white
skin. Then again, as Kola had chipped in, helpfully, AJ
had probably never met a white guy quite like Scotland.

'Chief said hi, did he?' replied AJ, giving no indication of whether or not he was impressed by that
association. He kept staring at me intently, which was

very disconcerting, especially since he was sitting less than a foot away from me.

I smiled weakly again, feeling exposed and uncomfortable. I picked up my pen then put it back down, wondering what to say to keep this conversation going. I'd only seen characters like AJ on TV programmes like *The Wire*; none of my life's experiences had really equipped me to be the Joint Assistant Librarian in the Big Spring Correctional Facility with a career crack cocaine dealer from the projects of inner Washington DC.

'Do you get laid much with that accent?' he suddenly asked – a complete change of tack.

'Not in here.' My quick response was rewarded with a slight grin from AJ.

'I mean in the Free World,' he qualified.

'Sure, between the accent and my boyish good looks,' I responded straight faced. AJ paused for a moment, then began to smile. Like a lot of the African–Americans I'd seen, he had a set of teeth a mother would be proud of, including the obligatory gold one.

'You're not a chomo, are you?' he asked, suddenly looking much more serious.

'I don't have a beard.'

'Or an AB?'

'No. No to both.'

'A'ight, a'ight,' AJ said, stretching his arms out on the desk before laying his head down on top of them and going to sleep.

About an hour later, he lifted his head up and carried on. 'Because if you is a chomo or an AB, then you and me will have a problem and I'll have to tell Miss Reed you can't work here.'

'Well, I'm not either!' I said. I'd been making some progress with my Spanish verbs in the meantime, and this was just irritating. AJ looked over at what I was writing.

'You studyin' Spanish?' he asked. I resisted the temptation to be sarcastic and instead just offered a grumpy '*Si.*'

'So am I,' said AJ.

'Well maybe we could test each other sometimes,' I offered. AJ carried on staring at me intently. 'Shouldn't you be teaching me the ropes or something?' I asked him, encouraged that he hadn't immediately shot down the idea of doing some Spanish together.

AJ stared at me once more. 'Shit!' he mumbled under his breath as he shook his head. 'Dude, do I look like a teacher!? A bus station is where a bus stops. A train station is where a train stops. And this here is my work station. You figure out the rest!' With that he lay his head back down and missed my smile.

I decided to push on.

'Shouldn't you at least explain to me how the library is organised?' I asked the back of his head. I still hadn't really come to terms with the laissez-faire attitude of both the cops and staff in Big Spring – no one really seemed to care much about anything. Everyone was just waiting, doing their own time and counting the hours till they went home. Everyone.

Looking thoroughly fed up as he raised his head again, AJ sighed then turned away from me towards the books. 'On this section over there, we have fiction,' then turning towards the other side of the room he continued, 'and over here we have the non-fiction.'

I had grabbed my pen and was writing this down.

When I looked back up he was staring at me. 'What are you doing?'

'Ahm, um, taking notes.'

'Notes?' responded AJ incredulously. 'You mean you can't remember where the fiction and non-fiction sections are?'

'Erm yes . . . no . . . I mean, of course I can,' I stammered. 'I just wanted to take notes for the rest of it.'

'Rest of it? The rest of it?' AJ echoed. 'Ain't no "rest of it". Over there we have fiction, and over here we have non-fiction. If someone comes in and asks you, "Where's the books at?" you say, "Over there we have fiction and over here we have non-fiction." That's it! If the book is fiction it goes there, and if its non-fiction it goes over here. And that's all!' That said, he theatrically placed his head back down onto the table and mimicked sleep.

I looked down at my scant notes, then looked up to the jumbled mess of books randomly scattered across the library. At first I felt bewildered but then suddenly elated – I had just found something to do. I was about to get up and start planning my assault on the books when AJ raised his head again.

'What?' I asked him.

'Can I ask you something?' he began in considered fashion. I had no idea where he was going this time, but had already realised he was the kind of guy that asked whatever was on his mind. That was why I liked him, I think, despite his rudeness.

'Shoot,' I said, unsure if that word sounded right coming from me, but thinking that's the way you might speak to someone who has been a crack cocaine dealer since he was a teenager.

'Does you like black people?'

'Sure,' I began confidently, without hesitation, 'but I don't like short people.'

AJ stared at me for a moment, contemplating that one before he broke out into a beautiful, face-filling smile, his gold tooth sparkling. 'Shh–iiitt!!' he exclaimed. 'That's funny!' he said, as he laughed and banged his hand on the table. 'That's good, Scotland! Don't like short people. You're funny!' He carried on laughing and hitting the table. This little outburst had caught the attention of a few of the other inmates who were staring over until AJ remembered his librarian role. 'What you motherfuckas looking at!?' he barked. 'You come here to read the motherfucking books or watch the mother-fucking floor show, motherfuckas?' The onlookers quickly recoiled into their books. Meanwhile, AJ's fury vanished as swiftly as it had appeared and he chuckled in my direction. 'We going be a'ight, Scotland, we going to be a'ight in the li–bra–ree!!'

Carried away a little, I made a reverse 'L' with the thumb and forefinger of my right hand.

'What the fuck's that?' said AJ doubtfully. 'That some kind of motherfucking Aryan Brotherhood sign you doin' at me now, motherfucka, 'cos if you're a . . .'

We both looked at my hand making a backwards 'L' sign. 'AJ – relax, relax,' I said, hastily. 'I was just doing an L sign . . .' It felt rather silly now. 'You know – that's the secret librarians' sign, dude.'

'Cool!' said AJ, instantly becalmed again as he started playing around with making the sign himself. 'Librarians!!' he cried out.

AJ and I didn't look back from that first day, and we spent a lot of time together even when we weren't working mornings in the library. He was tremendously insightful about prison life and its strange workings, although his manner got him into a lot of trouble with other inmates and the cops. He was very bright and sarcastic and it amazed me that a man with such inner resources and potential had only ever had one job in his life – selling crack cocaine. My upbringing had taught me that plenty of people stayed poor however hard they worked, but over the years I'd been in banking I'd developed the idea that everything sort of found its natural level. Bright people, strong people, talented people rose up – those who were less so, stayed put. But meeting people like AJ turned that idea on its head. In spite of his brains and wit, there was little chance of him 'working his way to the top' – as the American Dream would have had it – because he had no concept of being entitled to another life, much less any idea what he needed to do to achieve it. His greatest attribute was his sense of humour and he seemed really pleased when I told him he reminded me of Eddie Murphy. 'In *Shrek*,' I added – much to his disappointment.

. Friendships had different levels in prison, just like on the outside. AJ was a workmate – a joking and teasing partner, and later on, someone for whom I came to have immense fondness and respect. But there was something different in my relationship with Chief. He'd been a sort of mentor to me right at the start – and, I guess, like the relationships we form at the start of our lives, there was something more intense about the way we were with each other. A couple of times, I crossed the line with him – such as when I called out: 'Afternoon, ladies,' to him and Kola when they returned from their traditional native

Indian sweat-up session in the exercise yard. The two men eyed me closely for a while, then left me alone, later on calling me over to advise me on yet another point of prison etiquette.

'Never joke with someone you don't know, and never, ever, ever,' Chief said slowing down for emphasis, 'insinuate someone is a homo or feminine, or you'll get your Scottish face mashed up real bad.' I took the point.

And it was hammered home even harder by the fact that, later on that day, Chief told me casually, almost as if in passing, that he'd been praying for me out in the Yard. He and Kola would go to a sweat usually once a week, with the other 'Injuns'. They'd burn a fire and sit in a small wigwam that was permanently in place up to the side of the main yard, sweating away as they chanted, prayed or sang through the afternoon. I sat watching them a few times, envious perhaps of the brotherhood they had, and feeling more alone as a result. Given it was always over 90 degrees outside, I shuddered to think how much sweating they actually did in these meets, but Chief had told me he regularly would get to the point of passing out and hallucinating which, I surmised from the way he smiled as he said it, was the effect he was aiming for. I was taken aback at the idea that he'd put me in his prayers, and deeply touched.

I discovered his story later on, from Kola, on a day Chief had declined to go to the chow hall because he had taco exhaustion. He had served with pride, Kola told me, in Iran and Iraq, and he had also seen action in Afghanistan and Sierra Leone. Eventually, after eight years of service, his luck ran out and a night jump over Afghanistan went badly wrong for him when his parachute wouldn't properly open. Sure he was going to die, he said he stopped struggling and was prepared to meet the Big Chief in the sky, but some trees broke his descent and he survived. Unfortunately they also broke his back and crushed his skull. 'You don't actually need a working parachute to skydive,' Chief told me later. 'You only need a working one if you want to skydive twice.'

He would never skydive again. Fourteen months later, with an honourable discharge and a veteran's pension, he walked, stiffly and painfully, out of the life he'd loved, and into nothing. He had a broken body, and excruciating headaches that led in time to epilepsy. After the initial few hurrahs and welcomes-back on the Reservation, he hit the bottle – his fortunes taking a further dramatic downturn one night when partying with some friends around a camp fire.

They were joined in their revels by a couple of guys whom Chief didn't know, and one who soon started to taunt him about his strained walking style. Things deteriorated rapidly between the two of them, until the interloper foolishly pulled Chief's gun out from his trouser belt and started taunting him about his inability to use it. According to Kola, Chief immediately disarmed the man, 'pistol-whipped his ass', tied him up and dunked him in and out of the lake for a few minutes at a time for good measure. He then began to fire his gun over the wretched guy's head while performing a Zuni war dance around him. When the cops arrived, Chief was sitting calmly waiting for them at the fireplace, his captive still tied up and warming himself by the fire. As well as kidnapping and assault, he was charged with the further Federal offence of 'discharging a weapon in a reservation' – a big no-no which, combined with his other no-nos, got him fifteen years in the slammer. I couldn't help feeling his country would be better served if they'd given him fifteen weeks with a psychiatrist instead, but Chief was less easy on himself. 'There's no excuse for what I did,' he eventually told me. 'I got what I deserved. If it hadn't been that guy it would have been someone else – I was a wreck.'

Chief was a good example of one of the myths that lawyers and judges perpetrate about prison – that it's full of people claiming to be innocent. In my time in Big Spring, I met only three people who made that claim – the rest just 'fronted up' and accepted they were guilty. Chief was even sceptical of those three. 'In here, a clear conscience is usually the sign of a fuzzy memory,' he would say. They nearly all had complaints about how they were caught, or the details of the charge (even Chief claimed that he hadn't actually discharged his weapon), but most were serial offenders, and took the view that they were going to be caught sooner or later for something.

With AJ, Kola and Chief, I had at least met some people I could talk to, and that I liked, although relating to them was sometimes a struggle. I tried not to judge any of them, because I'd stopped feeling it was my right to. Fortunately for me, another good friend called Carlos, aka 'New York', was to arrive in the Range about a month after I got there, and was one of the last people in to make up our complement of eighty-two inmates in the Big Room.

New York was white, quite tall at around six feet, with short dark hair. As I watched him walk in one day from my vantage point in the corner, I knew immediately he was an old hand despite his relative youthfulness. From his swagger and the way he unpacked his stuff and made up his bed, he'd obviously been to lots of prisons – which meant he was a player or a troublemaker. He looked European, although I could hear from his accent that he was a New Yorker, from Brooklyn I guessed, thinking maybe he was Italian in background. I'd lived in New York for four years in the nineties, and Calum was born there, so at that moment I had more in common with Carlos than any of the other 1,500 inmates in Big Spring. I liked New York and New Yorkers, their abrasive style sitting comfortably with a Glaswegian from Pollok.

By then I was receiving a daily copy of *The New York Times*, courtesy of an Australian journalist friend of mine, Peter Wilson, who had also been doing a lot of 'under–cover' work to help me track Cara. It was often late, very late, and then would sometimes come in groups of five or six papers at a time. Sometimes it didn't come at all, but that didn't really matter – time wasn't an issue in prison and news didn't have to be up to date for it to be current in my world.

I took a copy down to Carlos a few days after he'd arrived and stood at the bottom of his bunk with it in my hand. He was sitting on his own on the top bunk, cross–legged, playing cards. Without looking up, and before I could speak, he said, 'What the fuck d'you want?' Maybe more Queens than Brooklyn, but definitely a confirmed New Yorker, I decided.

'Nuthin',' I began. 'I just thought you might want a copy of *The New York Times*.' I placed it up on his bunk, smiling.

Without looking up or stopping his card game, Carlos responded, 'Oh yeah?' He paused, studying one card for a moment, but still not looking up. 'And why would you want to do that?'

'I heard your accent,' I started. 'I guessed you were from New York or nearby and thought you might like it . . .' I trailed off, beginning to feel that this act of consideration was probably a mistake. I didn't know this guy; I couldn't guess that I'd like him or get on with him. I had to stop behaving as I would on the outside.

Carlos had by now looked up at me and held his hand out to take the paper. 'Huh. Tuesday's,' he said as he threw it to the side of his bunk. Today was Friday. Now he looked at me square on. 'What are you – a fuckin' chomo or something?' Deeply regretting my approach to him, I spluttered 'No!' as indignantly as I could and as I struggled for something else to say he continued, 'Well what the fuck are you then? A faggot?'

'Am I fuck!' I answered angrily, 'I was only trying to be friendly . . .' I was instantly aware of the stupidity of that phrase, and the stupidity of what I was trying to do. I was annoyed at myself. Normal civilities didn't work here; they were seen as weakness not a strength. I was annoyed at myself letting my guard down. 'Forget it!' I said and marched off back the thirteen steps to my bunk. Carlos went back to his cards while Chief, ever watchful, just shook his head.

'And you can shut up as well!' I called over to him as I passed his bunk and clambered back up onto mine. That started him laughing some more and shaking his head as he returned to writing one of his enormous letters. 'Yeah, put that in your letter as well!' I called over. 'I'm glad I entertain you, Chief!' I lay back on my bunk and stared at the ceiling.

'Oh you do, Scotty! You keep us all entertained.' I leaned up on one arm to see Kola grinning furiously himself.

I saw Carlos read *The Times* cover to cover over the next few days. 'Piece of shit,' I mumbled to myself. I noticed he spent quite a lot of time with Angel, who still hadn't gotten back to me on my papers, and Joker, who still looked quite capable of strangling me at a moment's notice. They always spoke in Spanish and I wondered if Carlos was a Sureno or a King – second-generation Hispanic perhaps. Whatever he was, he seemed an old practised hand at prison life – not a bumbling fool like me.

This was typical prison behaviour, though, from him and myself. Everyone watched everyone else in the Big Room. Who was talking to whom; who was arguing with whom; who had what; who went to whose bed during the night. Carlos wasn't being particularly aggressive towards me – just protecting himself, and showing everyone else who might be watching what sort of a man he was.

In any case, people who were after sex didn't go handing out free newspapers. It went on – I discovered that on my second night, when I took a trip to the latrines and found one pair of Hispanic guys pleasuring each other in a bunk, and another two going at it vigorously in the shower – but discreetly, according to rules I never enquired into. The Mexicans even had a phrase: *'Detras de la valla, el no es gay'* – 'Behind the fence, it's not gay'. Other racial groups in prison seemed to take a dimmer view of the activity – but that didn't necessarily mean they weren't indulging themselves.

About a fortnight after my first, failed attempt to strike

up a friendship with Carlos, I was lying on my bunk one afternoon, when the cocky bastard suddenly decided to acknowledge me.

'Hey Scotland?' he called out. 'D'you play cards?'

'You after another copy of *The Times*?' I responded disdainfully.

'Of course I am!' he exclaimed gleefully. 'So do you play cards or not?'

'No.'

'Good, then I'll teach you,' he said, without missing a beat as he moved over and stood at one of the disused lockers at the foot of Chief's bunk. 'You don't mind if we play here Chief, do ya?' he asked, shuffling the cards with a dexterity both impressive and unsurprising.

'Long as you wup Scotty's ass, New York,' replied Chief, barely looking up from this week's masterpiece, as I clambered reluctantly down from my bunk and began my first game of cards with Carlos. There was no apology, no attempt to explain – certainly no suggestion of him saying thanks for the loan of the paper. It was the male relationship stripped down to its purest form: Carlos had just decided to be friends with me – and so we were. I'd play every night with him from then on, while learning Carlos' unique perspective on the rights and wrongs of prison life and the life of crime. It was a card school in the truest sense of the term.

My relationship with my bunkie Ramon continued to develop well, because he was respectful and, for the most part, quiet. I practised my Spanish with him most days and also with Mendiola, an older man who had moved into the bunk just across from me. He was a kindly, gentle man in his early sixties, who had been in Big

Spring for over twelve years, and seemed to have no hopes of leaving. He didn't seem to have a job as such, but he got paid for fixing and mending things – including an old pair of training shoes, which he'd revamped with electrician's tape and some judicious stitching, and sold to me for the very reasonable sum of two stamps. They were around a size twelve, and you wouldn't get entry into a nightclub wearing them, but they were heaven-sent because they meant I could go up to the weight pile and gymnasium now and finally start to work out again. He'd also make simple wooden crucifixes from beads and laces which he'd bless in the Catholic church up near the Yard before selling them for a few stamps to the Hispanic inmates. I came back one day to find one left for me under my pillow – a gift offered without words. Mendiola was quiet and reserved, someone who seemed to be wrestling with some private inner grief, and I never knew why he was so fond of me. I would like to think I'd have been friends with him – and a number of others – on the outside, but I know that the pressures of overcrowded prison life had a lot to do with it. If someone slept, dressed, shat and ate within a few feet of you month after month, and they were quiet and clean and respectful and co-operative, then they were your friends. If they weren't respectful, then it didn't matter how much you had in common – they were your enemies. I hoped I didn't have any at that point.

14

BIGGLES

WITH A FEW PEOPLE AROUND WHOM I could consider as friends, and my job settled in the library at last, life was becoming almost bearable. I had begun work on re-organising the books alphabetically, much to the initial amusement of AJ, but by 'C' he had started joining me and that kept us busy and helped the time pass most mornings. Apparently, the books had been in alphabetical order years ago, but since so many of the inmates couldn't read (between 60 to 70% illiteracy levels, AJ reckoned – about double the level in UK prisons) they had decided there was no point. I was perplexed by this – surely people who couldn't read wouldn't go into the library in the first place?

I'd probably said this too triumphantly because he just shook his head and mumbled about me being a naive Scottish asshole. He liked to mumble things like that about me a lot, and he was usually right. He was in this case. Illiteracy was shameful for many of the men, and he'd known dudes that had been coming to the library for years and changing books regularly but who could barely read. 'It's a pride thing,' he said, in a way that made me embarrassed at all the opportunities I had had in my life.

'You have a Master's degree in Business, right?' he asked me one day as we shuffled books about. We were on the Ds by that point.

'Uh huh,' I grunted.

'An' you got a Distinction or some shit for that right?' he probed.

'Mmmm . . .' I concurred, regretting deeply that I'd ever shown him the stupid CV I'd prepared for Miss Reed.

'And you had another degree before that right?' he continued. By now I was down to nodding, understanding where he was going with this.

'Well, by my reckoning, that just about makes you the dumbest person ever to have set foot in Big Spring,' he announced triumphantly as he tossed me a copy of *Days of Our Lives*.

I couldn't help but lower my head a little and nod in agreement as I stacked another book away. The opportunities I had been given, and look what I'd done with them.

The hardest thing was still the heat – which seemed to be rising every day but was, according to old hands like Chief, nowhere near its peak. Another frustration was the mosquitoes, which gorged on my exotic Scottish blood every night, and spent the day dozing provocatively on the wall by my bed.

These were slightly less disgusting than the biting spiders and the cockroaches – all of which seemed to thrive in the fetid conditions of the Range. The female spiders had a vicious bite and would often nest in or around the cold steel frames of the bunks or the lockers. The inmates were genuinely freaked out by them, especially those who had been bitten already, and the earnest way in which they searched and re-searched their beds each night convinced me that this was one small spider worth worrying about.

The females had brown markings on their hairy backs, and the word was they laid their eggs just under your skin, the young ones eventually exploding out of your arm one day when you were least expecting it. I wasn't too sure about that, but I was certainly buying the rest of it, and completed a nightly inspection with Ramon around our bunks.

The cockroaches used to freak me out, appearing in a wondrous array of shapes and sizes every time I moved something while cleaning the toilet rooms. In the beginning, I'd spent half my time trying to kill them, but they seemed to be made of rubber, and if you did succeed in crushing one, the mess was ghastly to clean up. I overheard one of my bunkmates saying something one day about how the cockroaches were the only species to have survived ground zero at Hiroshima and Chernobyl, and after that I just decided to give up and try and get along with them.

Unfortunately, my peace treaty with the roaches was interrupted by two events. Firstly, I found one in my tortilla at lunch one day which was greeted by a shriek of terror from AJ. Two other big tough black dudes at our table all shrieked like babies as they realised I had half eaten it.

'Jesus, Scotland, you one dirty motherfucka!' said AJ,

standing up and looking at me with his hands held up at his chest in horror as if I had just sprinkled Tabasco on the beast. The other two guys were now also standing up, slack jawed and staring as I spat as much of it out as I could.

'Shit, Scotland!' one of them said. 'Why you done eat that shit for?' I ignored him and kept spitting out everything I could, convinced I could feel thirty of its little legs still rolling around my tongue and mouth. The reaction of the kitchen staff when I showed it to them confirmed to me that we usually ate such things in our tortillas without noticing. Without so much as a word to me one of the kitchen porters grabbed the half-eaten tortilla, scooped the residual parts of the cockroach out with a dirty forefinger, then handed it back to me. I threw it ceremoniously into the bin and walked away to the sound of uproarious laughter from the rest of the kitchen staff. I'd need to start cooking my own food, I thought, as I stumbled out of that lunch, suddenly not hungry anymore.

The second event pertained to one individual cockroach; I'll call him Biggles. I spent over an hour with New York strategising and chasing this unfeasibly large thing, black and red and about two and a half inches long, around my bunk one Tuesday afternoon before finally trapping it in a corner. By now, a growing crowd of well-wishers, including Chief, Kola and some more of the other Natives, had all crowded onto Chief and Kola's bunks, and were chipping in with advice and ideas while noticeably keeping well away from it. We had been in lockdown for nearly five hours at this point and this had been the most entertainment we had had. There had been some kind of retribution beating over in Sunrise. It was the sort of gang fracas of great interest to the 'players', but to most others (including myself) the three injured bodies – all apparently stabbed or 'shanked' – that we'd seen being stretchered out of the neighbouring bunk-house, signified only that another period of more intense boredom and frustration was about to begin. Was I becoming immune to such sights already?

For now, though, we were entertained with a beating of our own, and having surrounded our prey and asked everyone to keep quiet (thinking for some reason that might help), we started slowly moving in towards Biggles for the kill, with rolled-up copies of *The New York Times* in hand. It was a remarkably big cockroach, bigger than any I had seen or eaten. It seemed to know that this was it, the denouement, and contracted itself into some kind of ball, making me feel a little bit sorry for him. That feeling quickly changed though, when it lurched, contorted and suddenly metamorphosed into a different life-form altogether. Suddenly Biggles was airborne and flew right at me and New York.

'Ahhhh!!' we shrieked – I think half the room joined in as well – as it headed right towards us, my newspaper automatically swishing out at it. Nothing like as fast or nimble when airborne, it connected with the sports page of *The Times*, and was sent spinning in the direction of Chief's bed. The Indians all shrieked, then started clearing off the reservation far quicker than any cowboys had ever managed to shift them, and we all stood aghast for a few moments, taking stock.

'Where the fuck is it?' asked Chief, tentatively stepping back towards his and Kola's space. Kola was half hiding behind Chief, with his arms up covering his chest.

'Erm . . .' I pointed towards his messed up bed, deciding to say no more.

'Shit, Scotty. What the hell did you do that for?' He shot me an angry, aggrieved look, as if I'd just punched him. All the other Natives, including Kola, were looking at me just as accusingly. I turned to New York for solace, but he was looking at me accusingly as well.

Chief gingerly pulled his top blanket back. There was no sign of Biggles. A smart, as well as multi-faceted cockroach, he seemed to have cleared off in the melee. Chief started to strip the bed bare as the other inmates began to slowly disperse, today's entertainment over for the day. I had already stopped smiling. In the furore surrounding Biggles, I hadn't initially noticed John, the chomo, but as things calmed down and Chief strip-searched his bunk, I saw John lying prostrate on the floor near his own bunk, unconscious. Obviously someone had taken the opportunity of hitting him – from behind more than likely – as the rest of us had been focused on the cockroach hunt. Chief caught my eye-line and glanced towards John. I could tell, like me, he struggled with this, but we both continued with what we were doing – me attempting to write a positive letter back home, Chief to search for Biggles among his bedding. After a minute or two, John started to regain consciousness and for an uncomfortable few seconds he began to audibly moan, and my discomfort level heightened. I wasn't stupid; any attempt to help a chomo would take me beyond the wrath of even the gangs and I would have the entire inmate population to deal with. But I felt my inaction lessened me, stripped away my humanity. Maybe I would become like everyone else in here soon enough.

Mercifully, John regained his strength and his composure and stumbled his way to the bathroom – ignored, as was the rule, by everyone. I saw Joker looking at me and averted my eyes, a feeling of shame coming over me as, putting my letter aside, I lay back on my bed and tried to think of something else; anything else. My mind kept coming back to the same thing however: that the decision to put paedophiles and sexual predators into our unguarded, unmanned dormitory was a conscious one. That this was society's choice: to expose people like John to the random and almost constant beatings and abuses they knew – no, they wanted – the other inmates to inflict upon him.

I had often heard this argument made in newspapers and radio shows in the UK, that 'those kind of people' should be sent to a prison where the other prisoners 'will make sure their lives are a living hell' and I can imagine most of us, at some level, can see a certain attraction to that idea. But even if you put aside the degree of punishment someone like John should receive, it still left other equally troubling questions. What form of rehabilitation can ever work when you give inmates carte blanche to beat another inmate as and when they want to? How do you teach someone that violence is wrong if you implicitly suggest it's alright on certain occasions? John was put in there with the expectation that the other inmates would beat him and abuse him. When the judge sentenced him, he should have added: 'You will be placed in a facility where for large periods of the day and most of the night there will be no guards or officers present, but up to a hundred other inmates will have free access to you, where we expect you to have regular and constant beatings, possibly even leading to your death.'

By now, I'd seen John being hit a few times, usually by the same few people. There was nothing in their action that suggested to me their rage was anything other than indiscriminate – they were hitting John not because they were angry with him, just because they were angry. This was no moral crusade – John was an institutionally appointed punch-bag. He also fulfilled another important role for the inmates – he was the lowest of the low, a base point that allowed many of the inmates some solace. 'At least I'm not a fucking chomo!' was a frequently heard comment when the heat was on.

But I turned my back to John as he stumbled into the bathroom and everyone in the room got back to the extraordinary business of killing time.

Chief stripped his bed bare, and then stripped it again, mumbling my name all the time in disgust, but Biggles would never be seen again. Chief reckoned it took him three weeks before he could sleep again without scratching. As for me, after the giant flying cockroach, the extra protein in my tortilla, the fat mosquitoes and the biting spiders, even the noise of the rats running through the air vents at night couldn't affect me anymore. Like so much else in Big Spring, a 'world-class shithole' as New York called it, I taught myself to ignore it and just hoped my sanity would hold, even though that was getting harder by the day.

Killing a few mosquitoes who'd spent the night eating me just became part of my morning routine. I'd follow it by gazing out of the window, mumbling a quiet prayer to ask for the strength to get through another day, and taking a pen to mark another chunk of time served on the window ledge.

After a few minutes I would stumble down from my top bunk, careful not to disturb Ramon, whose 'privileged' job of clearing the bins at night (which took all of ten minutes) allowed him the luxury of a lie-in. Resisting the temptation to enter the ubiquitous queue for the toilet, I would hold on a bit longer until it was less busy.

If Mendiola or Big City were getting dressed at the same time as me, we would all have to negotiate this in the tiniest of spaces, each precariously balancing on one leg to put on a sock or pull on a trouser leg, not even room for a chair in the cramped spaces between the bunks. Often we would bump into each other, my sweating damp skin rubbing against theirs, and of all the things that freaked me out, *that* freaked me out the most. I hated it. I hated the lack of space. I hated the lack of privacy, I hated the feel of another man's skin slightly sticking against yours, his breathing, my breathing, the awkwardness of an intimacy none of us wanted nor could avoid. I found that the hardest thing; the part of the day when I had to really fight not to scream.

But I'd never scream. Instead, temporarily dressed in shorts and an old T-shirt, I would head to the kitchen and use the microwave to quickly cook myself some porridge and make myself a coffee. Occasionally Mendiola would have 'obtained' some fresh milk for me from the kitchen in exchange for three stamps – which should give you an insight into the quality of the training shoes he sold me for two – otherwise it was a powder mixture for both the coffee and oatmeal. With space at a premium, and people still chaotically milling around, I would climb back up onto my bunk, careful not to disturb either Ramon or to spill my coffee. Often I would just look out of the window and watch the birds swing into action as the other inmates would gradually stir.

Always at this time I would end up thinking of Calum and Julie and the other loved ones in my life; wondering where they were and what they were doing. It would already be lunchtime back home. Sometimes I would close my eyes and think of Calum, try to feel him, thinking that maybe if I could just concentrate hard enough I might in some way sense him; sense how he was feeling. Of course it never worked, but I seemed to get some comfort from trying. Occasionally on those early mornings I would allow myself to think of Cara too, but having no idea what kind of life she had, where she was, the kind of school she attended or what friends she had, I found it hard even imagining. Instead, all I could do was remember her. Her cheeky smile, her bravado, her strength and independence. Remember how close we were.

I rarely went for breakfast. They had oatmeal, but my own was better, and the sticky buns they gave out were an unwelcome temptation. Prison was stressful enough without clogging up my arteries. By 7 a.m. the room had begun to quieten down again, and I would head off to the bathroom and either shower or strip down to my shorts and wash in one of the hand basins if the showers were full. I'd come back to my bunk and dress, this time in my khaki fatigues, the standard wear for working hours. Packing up my Spanish language book, pens and writing paper and usually a few Sudoku puzzles, I would set off around 7.25 a.m. for work. Often I would meet AJ halfway and we would complete the rest of the journey together.

I would work through the morning, then head out at 12.05 with AJ for lunch, taking it in turns to eat on the 'white boys' side' (his words) or 'the dark side' (mine). With lunch over, I would head back to the Range and most days now change into gym gear and head up to the weight pile or the gymnasium. An hour or two later, I would be back and spend the rest of the afternoon 'siesta-ing', as I called it, or reading or writing some more. Some days I would just 'shoot the shit' with New York or Chief or whomever was around. Whatever I did, though, and however many people surrounded me, loneliness covered me like a jacket, and my heart was constantly in mourning. I accepted my life was terrible and that inside I was sad. It wasn't hard to see that nearly everyone there was. The challenge was just to hold on, to remind yourself that a better life awaited, if you could just navigate the challenges of Big Spring.

By 4 p.m. all the other roomies would start to filter back in, the filter a torrent by half-past. At 4.35 p.m. we had the second count of the day, followed by 'mail call', which had now become known as 'Mulgrew Call' because of the rising levels of letters I was receiving. For many, mail call was a daily, public reminder of how unloved, how forgotten, they had become. I felt I was the lucky one.

The doors would then be locked again until they started to let us out for evening chow, depending upon where in the queue our Range was. Typically we were first out, and the few times we slipped to lower in the queue, the drop in choice and quantity of food was marked.

After food there was 'free movement' until 9 p.m., and I would usually head up to the running track and walk endless laps around it until it was time to go back to the Range. Often I would meet New York or AJ up there, sometimes Turk the Knife, who had become a good friend, and once or twice a week I would play football with the Hispanics, showing them the wonders of the Scottish tackle from behind. I was sent off three times in my first four games although the second one was definitely harsh. Some days I would watch TV, but only once or twice a week. The TV room held about thirty-five seats comfortably with a few more spilling into the corridor. Getting a seat in there was like getting a box at the opera – a distinct kind of status symbol. The ground floor of Sunset had only two Ranges, smaller than the ones on the floors above – but still meaning that around 180 inmates were chasing thirty-five chairs when a big TV event was on.

If you wanted to watch uninterrupted – or unstabbed – you had to learn and keep to another set of rules. The Blacks tended to dominate the English-speaking rooms and would often have 80 or 90% of the seats. The Hispanics, meanwhile, would NEVER show any English-speaking programmes. So on some nights, the English room would actually be jam-packed with Spanish-speaking inmates eager to see some major sporting event, while next door, in a room of the same size, no more than a couple of elderly Mexican lifers dozed in front of an obscure Latin game show. The logic of that didn't matter. If you were to attempt to switch the game show to something in

English, you'd have the combined might of the Azteca, the East Texas Mafia and the Surenos to deal with.

Amongst the Blacks, the Native Indians and the Whites in the English–speaking TV rooms, the seats went first of all to the shot–callers. Even on a busy night, with no space and room temperature hitting 100 degrees, the shot–callers' seats would remain unoccupied unless they themselves were sitting in them. The rest of the seats, as far as I could see, were 'held' by those who over time had historically earned or gained them. There were no hard or fast rules except that there were groupings of seats that always belonged to the Blacks (around thirty), to the Natives (around three) and the Whites (around three). Often the seats were shared between two or three people, and these were typically what you'd call the alpha males in the Range. A lot of 'stuff' went on in the TV rooms – both the settling of scores and the setting–up of them – so many of the quieter inmates simply chose to avoid them.

The white plastic seats we sat on were stacked up each night just before lockdown. When the 4.30 p.m. count was completed and the doors opened for dinner, there would be a rush to lay out the chairs, and place a calling–card on a booked seat. I had a torn piece of the *Scotland on Sunday* newspaper with the word 'Scotland' printed next to a thistle (or poppy, depending upon your view). I shared this right to a seat with Chief and now New York, an arrangement which worked quite well as we all liked different things: Chief, movies; sport for me; and for New York, *Desperate Housewives* or anything else with remotely attractive women in it. Chief had originally inherited the seat from another Native three years earlier and held jealously onto it ever since – aware, as we all were, that you had to keep up occupancy to ensure some new challenger didn't come along and take it away. You wouldn't just lose your right to watch *Buffy the Vampire Slayer* if that happened – you'd lose face, and be signalling to everyone else the fact that you were weak and exploitable.

A seat-challenge happened to our little syndicate a few months into my stay. Some of the Aryan Brotherhood had been sniffing around for another seat for a week or two, so Chief, New York and I would always make sure one of us was using it. One night I was due to have taken the seat to watch a movie, but I had had to queue longer than usual to use the microwaves, so had missed the start of it. I heated up some popcorn, made some coffee and filled my water bottle. With the popcorn bag precariously held in my mouth and a drink in each hand, I started squeezing my way through the extremely tight spaces to our seat, getting in everyone's way and annoying them as I did so.

'Shit Scotland, get that big white ass of yours outta ma face!'

'Sorry, sorry . . .' I was mumbling through clenched teeth, still trying to squeeze through without spilling anything, and I had made it about halfway across the room when I realised our seat was occupied. Now I had a dilemma. If I went backwards, it would be a very public retreat. If I went forward, it was confrontation time. As I was contemplating this, I was still moving along, and before I really had time to think about it I was upon the interloper, coffee cup in one hand, water in another, with a bag of popcorn hanging precariously from my mouth. Right in front of me was an alumnus of the Aryan Brotherhood – the same short guy who had come to see me with SlumDawg the first day I arrived; the guy with 'Bob' issues.

He looked up at me and we both hesitated. Everyone else was waiting to see what would happen. With my hands full and my mouth clenching the bag of popcorn my options were limited, so I instinctively motioned for him to move with my head. He didn't. The coffee was in a paper cup and was beginning to burn my hand. There was no space to turn around, to move back, or to put it down. As I looked at the burning cup, a thought flashed into my mind about something AJ had told me, how inmates would use boiling water to throw onto a chomo's face if the mood struck them. The trick, AJ had cheerfully explained, was to load the boiling water with sugar first, as sugar sticks to the person's face, then burns through, permanently marking the victim.

I didn't take sugar or milk in my coffee, having decided that was a luxury I couldn't afford in prison. Nor was I seriously intending to use the coffee as a weapon, but with it burning my hand, I had naturally looked at it as these thoughts started creeping into my head. Whatever my intentions, it had the desired effect. Drawn by my gaze, my favourite AB, perhaps contemplating a sugar–inspired scalding of his fine baldy scalp, hesitated then quickly shifted and got out of the chair. Moving carefully away from me as my hand started to really burn, he looped round in front of the TV in full view of everyone, thus completing his humiliation.

For my part, I sat down, quickly rested the burning cup on the floor, and engrossed myself in the movie, as if I regularly stared down methadone-crazed, tattoo-skulled Aryan Brotherhood gang members, armed with nothing more than a cup of coffee and a bag of popcorn.

Inside, though, I was in turmoil. On the plus side, my credibility might have just gone up a notch or two – I had defended the seat and had given a good 'don't-fuck-with-me' type performance; albeit accidentally. On the downside, though, it felt like another life used up. I was stumbling through these things with more luck than reason, more Mr Bean than Mr T. Worse still, I had humiliated Mr Bob, possibly for the second time, depending upon how he took my refusal to join the ABs. It was a lesson I had learned as a boy in Glasgow – even when you have the upper hand you never humiliate someone; and if they are going to be humiliated, you try to do it as privately as possible. Public shame usually only led to one thing – revenge. It seemed every place and every situation in Big Spring carried some dangers.

More often than not – and precisely because such situations were happening there all the time – I would stay out of the TV room and play cards with New York. We would play for hours, just shooting the shit and talking to everyone around us. People would typically start meandering back into the Range around 8 p.m., getting things ready for the next day and chatting about the latest fight in the Yard.

At 9 p.m. on the dot, the count already completed, the door would be slammed shut, the lights dimmed. It would re-open ten or fifteen minutes later and then close permanently around 11 p.m., provided the count had gone without a hitch, but by 10 p.m., I would usually have crawled up onto my bunk, tired from the exercise, the heat and the tension of surviving another day. Closing my eyes, I would list my Ten Good Things: letters and books received; a telephone call made; good times with AJ, New York, Chief, Kola or whoever had been with me that day; a sunset; some fresh milk from Mendiola; a newspaper from home – and so it would go on. There would always be ten things. There would always be more than ten things, even in this terrible place. The negatives I would try to suppress, but I knew them nonetheless: I was using my lives up quickly; Angel still hadn't come back to me about the gang membership issue; still no word of Cara; and still no meeting with my Case Manager. On top of that, casually, during one hard-fought game of gin rummy, New York tossed in the news that he'd been chatting to some people in the Yard, and heard my name come up. Word was, apparently, that the Brotherhood were angry with me for disrespecting them, and intended to get even. The noose was tightening.

'Let 'em try,' I replied, just as calmly. New York scanned me carefully, but I let him see nothing. 'Gin,' I added, placing my winning hand down before him. New York stared at the cards, and from the cards to me.

'Lucky Scottish bastard,' he said with real warmth.

'That's me,' I answered. And for the split-second it took to say it, I believed it.

15

STAMPS

ONE OF THE LESS LIKELY PASTIMES in Big Spring was stamp-collecting – a by-product, perhaps, of the fact that unfranked stamps were valuable currency. I received letters from friends and well-wishers all around the world, and whenever I had a stamp of particular beauty, I'd pass it over to Mendiola, who would extract it painstakingly, using a small razor taken from a disused Bic.

Another keen philatelist was a Colombian guy I played football with called Polvora. His nickname meant 'thunderbolt' or 'firecracker', and had been given to him on account of how hard he could kick the ball. He had a ten-year-old daughter back home in Ancerma, near Pereira, Northern Colombia, and he sent old stamps to her for her collection.

Two friends of mine in particular, Phil and Melinda, would send me a different postcard every week from the different parts of Asia they travelled to, resulting in a small treasure-trove of gaily coloured exotic stamps, and I'd marked out Polvora's daughter as the ideal recipient for these. My own letter-writing done for the day, I decided to head down to the weight pile, and drop off the stamps on the way.

'*Para tu hija*' ('For your daughter'), I said simply, and placed them down on the bed, folded up in a blank piece of paper. Polvora looked surprised and tentatively opened the paper. His hands began to tremble as he gently thumbed through each stamp, seemingly more enamoured with each new one.

It was always the Latin Americans – the ones who collected the stamps, who did odd jobs for the other inmates for a tiny stipend – who sent money home to their families. For many of them, particularly those from El Salvador and Nicaragua, prison in Texas offered a better standard of life than being free at home, and often they had committed no 'crime' except to be over the border, trying to earn money without a visa.

The world in which a strong, tough man like Polvora could take so much joy in some old stamps was a world far removed from the one I'd moved in, so far that it was hard to believe they occurred on the same planet. One required the other, though – I was beginning to see that more and more clearly. The huge sums of money we'd moved around in my former life depended, some-where down the line, on the existence and desperation of people like Polvora. People with next to nothing, but who still had hope.

Polvora had still not spoken but was looking at each stamp in turn again. I was quite taken by his reaction and felt awkward as I started to move away. Polvora, so uncompromising on the football field, his face scarred by the unforgiving life he'd led, grabbed my arm and tried to speak, but became very emotional and choked on his words. He looked from me to the brightly coloured stamps, still holding my arm tightly as he continued to finger the stamps gently as if they were diamonds or pieces of gold. Still not releasing me, he looked right at me, searching my face and asked, *'Por qué?'*

'Mi hijo es la misma edad' ('My son is the same age'), I responded quietly, surprised by my own answer, as I hadn't really considered why I was doing it. I was suddenly shocked by the intense emotion that this scene had evoked in both of us. I felt sorry for myself, I longed to see my son – and at the same time I felt intensely sad for a man I knew had a ten-year sentence and would never see his daughter grow up, maybe never be a father. All Polvora had was things like these stamps to make his connection. Still touching the stamps lightly and without raising his head, he spoke softly, the effort apparent in his voice.

'Gracias, Escosais, gracias. Dios le bendice y su familia.' (Thank you, Scotland. God bless you and your family.)

I grabbed his shoulder tightly and nodded – two fathers joined in their pain, the longing to be home with their children, and the intense guilt from not being there, not being a proper father. Swallowing hard, I turned away and walked quickly out of the room, trying to force myself to calm down, and not really succeeding.

I headed out into the glaring sunlight and the boiling fucking heat and made my way through the various sections towards the weight pile, fuelled by anger and irritation – at the way things were, but mostly just at myself. Why did I have to get so involved with people?

It was free movement between twelve and one o'clock

and I figured it must be close to one now as I stepped up my pace, already sweating and thirsty from the heat and dust. The weight pile was quite busy, so I spoke to a few of AJ's friends and 'booked' the bench and a bar and weights for when they were finished. I walked across to the fixed bars and started a series of pull-ups, still thinking about my emotional interlude with Polvora. Was I angry? Was that what was fuelling me as I pulled myself up for ten reps with ease and in a manner I had never managed before?

'*Bueno Escosais, bueno. Muy fuerte!*' (Good Scotland, good. Very strong!) shouted a friend of mine called Toro, as he lined up along with six or seven others to use the pull-up bar.

'That's what ah'm talkin about Scotland,' said McKenzie, my erstwhile tailor, high-fiving me as I took my place towards the end of the line.

'Fuck this place,' I thought as I stood waiting in line for the next turn. 'Fuck these people for taking me away from my son.'

'These people' were everyone: judges, lawyers, politicians, weak witnesses, former colleagues, journalists. Even myself. My actions hadn't passed the morality test, I knew that. My biggest ever bonus was paid for cutting over a hundred jobs – making their lives suck while mine improved. I ran a Structured Finance Group whose sole rationale had been to take whatever accounting or tax rules that existed and find out how to bend those rules without breaking them, to maximise the financial benefit to our clients, and as a consequence of that, the financial benefit to us. Was that all wrong, or was it alright?

Did that mean I deserved to be in here? Perhaps so. But did Calum deserve to be without me? Did Cara deserve to be without me and her big brother? Did any of the people who'd judged me and testified against me and written about me and withheld the truth from me actually know or care what I'd done or whether this place was just recompense for it?

Suddenly I felt I hated all of them – the witnesses who wouldn't help; the politicians who didn't care. It was my turn again. I hauled myself up at the bar in a smooth movement. I started to say some of their names each time I pulled my body up. Ex-colleagues; lawyers; magistrates and judges – their names propelling me like rocket fuel, each one thrust me further up, my chin comfortably clearing that simple iron bar in my prison home in the middle of the desert in Texas. 'Fuck the lot of you,' I thought, as I finished my second set of ten reps.

'Wow, Escosais!! You motherfucka angry today!' shouted Toro, his English gently mixed up as always, and his handsome smiling face beaming right back at me as I moved down the line, high-fiving all the various lunatics, nutcases and criminal masterminds along the way. 'Get that shit out, man!' he shouted as all the other Latinos and Blacks in the line shouted and hollered as well.

'Yeah, yeah man! Get it out!' everyone cried. I was pumped. I was so pumped, feeling so angry, so physically powerful but still so powerless in this giant toilet I lived in.

'Yeah!' I suddenly hollered with a volume that amazed me, clenching my fists and throwing them into the air in an unintended impersonation of Rocky Balboa. 'Yeah,

yeah, fucking yeah!' I screamed as I banged chests, bumped fists and high–fived my way back up and down the line again, everyone now looking at me, the line joining in the frenzy.

'Go Scotland, you fuckin' hit it man. Hit it!' shouted McKenzie.

'*Vamos Escosais! Viva Escotia!*' they cried as I kept shouting and shouting.

'Yeah, yeah, yeah. Fuck the lot of them. Fuck every fucking one of them!' Carried away with the crowd, I suddenly felt so much better, so empowered. 'Better than any high–priced therapy session,' I thought, the energy still coursing through my veins as I looked for something to do.

'Git out of ma way!' I shouted as I theatrically pushed some of the laughing inmates out of their position in the queue – something I never would have dared to do at any other time.

'Git out of the motherfuckin' way, the Big Man is coming in,' I added, in that little known dialect of Americanised street Scottish, pushing the last two, large, black guys out the way, to continuous laughter and cheering around me.

'Come on Escosais, rip that motherfucka up!' shouted a laughing Toro as I attacked the push–up bar for a third time with even greater zest and vigour.

I flew into the first one, almost pulling my chest right over the bar to even more adrenalin–filled cheers. I launched into the second and got there reasonably quickly, as the cheers continued. The third was a struggle, as the shouting subsided, and by the fourth, I had hit the wall, barely able to budge my frame up at all, my arms starting to shake as I started straining to get my chin to the bar. All that adrenalin and emotion had surged off as quickly as it arrived. I felt knackered. Behind me there was silence.

'Look at that motherfuckin' white boy trying to get that large white ass up over that bar,' I heard McKenzie say, as I dangled there trying to contemplate my next move. 'Man that boy got a big ass, for such motherfuckin' skinny arms. He ain't haulin' that gi'normous ass thing up no further,' McKenzie continued.

'You OK, Escosais?' shouted Toro, the humour in his voice still apparent.

'Uhm, yeah,' I said, the effort of even just dangling starting to hurt. 'I'm just hanging out,' I added in a poor attempt at humour, too embarrassed to drop down.

The bad joke worked though, and Toro came running forward with McKenzie, Turk the Knife and a couple of others and grabbed my legs and started pushing me up and down to get me to complete my set of ten. '*Cuatro, cinco, seis!!*' everyone joined in, seemingly more people emerging to push me up to ensure I finished the set. '*Oucho, nueve . . . diez!!*' they all shouted and then cheered as I let go of the bar and collapsed onto Toro and McKenzie, laughing hysterically with the rest of them, having forgotten, for the first time, and for just the briefest second, that I was in prison in the middle of Texas. The wonders of group therapy.

When I returned to the Range it was quieter than usual, with just Mendiola mending a shirt for someone in his bunk and Chief, by the looks of it, writing another long letter. As always, he seemed to be concentrating on one thing while keeping an eye on many others, and after a few minutes he glanced up and said, simply, 'You're on the Call-Out list, Scotty. You're seeing your Case Manager in the morning. Miss Matthews.'

The fact that my Case Manager was a woman barely registered as I sprinted across to the Call-Out sheet pinned up on the Range noticeboard. '10 a.m., Thursday morning; Miss Matthews, Initial Case Manager Meeting.' Not exactly *War and Peace*, but I re-read it two or three times to make sure it was all correct.

Chief looked up again as I came back to my bunk. 'Mousey Matthews, huh? She likes you white dudes.'

'Why does it all have to be about race with you guys?' I asked, slightly irritated.

'Because everything is.'

Refusing to be drawn into that conversation, I headed off to my locker to get my best khakis and start preparing for my interview. My heart was racing. This was it: the first step; the tiniest, almost imperceptible first move towards Cara Katrina, towards home and out of this inferno. I got to my locker, still lacking a padlock since I hadn't made enough to buy one yet, and started searching frantically for my 'dress' khakis.

'Scotty . . . Scotty . . .' Chief called me softly as I went into a panic about where my best clothes had got to.

'What?' I snapped irritably, and span around to see him pointing at my khakis all immaculately pressed and ready on a hanger being held up by a grinning Mendiola.

'We figured you would be in a tailspin, so we took the liberty of paying Turko one stamp to do a top job for you. We know how serious you take your interviews,' he added drily.

That night I slept fitfully as I ran through the interview

time and time again in my mind. I thought back to some of the techniques Jack Black had taught me on his MindStore courses. Meditation was all but impossible in the hub-bub of the Big Room, but one of his tips was to visualise a critical meeting or situation going well, over and over again, and I tried that now as I lay awake excited and worried about my meeting in equal measure. I eventually slipped off into a dream, in which I seemed to be sheltering from an earthquake under a table, which probably had something to do with the fact that I was still reading *Shogun*.

I woke up and realised that the trembling and shaking was still going on. At first I thought that someone was shaking the bunk to awaken me or that maybe I had over-slept somehow and panicked about missing my meeting.

Gradually however, after removing the eye-mask I'd improvised from a pair of old socks sewn one end to the other, and the wads of tissue paper I used to block out the continual snoring in the room, I realised what was happening. I groaned and pushed the toilet paper back in my ears to try and block the sound of Ramon, my bunkie, masturbating languidly below me.

At least he was on his own, I thought, as I gave up trying to sleep and lay staring at the ceiling as he kept whacking one off below. I put my arm behind my head, turned to my little window and looked at the moon outside as I wondered how my life had ever come to this point. How do you end up lying here at three in the morning on a bunk bed in the middle of the Texas desert in a room with eighty-odd psychos, child molesters and gangsters, while your heavily tattooed cartel-leading bunkie is happily choking the chicken below you? Life can take some bizarre turns sometimes, I thought. All this for supposedly breaking my employment contract in London?

With Ramon seemingly struggling to reach a crescendo I thought back to the words Judge Werlein said as he sentenced me. He hoped that, since I had appeared to have lived an 'interesting life' thus far, maybe over the next few years I would have time to pause and reflect on the error of my ways. Maybe, I wondered now, this was the kind of moment he had in mind: in the small hours of the night, awake and listening as my heavily tattooed neighbour pleasured himself below me? Maybe the judge was right in his way, that this sort of thing would be a warning to others and ensure that I never dared to break my employment contract again.

Fortunately, after much huffing and puffing, Ramon reached the denouement and my bed stopped shaking. Within moments he was sound asleep, seemingly untroubled by the kind of thoughts that made me sleep even more fitfully for the rest of the night.

16

MISS MATTHEWS

I WAS UP EARLY AND DRESSED in my best khakis by eight, much to the amusement of my Indian chums. I waited nervously until the ten o'clock move, anxiously checking through my papers and re-reading my plea-bargain 'agreement' with the Government.

On the ten o'clock move, I walked the 112 steps down to the Administrative Office and waited in the corridor outside her office for some time. There were three other inmates to see her before me and I could sense from the body language, that for at least two of them the appointment mattered as much to them as it did to me. Would any of it matter to Miss Matthews though?

For many of the inmates, Big Spring was a real hardship post. Apart from the constant violence, and the dominance of the gangs, the prison was hundreds of miles from anywhere significant and sometimes thousands of miles from where an inmate had initially 'caught his case'. Like AJ, they'd often been sent here for a minor infraction of the rules elsewhere, or because they were

deemed to be violent. In a system dedicated to admin-
istering punishment, Big Spring was in a category all of
its own. With so many inmates in the US being poorly
educated and having limited financial resources, a
transfer to Big Spring often meant you wouldn't see your
family or children for years. Since recidivism rates were
best kept down when inmates retained a family structure,
the logic of this approach seemed questionable, but then
again, by the time you were sent to Big Spring, I realised
the system had probably already given up on you.

The first inmate stormed out of the office in great
distress, his annual ten minutes with the Justice System
over in a matter of seven. I began to feel increasingly
anxious, but I pushed myself to breathe, to relax and to
focus again on the meeting going well. Where was Jack
Black when I needed him?

Eventually my time came and I entered a surprisingly neat and tidy office. There were cuddly toys and
various child-like desk objects popping up everywhere
I looked, which took me aback, as did Miss Matthews.
A white woman in her mid thirties, she seemed timid
and mousey, with short dark hair in a bob and small
delicate features. She was wearing a frumpy high-
necked blouse, reminiscent of an old school teacher,
and she seemed even more out of place in Big Spring
than I was.

'Sit Mulgrew,' she motioned. She knew my name, I
thought. That was encouraging. 'Your name is Gary
Mulgrew,' she intoned, reading from my file. 'And you
pleaded guilty to one count of wire fraud and were
sentenced to thirty-seven months here in Big Spring, Texas.'

'Yes, that's right, but . . .'

She carried on, as if I wasn't there. 'Your sentence is due to finish on 11 May, 2011 at 10.30 a.m., although you could be released by 14 January of the same year if you have no infractions.'

Did she think I didn't know all this? Was this 'interview' actually meant to remind people lost in the US prison system who they were and how they'd ended up there?

'You were born in . . . Glass–gauw in 1962,' she went on. I had a strong sense that my ten–minute window was disappearing.

'Miss Matthews?' I interjected, softly, but firmly.

She stopped in her tracks and looked right at me. 'Yes?' She looked alarmed.

'I came to speak to you about a transfer back to England.'

'Oh,' she said quietly, looking around her desk as if she had mislaid something and then moving her hand protectively to the high neck of her old–fashioned blouse.

'Normally you would request a transfer at our next meeting.'

'But our next meeting isn't until next year, Miss Matthews.'

'Yes, that's right; in precisely twelve months from now . . .' she said firmly and with renewed confidence. 'At 10 a.m.'

'Wait!' I said more brusquely than I intended. Miss Matthews instantly recoiled, and I imagined her hand under the desk searching for a panic button.

I felt like the prosecutors were stiffing me again, reneging on the deal to get me home. But I knew if I got angry that would be the end of this meeting.

'If you look at my file,' I said, pointing a bit too force-fully at the file on her desk, 'you will see I have a deal, an arrangement with the DoJ to get transferred home. They promised.'

She had pushed herself as far back in her seat as she possibly could and was looking past me, probably for some help. Taking a large breath and using every atom of willpower I could summon, I eased slowly back from her desk and sat upright in my chair. I spoke very softly.

'Miss Matthews,' I began very carefully. 'A key part of my agreement and my decision to plead guilty was that the Department of Justice agreed to expedite my transfer home to England where I can properly begin the search for my missing daughter.'

I kept my voice on an even keel and seemed gradu-ally to be coaxing her back towards her desk and the open file.

'Unusually, expediting my transfer was specifically written within the plea agreement you have in your file,' I finished as I moved myself even further away from her desk, trying to appear as non-threatening as a 6ft 2 Glaswegian convict ever could.

Relaxing her grip on the neck of her blouse, Miss Matthews nervously edged forward and thumbed the file, before pulling out what I recognised was the plea agreement itself. She began to read through it. I stayed silent, my heart pounding as I waited for this most deli-cate of souls to reach the key passage of the agreement. I'd hoped the unusual nature of this deal might prick her interest, and it seemed to. Eventually she spoke. 'No transfer can take place if you are launching an appeal.' I stayed silent as she continued to read. 'You have started your appeal . . .' then a few seconds later, she added, 'No, you're . . . not having an appeal?'

'No, ma'am,' I replied gently. 'I waived every and all rights to an appeal now or at any time in the future. That was the specific condition the DoJ insisted on before they agreed to expedite my transfer home. I will always be guilty, ma'am.'

'And the judge allowed this?' she asked, her interest now seemingly piqued.

'Delighted to,' I responded, unable to entirely hide my disdain.

Miss Matthews read on. After a while longer, and by now perilously close to the ten-minute mark, she started to re-stack the papers back neatly into the file. As I waited for her to speak she stood the file up and carefully straightened it before laying it back down neatly on the table.

'The thing is, Mr Mulgrew,' she began, much more confident now. 'This agreement, while I accept it is real and it is in here as you say, it is also between you and the Department of Justice. I don't see what it has to do with me and the Big Spring Correctional Facility.' She tailed off, catching my stare.

I felt it all slipping away, my chance, my deal, my agreement, my hope. Panic started to rip through me, but I stopped it, pushed it back down and held my nerve. I leaned forward slowly and placed my hands on the file, near hers. I knew I was risking everything, but I needed her help and I needed it now.

'Miss Matthews?' I began gently. I paused and waited for her to look up at me and to speak.

'Yes . . .?' she responded hesitantly, but at least she was still with me.

'My agreement is with the United States Government, with the United States of America; a wonderful and honest country. They chose to bring me here, and they can choose to send me back.' She was nodding slightly now, and I took some comfort from this as I continued very clearly and precisely. 'You are an employee of the United States Government, am I correct?' She nodded her agreement. 'So you are required to honour that agreement I made with your employer.'

I finished, looking at her intently and willing her to agree. She sat back for a moment or two, then looked from me to the file. After a moment or two she reached, hesitated then reached again to her bottom drawer, pulled out the transfer form and began writing on it.

'You have to return this to me by next week, Mulgrew,' she said as she stamped it; my ten minutes nearly over and a party beginning in my heart. I thanked her as she momentarily held the form back and gave me an ominous warning.

'The transfer can take a year or two to come through, although as you point out, in your case Washington might expedite it. But if you have any disciplinary issues while you are in Big Spring or are involved in any rule breaches, even a minor infraction, your application is suspended until those breaches are resolved.' She was matter–of–fact again, on familiar turf. 'Simply put: stay out of trouble if you want to get home, Mulgrew.' She looked straight at me. 'Can you do your own time, Mulgrew?'

I almost danced back to the Range, elated at the thought that I had made even the tiniest of progress. However, only a few hours after that lift, as seemed to be the way,

Angel came to see me to discuss the unresolved gang question. Miss Matthews' wasn't the only prison department that had been working on my file, and whereas release and transfer dates could get moved further and further away, the 'who you running with?' issue wasn't going to go away.

'Stay out of trouble if you want to get home, Mulgrew.' That was what Miss Matthews had said. That was all Mulgrew wanted to do. And it seemed pretty unlikely that he could manage it if he was forced to join a prison gang. I tried explaining that to Angel – but to him it was like a soldier saying he couldn't go to war because he had to dig over his vegetable patch. My needs were negligible compared to the smooth running of the system.

'It's been decided you have to run with someone. We've been through this already.'

'Who says?' I asked, emboldened by my visit with Miss Matthews.

'I do,' said Angel sternly. 'And don't start manning up to me, Scotland,' he continued, 'or the Kings will have to kick your ass.' There was an edge to what he said, as there always was in any conversation here. This constant masculine posturing was draining.

'I'm just shittin' with you, Angel,' I said, glad my prison-speak lessons from New York were kicking in. 'So it's really just up to you?' I added, hopeful that might lead us to resolving things.

'No, jackass!' responded Angel, laughing at my naivety. 'All the shot-callers discuss it.'

'What – all you guys sit down together and discuss this shit?' Discussion, reasoned argument, was weird enough to envisage. Even more was the thought of these tattooed psychos – Latin, Native, Black and Nazi – all politely sitting round a table to work things out. Did they break for coffee? Was one gang in charge of the sandwiches?

'We've been discussing you,' Angel confirmed. 'Especially since that *Esquire* article came out.'

'*Esquire* article?' I echoed.

'You haven't seen it? You made the front cover,' Angel said, with a grin. 'A picture of you and your two buddies from the bank. It says you were responsible for that whole property crash, because you invented some kind of scheme called securitising or some shit like that, and you used it to fuck Enron, and you wiped, like, twenty percent off the value of everybody's home. That was some shit, that scheme of yours,' he added, almost admiringly, but also a little accusingly.

'Could I . . . could I see that article?'

'Oh sure, I think Juarez has it right now. He's the shot-caller for the Aztecas,' Angel replied affably. 'He likes the picture of you on the front cover.'

I gulped, wondering what Juarez might be doing with the front cover, but I was even more anxious when Angel leaned across and carried on, more quietly, 'But he didn't like what the article said at all. Juarez has a lot of real estate down the Baja, around the San Diego area all the way up to the Bay.'

'He has?'

'Yes. Juarez was really pissed when he first saw it. Wanted to come straight down and see you, but some of the other guys convinced him it was probably bullshit.'

'Who the hell reads *Esquire* in here, anyway?' I asked numbly.

'Hey – the articles are bullshit, but you get a lot of

high–class looking women in it,' Angel said, almost defen-
sively. 'No titties or pussy so the cops let it in.' We both
paused for a second to consider this.

Sex and death are, they say, the great themes in all
literature, and it wasn't many seconds before my thoughts
whirled away from whatever might be inside the pages
of *Esquire* to whatever might be awaiting me. So Juarez
had been persuaded not to believe everything the article
said. But would everyone else take such an enlightened
view? Was I a fool for thinking I could just plod along,
with my library job and my card games and my friendships, under the radar of the big players? Did I need
protection? Stay out of trouble, Mulgrew.

'Anyway.' Angel sighed. 'A couple of important people
want to talk to you . . .' He tailed off, scrutinising me
closely. His words caught me by surprise. I began to
speak but the words caught in my throat, as I did a
terrible job of repressing my fear.

'You mean . . . you mean the shot–callers?' I almost
whined, distressed by how quickly my bravado could
vanish.

'Let's just say a couple of people want to see you and
leave it at that, Scotland, alright?' said Angel again, all
confidence and menace. 'Someone will come for you in
a couple of days, OK?' he said as he rose to leave. 'And
don't discuss this with anyone else,' he continued as he
drew a surreptitious glance towards Chief's empty bunk.

'OK,' I responded, another lifeline gone and a wave
of fear engulfing me as I avoided his eyes. He just turned
and sauntered away.

17

CALLING THE SHOTS

I TRIED TO THINK OF A strategy for the meeting about my gang affiliation but I could come up with nothing other than to address the big players as succinctly as I could and try not to look like an idiot. I would explain my dilemma and see if they could sort it out for me. It wasn't a very sophisticated approach, but it was the best I could come up with.

The truth was, I was afraid of the shot-callers. I didn't know all of them by sight; they were just a faceless body controlling the prison and my fate within it. Other than Finn and DumbDumb, I'd never come across a real-life criminal before I was indicted myself.

After I was indicted, however, it was a very different story. Once the affair became public, a stunning array of acquaintances came forward and revealed themselves to have skeletons in the cupboard, from making unsuccessful drug deals to living off immoral earnings. It just reminded me how arbitrary the whole process could be – some people got away with stuff, others didn't.

Around this time I was very involved in building up a pub group in London through my consultancy company, Gambatte. Having had time to digest the indictment and talk to me about it, the other main partners, unfortunately named Crouch and Standing (Dan Crouch and brothers Giles and Gavin Standing) became great personal supporters, as well as friends and partners. They were the creative force behind our main bars, the Lock Tavern in Camden, and Brighton Rocks in Brighton. I dealt principally with the financial side of things and, mainly thanks to their innate sense of style and understanding of music, the business went from strength to strength.

One day, we had finished a meeting at our new venue, The Defectors Weld, in Shepherds Bush, when one of our lawyers, Ray, suggested we move on to a 'more up-market' place for another glass of wine or two. Gavin and Giles were busy and normally I would always make sure I picked up Calum from school in Brighton, but that night he was staying with my stepmother, Audrey.

I liked Ray a lot. He was a good old London boy, smart and always helpful and practical in dealing with the legal issues of the bars. He reminded me of Bob Hoskins – a little heavy set, with grey swept-back hair, overcoat sitting on his shoulders, and a cheeky grin. He was also another person I'd met after being indicted who didn't seem to judge me on the media version of the case.

'I know the perfect place for you, Mulgrew,' he said mischievously. 'Full of dodgy geezers – you'll have a right laugh.'

I could do with a laugh, I thought, after the stress of the extradition hearings, the panic about being dragged off to prison in America, the dread of having to tell

Calum. I was disciplined about not drinking too much, especially when I was in London, but I felt a few glasses of wine wouldn't harm me.

In the taxi over towards Mayfair, Ray told me that we were going to a private club that was more akin to the types of places he liked and he wished our pub group would open in the future. From the two well-dressed, enormous doormen with earpieces and stony expressions at the front of this Mayfair townhouse, I could see immediately it was the type of place we would never open. Not our market, not our niche. The doormen looked Russian and the whole place reeked of grandeur and opulence. It was surprisingly busy for a Tuesday afternoon and I immediately felt scruffy in my faded jeans, white shirt and black jacket. I wished I'd shaved too.

'I think I'm underdressed,' I said awkwardly to Ray, resplendent in his suit and tie and unnecessary overcoat perched on his shoulders.

'No, no,' he looked at me, smiling. 'You're perfect. Let's go upstairs. I want to see if any of the family are in. They'd love to meet you,' he continued, obviously enjoying himself. This was the first time I'd heard anything about it being a family affair, although I guessed I wasn't about to meet anyone's granny.

We walked up two flights of stairs through beautifully decorated hallways with a few bars and a dining area either side of them. There were beautiful women everywhere, dressed as if they were going to a dinner party. The men looked well-heeled and a number of them gave me the once-over. I was feeling very uncomfortable but there was little I could do except follow Ray, who was nodding and smiling at every second person he saw. I'd never been to a place like this and I found it fascinating. I'd always imagined gentlemen's clubs to be stuffy relics full of old Etonians in smoking jackets reading the *Financial Times* and bemoaning how the Empire had gone to the dogs, but this place was different. It had an edge to it.

Ray took me into a smoking room, where a waiter served me with a large cigar and a decent Burgundy. I'm not big into cigars, I would maybe smoke one every couple of years, but I welcomed the distraction; Ray was making me nervy. He always had great energy and a great sense of fun – just the kind of guy that could get me into trouble in an instant. He left me a couple of times to talk to people at the extremities of the room and I could see them looking over at me. I heard him say, 'NatWest Three' and 'Cayman Islands', which didn't help my increasing discomfort. Eventually he rejoined me.

'Some of the boys want to meet you,' he said, beaming his mischievous smile at me again.

'I'm not sure if that's a good idea,' I said, leaning forward, trying to look composed, and wishing he'd never forced the comedy cigar on me.

'Nonsense,' said Ray, slapping my thigh as he shouted out, 'Harry' to the man he had just spoken to in the corner. 'You'll love these guys and they're desperate to meet you!' He waved them over.

'All right, Gal? Pleasure to meet you, my son. My name's Harry.' Stocky and well built, Harry clearly had some influence here, as the merest flick of his hand brought a waiter scurrying back a few seconds later with a whisky on the rocks. 'Heard you've been in a bit of bovver, my son,' Harry observed, pulling up a seat directly opposite me and giving me a friendly smile.

We were immediately joined by four others and Ray introduced them all far too quickly for me to remember their names. They positioned their seats in a circle around our small table, and even though there was a round table there, I felt like I was in the middle. They all seemed to know who I was. When I spoke, they sat and listened as if I was the oracle, assessing me. What could they possibly want from me? Perhaps sensing my unease, Harry turned to Ray and began a side conversation. Soon the wine flowed as the conversation became more easy. The guy to the left of me (Mike, I think) talked mainly to me as the others argued over who was going to win that night's Champions League semi-final between Chelsea and Liverpool. Mike had less of a 'threat' about him, and his face and hands carried none of the telltale signs of a life of violence.

Suddenly the seating arrangements didn't seem so random. The wine had helped a bit and I was doing my best to relax and hoped I was masking how uncomfortable I felt. Ray had wandered off for a while and, as if on cue, Mike changed the subject abruptly.

'How much is it you nicked then?' he asked quietly.

'I didn't nick it,' I responded just as quietly, putting down my glass. 'Here it comes,' I thought as I shifted uneasily in my chair. I could sense that Harry was looking intently at me and a quick glance confirmed as much. He smiled at me and in that smile I detected genuine warmth. 'God,' I thought. 'They think I'm one of them.'

Mike pressed on. 'Yes, yes, of course. You never did it,' he said, smiling.

'No, no,' I said more forcibly and looking straight at him. 'I didn't actually do it.'

It always annoyed the shit out of me when someone patronised me either in saying, 'Of course you didn't,' or 'Oh, everyone says they're innocent.' How are you supposed to respond to that?

Mike saw how fervent I was but I am sure he'd seen that before. Everyone says they're innocent, right? I immediately regretted my emotion. These were not people to toy with. Again, I thought about how to make an exit. It seemed tricky.

'Sorry, Gal. No offence, mate. It's just I saw the indictment and the stuff in the paper . . . well.'

'I know, I know, Mike. No offence taken. The Americans have done a number on us, that's all. I'm sure it's not the first time.'

'Yes, you're right there. But normally that's because they want something else. What else could they want from you?'

He said this with a certain assuredness that suggested some experience. He was looking intently at me. Although the place had filled up and there was plenty of noise and talk around us, I sensed some of the others were listening in, but I didn't want to look. I considered his question. Could that be it? Was that why the Americans were after us? Could they genuinely think that we held the key to unlocking some of Enron's secrets, that we knew where some of the bodies were buried? Perhaps I was giving the Department of Justice way too much credit. Could they really be that stupid? The thought was an uncomfortable one. I changed tack and pace with Mike. I wanted to see what these guys wanted.

'I'm no technician, Mike. I can understand the basic mechanics of a structure, but don't ask me the details. I can sell the benefits, but ask me a day or two later and I'll be lucky to remember what it was called. My mind doesn't work that way,' I said much more assertively.

'Yes, but your mate Bermingham does,' he responded. It was a revealing response, as if acknowledging the sparring was over.

'But I doubt Bermo has much insight into what went on in Enron itself.'

'But he could deconstruct a lot of their deals . . .' He had done his research. Who had he been speaking to? I looked at him closely again.

'Possibly.' I hesitated, thinking it through. 'But I can't believe that they would go to all that trouble just to get us there. After all, they only needed to ask.'

'What do you mean?' he responded, seemingly confused for the first time.

'Well, they only needed to ask and we would have helped. We would have gone over there. We had already told the FSA that.'

'I'm not with you.'

'When we first went forward, self-reported. They asked us and we told them we would help them in any way we could.'

'You, you went forward to the FSA? You self-reported?' His eyes widened.

'Yes.'

'B . . . but why? Why would you do that?'

I looked at him quizzically for a moment. Perhaps no one would ever believe us, no matter how often we said it. What is it about the FBI or the Department of Justice that leads people to believe the nonsense they peddle? *Law and Order* has got a lot to answer for.

'Because,' I said, emphasising each word. 'We didn't. Actually. Do it.'

Mike sat back in his seat. His smile showed he didn't believe me, but he was intrigued by what I had said. Maybe he thought we were part of some grand double–bluff?

'You've got to admit that was a dumb thing to do?' he asked eventually, but I just shrugged my shoulders. I'd made my choices. It felt as if the oxygen and energy had been sucked out of the room. Mike stayed slumped back in his seat as I leaned toward my glass and gazed at the table. Going into the FSA was among the worst decisions I ever made, but regretting going forward was the same as regretting who I was.

'Gal, Gal?' One of the others – Dan maybe – shouted across to me and broke this awkward reflection. He was about my age, with a boxer's nose and noticeably large hands and features. Although he was wearing a nice suit, it just didn't sit comfortably on him. He looked like he was ready to bust out of it at any moment.

'Gal, you know how to handle yourself, right?' he asked, a large smile on his face.

I smiled back and shrugged my shoulders.

'Yeah, you do? Where's you from, Glasgow right? They're fuckin' well 'ard in Glasgow, right?'

'Was he challenging me?' I thought, nervously.

'Where do you get those scars? You don't get them for nuffin'!' he said, looking at my arms. I had rolled up my sleeves when I took my jacket off. I'd long stopped being self–conscious of the numerous scars on my arms.

'Oh, they came from a woman,' I said, smiling. (Technically

true, as it was a woman doctor who was responsible for a few of them.) That brought plenty of laughter.

'A woman? Told you he is not so tough!' said one of the others, who seemed Eastern European, and I thought was called Haider. There followed a twenty minute show-and-tell session that ran from various broken bones, scars and knife wounds to alleged bullet holes, all, allegedly, caused by wronged women – and, surprisingly, in Haider's case by a wronged man. After the tension of the last few hours, I was enjoying the release.

I noticed at one point Mike had slipped off to have a five-minute chat with Harry at the bar – no doubt filling him in on our earlier conversation. When they returned, Harry was looking at me more intently than ever. Out of the blue, Dan, having suddenly stopped laughing about the tapestry of scars on each of us, turned and said, 'Gal, what d'you do wif the money?'

'What?' I said, still laughing a bit at the latest woman-wound – which looked more like an errant BCG scar than a mortal slight.

'What do you do wif the money?' he reiterated in his strong cockney tone.

'What do you mean?' I asked calmly, though my heart was racing.

'When you stole the money from NatWest.'

'I didn't steal it,' I interrupted him.

'Yeah, yeah, whatever. But you got all that fuckin' money, right?' This was a new Dan, Dan the bruiser.

'Eh . . . yeah, yeah. I got it,' I responded hesitantly, wondering where he was going with this.

'And it was millions of dollars, right?'

'Right,' I said uncomfortably.

'And you 'ad it in the Cayman Islands, right?'

Man, they were well informed. 'Er, yes. It was in the Cayman Islands.'

'So what did you fuckin' do wif it then?' he asked again impatiently.

Everyone was hanging on every word.

'Do you mean how did I spend it?' I asked stupidly.

'Not 'ow you fuckin' spent it, you muppet. 'Ow you got it back into the fuckin' country,' he said, with a serious expression on his face.

'Oh, now I get it,' I said, putting my drink down. Money laundering. I nodded for a few moments, laughing at myself for being so slow up on the uptake.

'I transferred back into my account with NatWest here in London,' I said innocently enough.

'You . . .' he paused for a moment as he leaned forward and put his glass down. 'You did fuckin' wot?'

'I transferred it back to my NatWest account in London,' I continued. 'I phoned them and told them I had made a big off-shore investment with a client and that a large sum would be coming from the Cayman Islands in a couple of tranches.'

Quickly looking around as I spoke, I started to slow down as I realised the significance of what I was saying. I swallowed hard. Bizarrely, I had never thought of that before.

There was a moment's silence before Dan wrapped his large arm round my shoulder. 'Mate,' he said dramatically. 'That is . . . fuckin' quality. Fuckin' genius!!' he declared to the general approval of the rest of the troop.

'You've got some fuckin' balls on you, mate,' he continued becoming much more likeable again.

'Stealing their money one day, then asking them to 'old it the next. Fuckin' outstanding!' he continued, as he raised his glass once more to me.

'It's like robbing a fuckin' jewellers,' enthused one of the other guys to the rest of the group, 'and then giving it back a few weeks later and asking 'em to keep it safe for you!!' he said laughing. 'Fuckin' 'ats off to you, Gal,' he continued, raising his glass as well.

'B . . . but . . . but I didn't steal the money,' I said almost to myself as the conversation took off again, my legendary status becoming assured. I felt embarrassed, unsure, as the compliments about the 'size of my balls' and my 'cockiness' continued.

Eventually, thankfully, we went back downstairs to one of the bars. Ray had left earlier, still laughing at me as he said goodbye, and by now the Chelsea–Liverpool game was in full swing with the club's Slavic contingent seemingly well behind Chelski. The game was very boring, though, and I was looking to make my exit.

'Harry, thanks for your hospitality, but I have to leave,' I said, as I approached him with my hand out. He was talking to two other guys who looked like well–dressed businessmen.

'Give us a minute,' he said to them as he put an arm around my shoulder. 'Don't fancy any of the eye–candy?' he said motioning to a couple of elaborately dolled–up ladies sitting nearby on a sofa.

'Are they all hookers?' I asked naively.

'How can they be hookers if they're already paid for?' Harry asked, with a wink. 'There's a couple of rooms upstairs for the members' exclusive use, if you're interested.'

'No, no,' I said. 'Not my thing really. I'm picking my boy up tomorrow and I don't want to be a wreck for him.'

'None of this is really your "thing", is it?' he asked sympathetically.

'No, not really,' I responded looking right at him.

He nodded. 'Gal, can I give you a bit of advice?'

'Sure.'

'Don't go to Texas. Whatever happens, don't let them get you to Texas,' he said with some sincerity.

'I'll try not to,' I answered, a bit too glibly.

'No, no,' he said more forcibly, putting both hands on my shoulders. 'I want you to fink about somefing for me,' he said in a slight change of direction.

'OK,' I said, hesitantly.

'Cyprus.'

'Cyprus?' I said.

'Cyprus. Hundred grand. Special deal for you. Land for you to build on and a new identity. Passport, paper, credit cards, the full boona.'

'£100,000,' I repeated numbly, my head spinning at the thought of being Asil Nadir's neighbour.

'A one–off deal for you, Gal; you'll just cover our costs. I'm doing this because I think you're getting fucked by the Yanks and our own fuckin' government, and I don't like it.'

'Look, Harry,' I said, placing my hand on his arm and moving a little away to break the spell. 'I appreciate what you're saying and I appreciate the offer. But I'm going to fight them and I am going to win the extradition. If need be, I'll win easily in a court in Britain,' I asserted, still at that stage believing it.

'You're not listening to me, my son. You're never going

to trial in the UK; they know you wouldn't be found guilty, otherwise they'd have done you 'ere in the first place. They'll get you to the US then you will never make it to a trial. No one does.' That wasn't technically true, but I got his point.

'Cyprus,' he said again.

'OK, OK,' I said, suddenly feeling tired and over-whelmed and anxious to start the long journey out of London.

Harry re-asserted his grip on me one last time, his eyes searching into mine. 'Just promise me you'll fink about it. Fink about it. OK?' and with that he patted me on the shoulder, gave me a nod and turned away.

The evening after my last chat with Angel, I lay back on my bunk in Big Spring and wondered why I never did 'fink' about Harry's offer. I suppose I was fighting to regain my life, not run away from it. Besides, at that stage, maybe only a gangster could see what I could not – that I was screwed.

Someone came to collect me from my bunk around 10.30 p.m. The lights were already down; respectful of the rules of the Range, the messenger boy nudged me gently and asked me in a soft voice to come with him. I recognised him as one of Angel's guys. They had a whole chest-bumping, fist-clenching thing that they did and I'd often seen Angel chest-bumping and fist-clenching with this guy in the past. He was young, short, quiet, sharply cut and all business. I'd barely jumped down and he had already headed off. The door had been reopened after the count. It probably wouldn't finally close until around 11 p.m., but there were already significantly fewer people moving around; lots of inmates preferring the tranquillity of sleep to the perils of a few more hours awake in Big Spring.

I followed my escort through the main thoroughfare and up the stairs to the first floor of Sunset. Without checking I was still behind him, he moved swiftly through the first Range, Range 7. It was longer than our room, with even more people – maybe around 120 inmates. There were a few people moving around in the subdued light, but not many. It made me think of how submarine quarters would be at night-time.

We moved through another large, rectangular room almost 200 feet long, then continued to the end of it and on through a long corridor with a further warren of rooms either side of the corridor that acted as satellites of Range 8. I'd never been here before, and these sub-rooms were much smaller, housing no more than twenty or thirty inmates each, perhaps offering more discrete accommodation for the high-status prisoner. Some of the rooms looked as if they used to be offices or large storage cupboards, but all were jam-packed with this backwash of humanity. In the subdued light I could see no more than brief silhouettes, but the place reeked of despair and depravity. This was the net effect of America's choice to continue to imprison a large section of its underclass – now totalling 2.3 million men and women – or ten times the per capita rate of any other Western country. In a nation where a local mayor of a small town, a congressman or a senator could never be elected if they suggested any kind of softening on crime, this was the living, writhing result. My love affair with America had been easy when I was riding high as a smartarsed banker, but the entrails of this country were so much harder to admire.

The continued cutbacks in funding, and the insistence that philosophically prisons were about punishment – that rehabilitation wasn't a cure – meant that conditions would only get worse here, and the strain on space would grow ever greater. It also meant the gangs could not only flourish, but begin to occupy the 'policing' vacuum left by the over-stretched cops.

There were no closed doors to any of these rooms, but the narrow corridors connecting them twisted and turned in various directions, giving each off-shoot some sense of isolation and privacy. I couldn't imagine the cops would venture down here very often, and by the time they did whatever 'stuff' was taking place would surely be over. One more turn took me to a very congested corridor, outside what seemed to be the final room in this network. There were Native Indians, African-Americans, Mexicans, Salvadorians, Nicaraguans and Colombians all milling around or kicking back outside – a multitude of guards, it seemed. Among them I saw SlumDawg and at that moment I knew I'd reached the shot-callers. As I slowed down and started to ease past them, my messenger stopped at the door to the room and turned to face me, flicking his head to motion me to enter. The last person I had to squeeze by was SlumDawg – unpleasant both because of our proximity and the fact that he reeked of alcohol.

The room itself couldn't house more than ten or twelve inmates – and must at some stage have been a storage closet instead of a place where men spent their lives.

'Hey Scotland, how are you doing? Come on in,' Angel

called out, jovially fist-bumping me and offering no further introductions as I squeezed my way in. There were probably eight or nine other guys in the room, some sitting, some standing, some looking at me, some not. It was hard to get a handle on them since none of them introduced themselves or offered their fists for a bump. No one seemed interested in the pleasantries. There was a seat between them, right in the middle, which Angel motioned for me to take. I hesitated; I would be right in the middle of a tightly congested room with people in the front, around and behind me, many of them standing up as I was sitting down. That intimidated me. I moved forwards, but then foolishly hesitated again.

'Go on, Scotland,' Angel said, his sardonic smile taunting me as he motioned me towards the chair. Getting a grip of myself and allowing my fears no airtime, I moved smoothly through the faceless gathering and sat down. I was trying to attach shot-caller to gang, but that was difficult since four were Hispanics and looked more like bingo callers than shot-callers. I smiled at the tubby little round one right in front of me. He didn't smile back. He had a tattoo of a hand with two fingers held up in a V-sign on his shaven head which I knew was the West Texas Syndicate insignia. He had some papers in front of him which, having finished staring at me, he began to read again.

No one spoke for a moment, and I realised they were waiting for TexMex to finish whatever he was reading. A second look confirmed it was my papers, even though they had already been returned to me – which meant, incredibly, that the gangs had access to a photocopier. Was there a Gang Admin Centre somewhere in this warren? I realised I had seen TexMex a few times before. I had noticed him talking to the guards and once in the guards' office in the ground floor of Sunrise. It had stuck in my mind because you seldom saw anyone converse much with the guards and it was unusual to be so openly chatty.

Angel smiled, as did the man I took to head the Native Indians, before my eyes settled on a white, hairy, crazed-looking guy – who I guessed was the AB shot-caller. He was big, very big, like an overfed biker, and unusually healthy looking for a member of the Master Race. I averted my eyes from his quickly, way too quickly I realised, in a movement that could easily be construed as showing fear. I tried not to lose my composure, but now I felt awkward about where to look. Just swallowing seemed to take on a magnified significance, as I become painstakingly aware of my every movement, my every breath. Feeling I was crumbling under their gaze, I tried to re-assert control over myself and to at least raise my gaze again to this assortment of hardened criminals. Doubts started creeping through my mind: what was I doing here? I was a fraud. I was afraid. What did they want from me? My neck felt stiff, as if my head weighed a hundredweight – had anyone noticed?

I battled for control of my fears and forced myself to look at the AB leader again, who was now leaning over talking to one of the other shot-callers. No one seemed to have noticed my mini-crisis and I began to relax a tiny bit more as I started to assess the AB shot-caller in detail. He was a big guy alright, and my eyes were drawn to what seemed like the same tattoo across his chest that I had seen on my first day in Big Spring when the ABs were on their recruitment drive. Another Bob hater, I thought, mystified by their bizarre relationship with Bob, until the big man turned towards me and the full stupidity of my mistake was exposed to me. The tattoo didn't say 'Bob Hates Me' but 'God Hates Me'. I replayed the bemused look of SlumDawg and his sidekick as I'd told them to take their gifts and 'give them to Bob', mistaking the key word thanks to the neckline of his low-slung vest. What an idiot I was, I told myself, feeling more confidence drain from me; an idiot abroad. Why hadn't I just kept my mouth shut?

'This ees strange,' said TexMex eventually raising his head, and looking at the other shot-callers. 'All that money and so short?' He meant the length of my sentence – or rather, he meant that I must have squealed in order to get one so short.

'*No estoy un rata*,' I said slowly, my Scottish accent rolling over the word '*rata*'. Perhaps it was the fact that I'd used Spanish, perhaps it was the sincerity behind my words, but it seemed to have the desired impact. Angel spoke quickly to TexMex and the other Hispanics in Spanish – too quickly for me to understand, but he was stopped abruptly as the AB shot-caller suddenly bellowed, 'Eng-glish!' adding, 'Come on, Angel, you know the rules about this shit.'

Angel smiled and grimaced at the same time, in a way only he could.

'Okay,' Angel began. 'We only speak English in this meeting. You know the deal, Scotland. You've caused too many waves since you got here and we need to sort out who you are going to run with and whose protection you fall under.'

'Yeah, protection at a price,' I thought, as his words confirmed all my fears as to the purpose of the meeting.

'Well, he ain't running with us!' began TexMex. 'Don't care how good his Spanish is, he no is one of us.'

'And he sure don't look like one of us,' rumbled the African–American shot–caller, a scholarly looking elder with glasses and a full beard.

As one, like the crowd at a tennis match, everyone looked at the Aryan Brotherhood representative. He didn't look all that keen on me either, but I wasn't going to give him the chance to speak.

'I want to walk alone,' I said, to a general intake of breath. 'I'm Scottish. I'm not from here, and I don't want to get involved in anyone else's shit.'

'You know you can't do that, Scotland,' a sympathetic Angel said, to general nodding. 'I understand how you feel, but you stand out too much and you keep inter-fering. Everyone who shows has to run with someone.'

'OK then,' I said, suddenly having a brainwave – or possibly just signing my own death warrant, 'then I will run with a gang . . . Mine,' I said more quietly as my resolve faltered.

I paused then said '*Los Escosais*' with renewed authority. 'The Scottish.'

This elicited almost immediate laughter and a bigger than ever grin from Angel. The talkative black shot–caller slapped me on the back as he laughed. 'A Scottish Gang, that's a new one, Scotland! Who's gonna be your shot–caller?'

'I'll be the shot–caller,' I responded calmly and seri-ously. 'If anyone wants to fuck with me, then they've got to clear it with me first!'

More chuckles. The tension seemed to have vanished from the stifling little room. Only the fat biker was looking brooding. 'You can't be serious,' said a smiling Angel, through twinkling eyes.

But I was – and the more I thought about the idea, the more I realised it could be my safe passage. 'Look, I'm not here for long, I will keep myself to myself and I will still technically be in a gang . . .' I prompted, searching desperately for a sign of acquiescence in one of their faces. I didn't see any – only, as the laughs faded, increasing scepticism.

'Come on,' I implored. 'This is the best solution.'

The breakthrough came from TexMex. The slightest tilt of his head, the smallest incline of an eyebrow. I seized on it.

'*Por favor?*' I said, more quietly, looking straight at him as if no one else was in the room. '*No quiero ser con los hombres blancos*' ('I don't want to be with the whites') TexMex nodded.

'What did he fucking say!?' growled my biker friend, leaning aggressively towards me and pushing my shoulder. 'What did you fucking say? What did he fucking say?' he demanded again.

'Get your hands away from him,' interjected Angel with a steely calmness. 'You know the rules about touching people in here.' *In here*, I thought. No telling what revenge the Brotherhood might exact somewhere else.

TexMex raised the palm of his hand to him for quiet and it had the desired effect. He seemed the least likely to be in charge, short and chubby with a round bald head and no neck. He looked like a snowman with skin, but since Mexicans dominated the Yard through sheer scale of numbers, he clearly held sway here. 'A gang of one?' he queried in perfect English, clearly still thinking it through. Angel grinned some more at this comment, giving me encouragement.

'We're OK with it,' said the Native Indian leader suddenly.

'It's cool with the brothers, too.'

'Aw, this is bullshit!' shouted the AB. 'Total bullshit!' He stood up and, ignoring me, stalked out of the room.

'Oh, just ignore him,' said Angel, slapping my thigh as he sat down in the fat Aryan Biker's recently vacated seat. 'Looks like we've got ourselves a new Scottish shot-caller!' He smiled, although I sensed none of the others quite shared his enthusiasm.

'Just remember, Escosais,' said TexMex solemnly. 'You walk alone now; you stay out of our issues, our problems. You do your own time. Any interference and there will be no protection for you. You understand?'

'I understand. I will respect how the gangs operate and will keep out of everyone's business. You won't notice me.'

'OK. And by the way,' TexMex added as he started to get up, signifying the meeting was over. 'If I were you . . . the last thing I'd do is ignore him.' He motioned with his head in the direction taken by the disgruntled Aryan. 'I would watch him like the hawk.'

He left as the African-American leader fist-bumped me and smiled. 'Who knows, Scotland, we may even get some more of your guys here one day,' he laughed.

'Yeah.' I smiled back as I stood up to leave, relieved that it had gone reasonably well. 'If any pasty-looking white guys with ginger hair show up, they're mine.'

18

TANK

WITH NOTHING ELSE TO DO NOW but serve my time and watch out for vengeful Aryans, life as the Scottish shot-caller settled into a monotonous routine of letter-writing and weightlifting. AJ and I had got as far as 'J' in the fiction section of the library and even Miss Reed had noticed what we were doing, although what she thought of it remained a mystery. The gang issue had gone away for the time being, but the sights and sounds and smells of prison life were no less oppressive. I never allowed myself to forget that I had another life elsewhere, outside, and while that made my time harder to serve, it also, to some extent, kept me going.

One hot day, deep in the middle of the brutal summer heat, I headed out to the weight pile in my new training shoes. These, my coffee and my porridge constituted my only worldly goods – whatever remained of my meagre income being spent on phone calls and stamps.

Communication was a lifeline to the outside, an umbilical cord keeping me linked to the world I intended to rejoin. But this only worked when the news was good or routine. Bad tidings seemed to hit me – and other inmates – more than they could have done on the outside, perhaps because of all the time you had to sit and dwell on them, and also because there was nothing, absolutely nothing, you could do about it.

I'd been hit by some terrible news about a good friend of mine, Paul Kavanagh, who, the week previously, had tripped going up some steps with his hands in his pockets, and died instantly, aged forty-three, of a broken neck. It was a senseless death – proof that however hard we try in this life, however good we are, we can still be snuffed out in an instant. For me, the fact that I hadn't said goodbye to Paul – and the fact that life and death seemed to be going on elsewhere, without me – was especially painful.

I made my way slowly up to the weight pile. It was in a partially covered area at the top of the prison grounds, nothing more than a tin roof suspended on a couple of wooden beams. It gave it the look of a real man's gym; the floor was concrete and other than the tin roof and a little mesh fencing around it, you were basically exercising in the Texas desert.

It was just before the main running track, although you seldom saw anyone running there because of the heat. Just behind the running track were the handball courts – always busy, whatever the temperature. I'd been told three people had died there from heat exhaustion the previous year, and I had visions of them just dragging the bodies off to the side of the courts so they didn't get in the way of the next match. The games were fiercely contested, with a lot of money made and a lot more seemingly lost. In the middle of the running track was the dust bowl of the football pitch, where I had tried to introduce Scottish football techniques to unsus-pecting Mexicans a couple of times a week. To the left of the weight pile was a large indoor gymnasium, used principally for never-ending games of basketball, although one inmate Turk the Knife had told me, shyly, that he had done yoga classes there in the morning. 'Very early,' he added, 'so no one else sees us.'

The weight pile occupied a fairly large area, probably about fifty metres square, and all the weights were loose – no machines – although there were benches for bench pressing and support bars for squats. New York had told me that there used to be much more equipment but after a series of television programmes by Barbara Walters on how 'luxurious' conditions were in US prisons, the relevant government department had declared that anything broken would either have to be repaired or thrown away. It would not be replaced. Ms Walters had also expressed concern about inmates getting a five or ten year sentence and spending that whole time using gym equipment and 'getting bigger' – so that they could wreak even more havoc and destruction on the good people of America on their release. She had a point.

I had passed the weight pile a number of times when I initially arrived at Big Spring, but had felt far too intimidated to enter. It was predominantly populated by the Blacks, and some of them were, for want of a better word, huge. As with the TV rooms, there was a clear but unwritten etiquette on how to stake a claim to the equip-ment, how it should be used, and for how long, and when it should be handed, without hesitation to someone else. Not knowing the rules, I was worried about falling foul of them and ending up with a barbell planted between my ears. Another reason I was intimidated was the sheer size of the weights the average pile–dawg lifted.

Eventually, I took some lessons from New York in how the 'pile' operated. After watching him a few times, I tried it alongside him, and then, when his job and his daily routine changed, I had a variety of companions. Some days, like today, I went there on my own.

The pile was quiet today and I managed to find a bench and a bar and a loose collection of weights in one corner to work with. Starting at a meagre 50kg, I started to bench press, moving up to 60kg after one set. After ten minutes or so Tank from the clothing store came over to me as I was taking a breather and drinking some water in the intense heat. We bumped fists. I was hot and sweating, the exertion and the heat beginning to catch up with me.

'Hey, what's happening Scotland?' Even though I'd seen him around the Yard a few times after he'd given me the pillows on my first day there, I'd never really appreciated just how big Tank was until now. 'What an apt name,' I thought, surveying him.

'How you doin', Tank?' I responded in between slugs of water.

'You gettin' big there, Scotland!' exclaimed Tank, nodding with an ironic smile in the direction of my tiny biceps.

'Yo, Scotland!' shouted over McKenzie, himself a regular visitor to the weights. 'Is you flashin' them guns in this weight pile? Don't go flashin' them guns at nobody, you hear me? You flash them guns, you gonna bring every motherfucka down here lookin for some action . . . you know what I'm saying?' As always I nodded back vaguely, hoping that was the right response to whatever he was saying.

'You workin' out alone, Scotland?' continued Tank, then not waiting for a response added, 'Can I work out with you?'

'Sure Tank, but you do much heavier weights than me.'

'Oh, that's no problem, Scotland. I'll just add some on a little here and there.'

We worked out for an hour or so, Tank swopping from my meagre 60kg to his 100kg, then 120kg. I started to struggle after a while, but Tank was full of encouragement, spotting me and shouting, 'That's all you, Scotland. That's all you, baby!' as enthusiastically as if I had just clean and jerked a new Olympic record. He kept giving me tips on the proper position for my elbows and back and even though I was rapidly running out of gas, I enjoyed training with him, and just chatting about nothing in particular. It helped to get my mind off Paul, and the lonely, senseless way he'd died.

After a while I was done. 'I'm spent, Tank,' I panted. 'I've got to get heading back in the next movement.' I was aiming to get back to the Range in the 2 p.m. window and have a well-needed shower. As he was adding another 20kg to his weights, and I was wiping my face, Tank looked up and asked quietly, 'Hey Scotland, could you help me out with something?'

I hesitated. This was a leading question in prison, and flew in the face of the inmates' survival mantra: do your own time. 'Possibly . . .' I replied, my hesitancy clear.

'I'm in a bit of a jam,' he began slowly. 'I need a couple of books of stamps, just to see me through to next Friday.'

I said nothing, and Tank offered no more. Just then the movement bell sounded, as if to add to the pressure of the moment. This was bad. You didn't want to borrow from or lend anyone anything in this place. That made them or you beholden to each other. And beholden, as AJ often said during his many sermons on prison life, was the doorway to trouble.

'I'm not sure,' I began slowly. 'I don't like to lend to anyone, you know, and I'm not sure if I have any spare.' I was lying. I had ten books of stamps in my locker.

'Oh come on, Scotland. Everyone knows you write about a hundred letters a day.'

By now he had moved closer to me, and although he was not attempting to intimidate me, I was feeling the pressure.

I liked people too much. This had always been my Achilles' heel. I trusted them too much. Or rather, I wanted them to like me too much. Saying no was a problem for me. Thanks to my past, my childhood full of difficult separations, I was a classic needy type. I had developed an uncanny knack of empathising with people and getting on their right side. I used a combination of humour and kindness and sometimes just sheer unfettered manipulation to try and get people to like me, to get their attention and acclaim.

'Look, man,' continued the Tank, perhaps sensing my inner turmoil. 'I give you my word. I'll get it back to you by next Friday. Ask anyone in this Yard, when the Tank gives his word, that means something. After all, a man's nothin' in this Yard if he doesn't have his word.' I looked right at him, taken by his sincerity. He stared back, unflinching and confident.

I'd warned myself about this. Warned myself about my weakness, the sad, blind trust I invested in people, in the hope that they would like me. That's how I had operated all my life; that was how, in prison speak, I liked to roll. But this was prison, this was different. People would take advantage of me in here. That's what my eldest brother Michael had specifically warned me about, and Julie too. That's what Giles had sarcastically predicted would be my downfall – trying to be Mr Popular in prison. I was too trusting, too soft, too easy on the outside maybe, but I understood the score in here. I ought to by now.

Tank was still looking at me.

'OK then, but repay me by next Friday,' I responded, having completely ignored the logical traffic in my mind. Regretting it instantly, I added, 'Don't let me down, Tank!'

'I won't, Scotland. I got you covered. I gave you my word.'

'Alright man,' I said, bumping fists with him, telling myself that people were basically good and I was right to trust him. The bell sounded again for final movement and I grabbed my stuff, and Tank lay down again and started bench-pressing 140kg like they were bags of sugar.

It only took a couple of days for AJ to find out what had happened. He had popped out of the library for a few minutes to collect some more writing paper from the Range. As he came back, I noticed he was moving much faster than his usual languid stroll, so I knew something was up. Perhaps another shakedown or a shanking. But he didn't look irritated or on edge. He just looked angry. Angry at me. He slumped down into the chair beside me.

'Man,' he began at almost a whining pitch. 'Don't you listen to nuthin' ah say to you, white boy?' The use of 'white boy' was usually a bad sign. I waited for him to continue. He seemed really annoyed. 'I told you. I spe-cif-ically told you. I warned you. Didn't I warn you?'

I found myself nodding, even though I had no idea what he was talking about.

'Man, I knew I didn't want to work with no green-behind-the-ears white boy,' he started turning away from me and looking for something to throw around. 'I don't wanna be dragged into your shit. You want me dragged into your shit, Scotland? Is that what you want, man? Because I don't do none of your, "It's OK, I'm the Scottish shot-caller" white-boy shit?' It was a passable Scottish accent.

'AJ! AJ!' I shouted, grabbing his shoulders as he turned to face me. 'What the fuck are you going on about!?' I was getting tired of the theatrics.

He stopped and stared at me for a moment. 'Did you give Tank two books? Tell me you didn't give the Tank two books of stamps?'

'Oh!' I responded rather sheepishly. 'That.' I looked away from him. Now I knew.

'Shit!' AJ replied.

'He said he was in a jam and I lent him two books. He gave me his word that he would give me them back. He's an honest guy, right?' My conviction tailed off as I listened to my own words.

AJ looked right at me again, astonished. 'An honest guy? An honest guy!? Shit Scotland! Do you realise where you live? Have you stopped to look around you for a minute, and remember where you are, you dumb motherfucka . . . Shit!' he said once more, looking away from me, then refusing to talk to me any further. He continued to sulk for the rest of the morning session, thumbing through stylish magazines and mumbling things like 'dumb motherfucka', 'shot–caller my ass' and '. . . right back to Scot–land' without speaking to me further. When the lunch bell sounded, he was straight up from his seat and started heading out, but at the last moment, he stopped and turned to me.

'Scotland, you better make sure he gives you those books back,' he said with a look of woeful severity. I just nodded back, not wishing to offend AJ, but still feeling he was making too much of it.

The fact was, it was already Thursday, the day before Tank had promised to repay. And then Friday came and went and he didn't show up. Perhaps I should have gone to find him at that point, but I didn't know what I would say to him if I did. I imagined me standing there like an idiot in front of this man–mountain, meekly asking for my stamps back. He'd probably laugh at me and, even if he didn't, the simple truth was that I was scared of him. In spite of having friends, and knowing the lingo, and being the shot–caller for the US Penitentiary System's smallest gang, I was still afraid of most of the people in the prison.

Another week passed and still no sign of Tank or the stamps. Thankfully AJ had dropped the subject, and although it continued to niggle at the back of my mind, I comforted myself by thinking it was only $6.40 worth of stamps. Hardly worth dying for. I would just ignore Tank in the future and definitely strike him off my Christmas card list. I'd forget about it and chalk it down to experience. But things aren't that simple in prison.

A few weeks later, AJ was back at me, but this time the message was more serious.

'You need to deal with the Tank, man,' he said suddenly as he sat down beside me one day. 'Everyone in my Range was talking about it last night.'

'Quite the sewing circle up in your Range, isn't it?' I quipped, trying to mask my annoyance that the subject hadn't gone away.

AJ frowned. 'Word is out, Scotland. Word is you ain't no shot-caller. You a soft touch. Tank jacked you for a couple books and you ain't doin' shit about it. That's the word. That you don't have the balls.'

'Yeah well . . .' I mumbled, feeling threatened and annoyed at myself for trusting Tank and creating this mess. 'It was only a couple of books and I can't do anything to screw up my transfer.'

AJ was on top of me for that response straight away. 'Shit, Scotland! Don't be such an asshole.' He was angry now. 'It wouldn't matter if you gave him one stamp and he didn't give you it back. You can't allow that to happen. And don't forget sump'n. You walk alone in this Yard. You got no backup, Mr Fucking smartass Scottish shot-caller. Even the ABs wouldn't have let this shit happen to you. You were so fucking clever with that, weren't you? Well, they know you're isolated and now you've just shown them you're an easy-touch bleedin'-heart white boy all on his own with nothin' to back it up.' Leaning right into me, pointing his finger at me, AJ was more pissed off than I'd ever seen him. With anyone. And that was saying something. He followed it up by slapping me on the head.

'Alright, alright, for fuck's sake!' I said, annoyed. 'I get it about the stamps. I get it! Now what the fuck should

I do about it?' I knew he was right. I had seen it in operation. I knew that if the word got out you were a patsy or a soft touch, you'd be a target for every low-life gang-banger in the place. I'd seen people's entire commissary – their weekly supplies from the prison shop – being handed over: unopened letters, books, radios, sneakers – you name it, they took it. If they wanted it and you weren't prepared to fight for it, they'd take it.

'I'll tell you exactly what you're gonna do. You're gonna get your stamps back, or you're going to get your ass kicked trying. That's what you're going to do!' screeched AJ, seemingly more annoyed with me by the second. As I started to digest that thought he went on, 'What the hell were you thinking? You s'posed to be a motherfucking banker dude, and you don't know shit about lending! Didn't you tell me good bankers only lend to the people who don't need it? No wonder the fucking world e-fucking-conomy's gone to shit, Scotland; it's got motherfuckers like you running the show!'

I almost smiled at that – somehow, AJ always hit the nail right on the head – but for now, I was just overcome with misery at the thought of what lay ahead. Doing nothing was not an option.

'This is how it's gonna work,' AJ said, 'and there ain't no other way, so just listen. You need to demand your stamps back, and you need to demand them back now, someplace when everyone can hear you. He'll tell you to go shit, then you have to try and at least get one good hit on him, before he busts your ass into sorry little pieces. Then when you come back from the infirmary and after a few weeks in the Hole, things will be cool between you and Tank and you'll have respect back in the Yard because they'll know you're no easy touch because you were prepared to go toe-to-toe with the Tank.'

'That's a plan??' I said, feeling genuinely afraid. 'I'm trying to get home, AJ. I can't get into a fight.'

AJ lapsed into a haughty silence and left me, for a while, sitting with my head in my hands. I knew he was right. I'd lent hundreds of millions of dollars throughout my career; I'd even once arranged a short-term bridging loan of $3bn to allow a major British utility to be acquired. And yet two $3.20 books of stamps looked like being the worst loan I ever made.

Eventually, when he felt he'd made enough of a point by ignoring me and thumbing through his magazine, AJ put it down and spoke again calmly. 'If you don't fight, Scotland, then you ain't gonna be worth shit in this Yard. You'll be somebody's bitch by the end of the week . . . and me, Chief, New York or Toro won't be able to do nuthin' for you. Your transfer will never happen anyway because you'll find yourself in trouble just about every day.' He let this wisdom sink in for a while before continuing. 'I'll be embarrassed to be associated with you. You'll bring shame to this here library, and to librarians everywhere.' That was stretching it a bit, I thought, but I could see his point. I took a deep, weary breath – the breath of a man who has at last appreciated the size of the mountain he has to climb.

After a while longer I turned to AJ again. 'OK, here's what I am going to do,' I hoped I sounded more determined than I felt. 'The NBA semi-finals are on right now, yes?'

'Ahum,' AJ nodded.

'The Lakers are playing tonight and that's Tank's team, right?'

'Ahum.'

'So he'll be watching it?'

'Yup,' said AJ, 'prob'ly betting your stamps.'

'He bets?' I asked, surprised.

AJ lay his head on the desk and banged his fist on the table for effect. 'You dumb Scottish, skirt–wearing asshole. You didn't even know that? You didn't know the Tank is one of the major gamblers in this place? That's his bag man, that's his thing . . . tell me you at least checked that out?' he pleaded, looking right at me. My stony, scowling face told him his answer. 'Jesus,' he groaned, resting his head once more onto the table, 'how did you ever get this job?'

It was the CAMPARI test. Banking class number one, day one, lesson one, that's what they taught us – assess every loan under the CAMPARI mnemonic: Character, Ability, Means, Principal, Amount, Repayment and Interest. I hadn't applied even one of those criteria to Tank; I hadn't even started that process. Instead I'd invented the new mnemonic SLAAB: Seemed Like An Alright Bloke. What a banker I'd turned out to be.

'So Tank will be watching the TV tonight,' I went on. 'And the room will be packed?'

'Yes,' AJ responded mournfully, seemingly losing his belief in me by the minute.

'OK. So at half–time, I . . .'

'End of the second quarter.'

'What?'

'We call it the end of the second quarter.'

'Whatever. At the end of the second quarter, when everyone leaves to get coffee and stuff, I'll grab the remote control and when the game restarts and everyone including Tank settles down to watch it, I'll switch the game off and say it's not going back on until Tank returns my stamps!'

I wanted to say 'darrraahhh!!' but resisted the temptation and just grinned instead.

'Are . . . you . . . the . . . dumbest . . . stupidest . . . motherfucka . . . in the entire history of prison?' AJ began slowly, shaking his head with genuine emotion. 'Have . . . I . . . wasted . . . all my time on your sorry white Scottish ass? They will beat you up so bad that they won't even bother taking your sad motherfuckin' body back to little old Scotland to your mamma. You come between those dudes and the play–offs and you are a dead Scottish guy. Shit, they'll kill every other dumb-assed Scottish guy who is dumb enough to stray into Big Spring prison for a hundred years in the future!' He would have gone on I think, but I stopped him.

'AJ,' I said, as I grabbed him. 'I was joking. I get the point. I'll deal with Tank. I'll deal with him tonight.'

'You will,' AJ concluded, ominously.

The NBA play–offs meant the TV room was packed for more than an hour beforehand, and rowdier than usual as it was the fifth game in the play–offs, and vital in a way you had to be an American to understand. I wasn't exactly going to be watching the match, anyway.

The last time I had faced an incident in the TV room – with the Aryan in my seat – I had survived by stumbling through things before I had time to really think them through or to fully contemplate the ramifications of my actions. This time it was different. This time I had had plenty of time to think it through and I had a good idea of the ramifications. My choices were stark. Ignore

Tank, make no attempt to get my stamps back and lay myself open to what would almost certainly be a systematic programme of extortion – if I was lucky – and if unlucky . . . well, at that point I would move deep back into my 'fucking catastrophic' list of rape, sodomy and being someone's sex toy for the next few years. The alternative was to publicly have it out with Tank, try and lay one shot on him, then hope that the subsequent beating he would be required to inflict on me for the sake of his own credibility wouldn't end up causing me any permanent damage. I didn't want to end up as one of those 'Thriller' extras who answered the chow-call each evening, hobbling down on my crutches to get some cockroach burritos before the great stampede consumed me.

Neither scenario seemed to assist my chances of staying out of trouble – the one definitive and useful piece of advice I'd been given by the authorities. 'Do your own time' was the saying. Stay out of trouble = transfer home. Trouble = no transfer home. There was a third option, going to see Tank and requesting a relatively 'tame' beating, but it all came back to the same thing. So much here was about how you fronted it, and I risked making things much worse by trying to take Tank into my confidence. I needed to face him. I needed to front up. I'd made such a hoo-ha about being in the Scottish gang of one; now I had to live up to that billing, organise myself a respectable beating and hope that the cops would take a more enlightened view if I was the victim rather than the perpetrator.

Tank was in the room and had nodded over to me when he came in. AJ was there too, looking nervous. My heart was racing and the waiting was agony. It was too noisy during the game to hear much of what anyone was saying, muffled as it was by our earphones from the radios we needed to hear the sound. The game was tight and the Lakers were losing, which seemed, to my dismay, to make Tank more agitated. Eventually, the second quarter ended and people started taking their headphones off and either standing to stretch or heading out for coffee or food. Tank got up and made a move towards the door. It was now or never.

'Eh, Tank!' I shouted loudly, still seated, deliberately looking not at him but forward to the TV. The murmur died down almost instantly.

'Tank!' I shouted again, on autopilot now and still not looking at him. He turned around and looked at me, seemingly surprised. Before he could speak, I faced him and as forcibly as possible, with as strong a Scottish accent as I could muster, I said, 'Where's my fucking stamps?'

Tank looked aghast, genuinely surprised, and everyone looked from him to me and back again.

'I got you, Scotland, I got you covered,' he replied, hesitantly. Before he could continue, I spoke brusquely to him once more.

'Just get me my fucking stamps,' I said, jabbing my finger at him with all the menace I could muster, as I looked square from him back to the TV and placed my earphones ceremoniously back into my ears. An age went by as my heart pounded.

From the corner of my eye, I could tell he hesitated for a second and I thought he was contemplating a lunge for me, no doubt to compress me into a Scotch egg, but thankfully the huge man hesitated just a second or two longer and then ambled out. I didn't sigh with relief or give away any emotion, but I noticed my hand was trembling violently. It shocked me, until I thought about just how scared I actually was, and how little I was looking forward to my self-induced Tank beating.

I caught AJ's eye and he nodded me the type of nod you give someone when they volunteer to be shot first and you realise you're going to miss having him around.

I'd figured Tank wouldn't do anything in the TV room, so in many ways this was the easy bit of my master-plan. He didn't want it known that he didn't pay anyone back, or else his credit – if he could still source any in here – would be in ruins. No, he was going to wait a day or two, maybe a week, before he broke my body into little pieces. Hopefully he'd do it somewhere quiet, and AJ said that as long as I still could walk and check myself into the infirmary, the cops would respect me if I said I fell. Not much of a plan, I knew, but that was all I had. At least I had sent out a public message, though, that I would defend myself. But the whole thing – the whole charade, the games, the rules in this place – felt overwhelming; so hard, so dangerous and so frightening. As I sat there, trying to stop myself shaking, I reminded myself again of the prize: home. Cara, Calum, Julie and her kids Issi and Jamie, my mum, my brothers, Celtic games, watching Scotland getting gubbed at rugby, my family, my life. All of that was worth taking a beating for – for that I would take ten beatings and more.

Half-time in American sport takes an age, so I decided to pop back to the Range to get a water refill. As soon as I emerged from the TV room towards the Range, Tank was in my slipstream.

'Hey Scotland! Scotland!' he called after me as I walked

quickly toward the Range. Ignoring him while mass hysteria broke out in my mind, I got myself into the narrow corridor that snaked round toward my Range. Tank's massive, paw-like hand gripped my right shoulder.

I thought about elbowing him straight off, like I'd practised with Sergei, but we hadn't practised that with a ten-foot gorilla. I would only bounce off his chest. He was supposed to beat me up in a couple of days' time, not today, dammit! I wasn't ready! I had football tomorrow and I also wanted to have some quality time to say goodbye to my face before he rearranged it. I was breathing heavily as I turned around. So was Tank. In the close quarters of the corridor – we could both touch the walls either side of us – Tank seemed even more intimidating than before. The walls made me more afraid, as I thought about how easily he could smash my head against them, but I was trapped.

'Scotland, what's wid choo?' he started.

'I want . . . I need my stamps back!'

'I said I had you covered, Scotland. I said I had you covered.' Here we go, I thought, and steeled myself to try and belt him. He went on. 'Why'd you have to disrespect me in front of all those people?'

Keen to get on with my losing fight, for some reason that question really annoyed me. It was as if he was suggesting this was all my fault. 'You fucking disrespected me!' I shouted at him. 'You gave me all that shite about how you're nothing in this Yard if you don't have your word and you promised me, you fucking promised me, you would pay me back no matter what, and how everyone in this Yard "respects the Tank" and how I can count on you and your word is your bond and all that shite . . .' I was past caring by this time and without realising it I was jabbing my finger into the Tank's chest as he towered over me. 'You fucking know I walk alone on this Yard and I am in a gang of one and if I don't face up to you then I will be for shit round here and the ABs will have my arse . . . And I fucking liked you as well, ya twat and I thought you were a good guy, but now I'm going to have to fucking fight you . . .'

My accent and my anger probably made most of this indiscernible to the Tank but still I stuck up my fists and assumed the position Sergei had taught me, suddenly desperate to stick one on him.

'. . . and you're going to kick the shit out of me but that's still better than having those ABs own me, and this is all over two poxy books of stamps worth six dollars, and forty fucking measly fucking cents, ya fucking cunt . . .' I tailed off, my fists still up, no breath left.

Tank looked shocked. Not scared. But shocked. He held up two, table-sized hands in a stop sign. 'Wow, wow . . . hang on there, Scotland; slow down! Man, you talk fast,' he said, still with his hands raised. We both breathed heavily and I jockeyed for position a bit so I could stick one on the big prick.

'A'ight, Scotland, a'ight. Fuck's sake, dude. I'm feeling you. I'm not quite understandin' you with that Scotch of yours, but I'm feelin' you. I don't want you beatin' up on me or nothing,' he added, as a smile began to spread across his face.

I was breathing very heavily and with my anger subsiding the corridor felt narrow and claustrophobic again. 'I'll get you your stamps back this week, Scotland. And I'll give you two extra for loss of time,' he went on, much more soberly. 'But you make sure everyone in the Yard knows Tank pays up and covers some extra if he gotta.'

I looked at him for a moment or two, my fists still at the ready, before slowly nodding in agreement, still peering up at him. He playfully slapped my face a couple of times. 'You was gonna take a shot at me, wasn't you?' he asked, genuinely intrigued at the thought of it. I simply looked up at him and nodded, not sure if I would have ever mustered a shot at him. 'Well, I'll be . . .' he mused, seemingly rather pleased with the thought. 'Good for you Scotland, good for you!' He smiled. 'You know I would have had to whip your ass though, right?' he continued, more of a statement of fact than a question.

I felt so exhausted, so drained, I just nodded again.

'You got some balls on you, Scotland!' Tank concluded, appreciatively, and with one more playful slap he lumbered off. I shuffled in the opposite direction, back to my bunk, where I lay prone for hours, just staring at the ceiling, not knowing whether to laugh or cry.

Two days later my books of stamps were returned, with two extra stamps for good measure. I barely spoke to Tank when he delivered them to me; I just grunted 'thanks' and turned away from him to face the wall again. I had something more important to contemplate. In my hand I looked again for the hundredth time at a picture of my daughter. My now seven-year-old daughter. Her picture had arrived.

19

RAIN

FOR THE NEXT FEW WEEKS, THE picture of Cara dominated much of my thoughts. When I'd first received it, it had shocked me. She looked so different, so much older than the most recent pictures and memories I had of her, when she had just turned five; an angelic smile when we went to buy flowers for her granny in Crail in Scotland; or a cheeky grin on her birthday. The difference in her made me sad and anxious; bringing home to me even more that precious moments with her had already slipped by, that my wee girl was growing up without me. I needed solitude; somewhere I could be on my own to grieve my sense of the years lost already. To grieve the loss of my daughter, the loss of my son and my failure as a father – but there was nowhere for me to go. Only this incessantly noisy, crowded room.

It was a Saturday, the visits were finished and we had 'free movement' until around 5 p.m., when they would complete a count then start the dinner rota. I had taken refuge in the Range, where the air–conditioning remained sporadic at best, but offered at least some respite from the heat. It was one of those slow, torturous days in Big Spring when life seemed to be what other people lived. Monday was a government holiday, so the prison would be effectively closed for a long weekend – and on days such as this, despair could creep up on you suddenly.

I was writing a letter to Calum, which wasn't helping my feeling of melancholy and despair. It was his birthday soon, and Chief was completing a drawing for him which I was sending him as a gift. He would be thirteen years old, becoming a teenager – a target date I had always set for coming home, when I foolishly believed we were going to trial to win. I wanted to sound cheery in the letter and the card, but missing his birthday just felt like another entry on the failure list as a father. My poor boy got me as a dad. I felt I should be apologising to him rather than telling him how much I missed him.

This was one of the 'real' Big Spring days, mind–numbingly boring, with nothing happening other than the usual spats and power displays. Treading time in significant discomfort, and solitude among the multitude. Bryan Ferry had been wrong when he sang that 'Loneliness is a crowded room', or at least he had been slightly inaccurate. 'Loneliness is a crowded room full of Mexicans,' I thought as I lay there gazing at my excitable roommates.

Yesterday we had had another spontaneous 'shake-down' by the cops. 'Shakedowns' were about the only time they seemed to involve themselves with the inmates' lives in Big Spring – if involvement meant picking up your stuff and hurling it across the room while shouting at you. They had removed books from my locker, because I'd had six in there, and regulation 4(ii) sub-section 8 of the Correctional Rules for Big Spring Correctional Facility said that I could only have two at a time. Fortunately this breach wasn't a Federal offence so I wouldn't be getting extra time for it.

The cops weren't looking for books, though, and they had found what they termed a 'shank' or weapon, but which Alex, the unfortunate inmate under whose bed they'd found it, termed a 'can-opener'. Alex bunked about fifteen feet away from me and also played left-back for our football team, so his disappearance off to the Hole was a disappointment for all of us. I couldn't imagine him – this mild-mannered, slightly boring bloke – using a weapon, but then as you got to know people more and more, it was harder to see any of them as criminals. Alex came from French Guyana and had a shock of red, gingery hair. We called him 'the Axe' – not because of his penchant for chopping things into pieces, but on account of his violent tackling on the football pitch. Or at least that is why I assumed 'we' called him the Axe . . .

I had seen the cops find the implement and I was struck by two things. Firstly, what a very stupid place to hide it, under a bed, and secondly that Alex must have been planning to open some industrial-sized tins. It had a six-inch handle and about a four-inch blade – made apparently from a number of tuna cans welded together. Its existence under Alex's bed confirmed the uncomfortable truth of how little I really understood about what was going on around me.

I pushed Calum's card aside for a moment, lay back again and wondered when all of this would ever end. There had been some news on my transfer. I had filled in a few more forms and signed a few more papers, but progress was sporadic. Julie had written to me and said that pressure was being applied from the UK to bring us home, but I had no confidence in any politician other than Menzies Campbell. Only Sir Menzies had stayed resolutely behind us and I think truly understood the inadequacies of the US judicial system, having practised law himself in the United States many years earlier. His support never wavered and I knew he would continue to help as much as he could. Julie told me that David had been moved and I took that as a positive sign that a move for me might also be imminent. All repatriations to England took place from New York, so David being moved could be an indication of something afoot.

Chief kept reminding me that the journey through the US prison system would take me many months after I left Big Spring, and would, in fact, be many times worse; but it was hard to imagine anything worse than this soul-destroying purgatory. And the way I saw it, even one step towards home – towards Calum and Cara and the rest of my loved ones – was progress.

Even though there had been so much publicity around our case when Enron had first collapsed, I had thought Calum was immune to it. That naive view changed one day when I was dropping off Angus, one of Calum's friends, at his house in the village next to us. I took turns at the school runs some evenings with a couple of other parents whose children attended the same school.

Laura had become increasingly isolated since the news of the Enron collapse had broken, and believed everyone was looking at her and talking about her, so she stopped doing the school runs. After years in the City, I found them quite enjoyable.

Angus's mother, Edith, had invited me in for a cup of tea, somewhat conspiratorially, as seven-year-old Calum rushed off to play with Angus in the garden.

'What does Calum know about your possible extradition?' she asked, when we had settled into the kitchen.

'Nothing.' I was surprised by the question.

'You might be mistaken about that,' she began.

'Go on,' I said, feeling uncomfortable as I watched him play in the garden with Angus.

'Yesterday,' Edith went on, 'when I picked the boys up, I congratulated Calum on the school play, you know, because there was a picture of it in the local paper. And then Angus piped up, "Oh, I saw your dad in the paper, Calum." I froze. And I looked at Calum in my rear-view mirror, but he just seemed lost, gazing out of the window. And then Angus said, "They say he stole one pound from someone."' Edith told me that part with a smile on her face. We looked out at the pair of them, hurtling round the garden, so innocent.

'Anyway,' continued Edith, eyeing me intently. 'Then Calum said, "Yes, the Americans are after my dad for something he didn't do."'

My heart sank and I leaned my head against the window, still watching him play.

'And then he said, "They might come during the night but I've made a spear to keep under my bed to get them if they try to take my dad."'

Edith stopped talking. I couldn't look at her. I never thought he was so aware of what was going on, but I suppose with all the phone calls and hushed conversations there was always a good chance of him picking up something. I chided myself for not being more self-disciplined around him. The thought that he was trying to protect me made my heart feel like it was going to burst.

Later, when we returned home, he and I went hunting chestnuts in the garden together. I said nothing to him about Edith's revelations, but I watched him more intently than ever. He seemed to be playing happily enough, and I almost convinced myself that he'd perhaps just been joking with Angus and Edith. Later that night, I read him one of his favourite stories and told him a couple of tales about William Wallace, the great Scottish warrior. Like all kids, he pushed for a little more, but I stuck with our routine then sang to him a little. My singing was rotten, but he and Cara used to like it, so I'd usually oblige. It was one of the (admittedly few) great things about being out of work awaiting extradition to a US Correctional Facility – you got more time with the kids. I held one of his hands while I stroked his head with the other. And five minutes later he was asleep.

I watched him for a while longer, just the ticking of his luminous bear clock breaking the silence of his darkened room. I loved the smell of his room and the sense of comfort in it. Thinking again of what Edith had said, I gently released his hand, and went down on my knees, quietly feeling around under his bed. It didn't take me long to find what I was looking for, a long bamboo stick with a plastic 'bayonet' Sellotaped to the top of it and some feathers stuck halfway down the bamboo. Nothing like as dangerous as Alex's shank, but definitely Calum's spear. I held the flimsy weapon in my hand and looked again at my beautiful boy, trying to defend his father, but now fast asleep.

Six years later, on my bunk in Big Spring, I thought of what must have been going through my boy's head as he made his spear to protect his dad all those years ago, and the thought that now, even though he was just turning thirteen, that fight had lasted almost half of his lifetime. Where would his next birthday card be sent from? By then he would be fourteen and I would have missed so much of his childhood. I had to start heading home soon, or my loss, his loss, our loss, would be incalculable.

I sighed, feeling a trickle of sweat roll down my back. I sat up and tuned back into the chaos around me. Most of the other guys were still kicking back, either sleeping or playing cards or arguing over something. Chief was lost in the finishing touches of Calum's drawing and I hadn't seen New York or AJ all day. A few bunks across from me, Adam, who had entered Big Spring the same day as me so many months earlier, had been agonising over a letter to his ex-girlfriend. I had heard him ask about six or seven times how to spell words like 'bitch', 'cock-sucker' and 'destroy' – so I doubted he'd parted on cordial terms with this particular lady. A light-hearted argument had now developed over how to spell the word 'strangle' – the two leading protagonists being a member of the Aryan Brotherhood, and a tubby, Buddha-like Hispanic guy called Amadeo. I had never seen him leave the Range and he had a huge tattoo of the decapitated head of the King of Spain – the sign of a Sureno – over his engorged belly. Unfortunately, he had clearly expanded his waistline after getting the tattoo because the King of Spain, as well as suffering the misfortune of being decapitated, had had his nose and forehead significantly stretched. This gave the unfortunate king a look closer to Gerard Depardieu in *Cyrano de Bergerac* – a frequent downside of prison tattooing. As stomachs expanded or arms and legs grew to ridiculous sizes from too much gym time, once perfectly proportioned body art would get distorted, and take on a myriad of bizarre forms.

Adam remained torn between the Aryan 'S.T.R.A.N.G.I.L.' and the less prosaic Hispanic 'S.T.R.A.N.G.U.L.L.', when Amadeo gestured excitedly towards me. 'Ask Scotland. He knows all kinds of shit!' Several heads turned my way.

Ignoring the possibility that the FBI might charge me with being a co-conspirator to some poor girl's strangulation, I rapidly fired off my response. 'S.T.R.A.N.G.L.E.'

There was silence for a moment as Adam, Amadeo and the Aryan Brother just gazed at me, at first sceptical, then finally dumbfounded.

'Wow,' said Adam eventually, with genuine admiration. 'How do you know so much stuff?'

I shrugged my shoulders then lay back on my bunk and sighed. What the hell was I doing here? I was considering having another go at the letter to Calum when New York bounded into the room, full of the joys of life, calling over to me as he strode towards his bunk halfway down the Range. 'Hey Scottie. Scottie?'

'Yo!' I responded, my paltry attempt at jail-speak raising a wry smile and a shake of the head from the ever-observant Chief in the corner. It was a constant battle to seem outwardly positive when inside my spirits were flagging so badly.

'I thought you'd be out there, man,' exclaimed an excitable New York as he ripped off his clothing, getting ready to go to the shower. He had clearly been working out again.

'Yeah?' I queried, having no idea what he was talking about. 'Out where?'

'In the Yard, man! It's raining!' New York replied as he reached for his toiletries from his locker. I didn't even wait for him to finish – just leapt right off my bunk, grabbed my T-shirt and was heading for the door.

'Hey, Scotty,' a serious-sounding Chief shouted after me.

Raining! It hadn't rained in over four months, and before that only twice at night – soaking the floors, but not giving us any relief.

'Scotty, hold up . . .' I briefly heard Chief shout again as I left the Range, determined to get out into the rain before it stopped, and completely overlooking the concern in his voice.

I paused at the front of Sunset and looked out into the gap between the two buildings, seeing an almost imperceptible light mist of rain falling steadily. I had read once that there were forty-seven different terms for rain in the Scottish vernacular, something I could well believe, having been drenched, drowned and sodden all too often growing up in dreach Glasgow, but I'd never seen rain like this. I'd often wondered why we hadn't just switched to the German word for weather – '*Wetter*'. It seemed a far more appropriate word for the west coast of Scotland – we don't have weather there, we just have wetter.

I put my top on and started to walk up to the Yard, positively revelling in the fine, misty spray that passed for rain in Big Spring, Texas, my spirits suddenly soaring. Texas mist, not Scotch mist, but it would do for me. It had a cleansing, serene quality and I stopped for a moment just under the bird house and turned my face to the air, letting the tiny droplets fall gently onto my face. I felt almost free and completely refreshed. There was a slight breeze, another first for Big Spring, yet it was still warm and the overall combination was intoxicating. I felt elated; I felt connected to home; I felt blessed to experience this simple pleasure in such a dire place.

I walked quickly towards the gateposts separating the main housing blocks from the path, up past the church to the Yard. I had been relatively oblivious to anyone else, although it had occurred to me that everyone seemed to be heading back in, even though the move wouldn't be called for a while yet.

'Bunch of pussies,' I thought. 'It's just a wee bit of mist. It's barely even raining.'

I held my hand in front of my face. The rain was so light it was drifting, giving the whole moment a surreal quality. Still people passed me.

'Scotland, you'd better done not go up there,' an unrecognisable voice called as its owner hurried by me.

The place was emptying fast. Some of them were covering their heads as they ran, a sight which fuelled my disdain further, and by the time I reached the running track there were only a few people ahead of me.

I hadn't seen them initially because they were standing at the one covered spot that abutted the running track. The running track was on the top of a gradual incline, so since the covered section was slightly hidden from the main Yard, it was a regular gathering place for gang meetings and retributions. I could tell immediately, from the way the two chief protagonists were standing facing each other, surrounded by a ring of a dozen or so gang-bangers, that violence was in the air. My mood immediately changed, and my heart started to race. I was in the wrong place at the wrong time.

I was already only fifty feet away, but at that moment, I had a chance, a brief chance, to turn around and walk away without anyone being the wiser. But I hesitated, not in movement, but in thought – the wrong combination, because by the time I had decided to turn around my legs had carried me further on, level with the little crowd, but just to their left on the running track.

I saw sunlight glinting on a bald head. Aryan Brotherhood, my favourite guys. There were around ten of them, encircling some poor guy who was facing up to my old pal SlumDawg, the AB's enforcer. He dwarfed his victim, and I noticed how relaxed his arms were and how large his hands seemed as they dangled loosely by his side. Always fear the man who looks relaxed prior to combat.

SlumDawg had a face wracked with pockmarks, a mind ravaged by crystal meth. What he lacked in teeth he now made up for in hair, blonde hair, masses of it covering his head and face, but more in patchwork than in any consistent fashion. Pasty white and very thin, he looked like a mutation of his beloved white gene pool, fucked up by centuries of inbreeding in the Tennessee Blue Mountains. I'd barely heard him speaking since he visited me on my first day in Big Spring, but had seen him on the same 'stoop' at the side of the Yard most days, sitting idly and growing new bits of blonde hair. New York, unaware that we had 'history', had furtively pointed him out to me and told me he was one to steer clear of – the Aryan Brotherhood's weapon of choice when retribution was called for. I'd often thought he and I would end up having more dealings with each other. But not like this.

I was anxious to walk on round the track before I drew any attention to myself. I looked ahead and kept moving. I was just slightly ahead of them now, but temptation got the better of me and I turned to glance over my shoulder. With perfect timing, I saw SlumDawg swing a haymaker – round and wide and clean into the face of his victim, who had made no attempt to defend himself. I caught a clear view of the man's face as he began to fall to the concrete floor. The first punch had knocked him out cold. His head cracked onto the solid surface, the sound unusual but unmistakeable.

I recognised him, but I didn't know his name. He was a good handball player, and I'd often seen him on the courts there. I'd never even realised he was an AB – he didn't seem the type – even though he was white, tall and angular. I remember him as always smiling. He wasn't smiling now. I realised I had stopped and was standing staring, mesmerised by what I had just seen. Everything seemed to have slowed down and I knew from the mechanical, precise movements of SlumDawg and the other ABs that this retribution had only just begun. I couldn't move, as if my feet were set in concrete, and I knew then that I was going to stand there and watch; that I wouldn't move now even if I could. A thought entered my head that I wouldn't initially acknowledge, but which forced itself to the fore. 'They are going to kill him.' I nodded; maybe I nodded, I don't know. My mind was spinning and I continued to stand spellbound, useless, as SlumDawg surveyed his victim. He was lying peacefully as if asleep, on the concrete floor of the shelter. As SlumDawg walked around him, it registered with me that he was already bleeding from the head. I say registered, because I remember clearly seeing the blood flow off the concrete and onto the dust that preceded the running track where I stood, but I don't know what I thought about it; what my view of this was. It felt like I was watching a TV show. But I had no way of changing channels.

SlumDawg was circling his victim and, having received some words of advice from the other gang members, he quickly and confidently crouched down over his victim and peered closely into his face. Then, with a gentleness both surprising and chilling, he held his victim's chin lightly in his left hand, turning his face smoothly one way then another. Kneeling over the flaccid body, and having adjusted his position so he was now crouched above the chest, he scrutinised the man's face once more, as if considering how to best maximise the damage he could inflict on his unconscious victim.

I felt chained to that spot. Mouth open, I glanced away from SlumDawg for a second and saw the looks of relish on the other gang members' faces. Still I stood there helplessly. This was breaking the rules of humanity, but still I couldn't move.

The second blow was as sickening as it was sudden, the third and fourth rammed into this nameless soul's unprotected face with such force it felt as if they must burst through to the concrete below. A fifth, maybe a sixth, maybe a seventh, I don't know, maybe even a tenth blow fell onto his unprotected face and head, interspersed all the while with the occasional gentle adjustment from SlumDawg as he repositioned the head in order to target any undamaged features. And there I stood, too shocked to speak. Too horrified to run away. Too beaten to intervene.

There was nothing but silence, punctuated by the sound of SlumDawg's blows and a man's face breaking. No sound from the other ABs, just silence for seconds; maybe minutes, maybe someone's lifetime; until suddenly and violently a scream emerged. An agonised, frenzied scream.

'FUR FUCK'S SAKE!'

They all turned and looked at me. SlumDawg, still perched over his unconscious victim – a body now with no recognisable face – looked up at me, his fist still bloodied and at the ready. He turned and looked at the shot–caller for guidance, but he was too busy staring at me too. I recognised him from our meeting a few months back, my hairy biker friend. After a second or two, he sneered at me and motioned to SlumDawg to leave. Carefully extricating himself from the lifeless body below him, the enforcer stood up to his full height, smiling as he surveyed the wreckage of his work; his pride sickeningly obvious at the probable termination of another man's life. I didn't wait for them to leave. I turned around and started to walk away around the running track, my body trembling and my legs almost failing me.

'Fuck these people!' I said out loud, my breath rasping and my heart pounding. I was walking even quicker now but turned my head to view the scene behind me. The man had not moved, not one inch, while the rest of the ABs were dispersing rapidly. I was walking the wrong way, deeper into the running track and further from the safety of the Yard. I walked faster still in the wrong direction – just desperate to walk away. 'Fuck that guy!' I thought. 'It's not my issue; it's not my fucking concern.' I was scared; I was sickened; I was disgusted. Disgusted with myself. Here I was walking away again. Being a coward; just like I had done with the rat in the Range, just like I had done all those years ago with my brothers, when I hid with the girls behind the storm doors from DumbDumb and Finn. In here for fraud. And rightly too. I was a wanker, a complete fraud.

But this wasn't my fault. It was the other guy's fault – whoever he was, and for whatever he had done. I was going home. I had to go home. I had to get to Cara and had to help my son. I looked back. The guy still hadn't moved. 'Shit, move you dumb arsehole. Fucking move!' I said under my breath. I stopped walking and turned and stared at him. I could feel my heart pounding. No movement. 'Move, you dumb fuck!' I shouted. I was still completely alone. Everyone else had known what was going down; everyone else had made sure they saw nothing. Chief had even fucking warned me.

'Well, fuck him. Fuck them all!' I turned away again and started to walk further around the track. I'd made my promises; I'd told Calum I would come home. Promised every night to do whatever it took to find Cara. I was getting transferred out of this hellhole. Leaving. Going. Now.

I was repeating these points over and over again, trying to drown everything else out. I stopped once again and looked back the hundred metres or so. It occurred to me that in my haste to get away from SlumDawg, to get away from the body, I was still moving the wrong way. I needed to walk back down past the body. Fuck, he still hadn't moved. Worse, a voice inside me was saying over and over again that there was something wrong with his position, with the way he was lying. His head was right back – the prime position in which to swallow your tongue or choke on your own blood or vomit. 'At least move your fucking head!' I shouted. I looked around to see if anyone was coming near but there was no sign of anyone, other than the inmates milling around down the hill towards the main yard. The ABs were long gone. No cops, no anyone. Just me alone on the top of this running track and this . . . this dying man.

I stood still for a further second. 'Fuck him. Forget him. Fuck him!!' I chanted, tears welling up in my eyes. I walked determinedly away. Two steps later I stopped. 'He might be dying!' a voice inside pleaded. I turned again, not knowing what to do – to walk or stay; to help or to run away? He still wasn't moving. What could I do anyway? I was just an idiot from Glasgow. I was out of my depth in the Texas desert; a danger to myself, a danger to others.

Without even consciously making the decision, I found that I'd started back towards him, moving quickly. I had no choice, I realised – I just had to help him. If I didn't, then I would have lost my basic humanity; I would be lost myself. There would be no point in my going home then; the person I had been would be gone forever. It had a sudden inevitability about it and as I continued to think it through I realised I was moving rapidly towards the body on the ground.

He still hadn't moved, so I ran the last few yards to the prostrate and bloodied figure. I quickly crouched beside him but then recoiled as I went to touch him. I saw he was breathing but his face was horribly misshapen and tilted at an alarming angle. The area around his eyes was badly swollen and the bottom half of his face had collapsed, his chin effectively missing. I tried not to look at him, sickened at the sudden, ludicrous thought that part of him might come off in my hand. I looked around again, anxiously checking that no one could see me and that there were no cops around. There was blood everywhere. My eyes took snapshots that would haunt me for years to come. They haunt me still.

From my vantage point, I could see what looked like a cop near the far away perimeter fence, too far to see me, but he could be within vision in moments. I had my hands now on the victim's torso as I crouched over him. He had lost a lot of blood, too much blood, but I tried to ignore that and figure out how to move him.

His body was warm and surprisingly heavy as I tried to pull him forward towards me. I couldn't budge him the first time, as I was too tentative and worried about hurting him further, but another glance down to where the cop was walking near the perimeter fence galvanised me, and I yanked him over as my panic began to deepen. His arm, lifeless and bloodstained, flopped onto my legs, limp and clammy and heavy. My heart soared as he spluttered and spat, an explosion of air finally escaping from his lungs. I tried to check that his airway was unobstructed, but the destruction to his face made it almost impossible to tell exactly where his mouth was. The touch of his brutalised mouth disgusted me, but I found it and managed to force open a gap with my fingers. I leaned forward towards him and put my ear to where his jaw hung limply on the concrete. He was breathing still; barely, but breathing, definitely breathing.

The cop was now walking in my direction, although still not looking my way. I hauled the victim's legs forward into the recovery position just as I had been taught all those years ago in my First Aid classes. I real-ised I was crying, a fool in hell's arms. He spluttered again, alive, but as I started to rise from my crouched position I saw how horribly misshapen the back of his skull had become. It was hopeless. I desperately wanted to help him, to hold his hand, to touch him. But I couldn't stay. I blessed him quickly and my prayer for him contained only the words 'please God'. Panic began to envelope me. I looked up again and saw the cop getting ever closer. I crouched over the body, my hands still resting on him, but my eyes trained on the cop as I waited for my opportunity to move. He groaned again. Maybe he would live, maybe it wasn't too bad, but I tried to block these thoughts out of my mind; I needed to make my move. The cop looked toward the fence and I was up and away. Not running, but walking as fast as I could. Walking alone.

I arched my path rather than take the direct route to the gymnasium, so I would have the cover of the two-tiered benching around the running track, never taking my eyes off the cop until he was fractionally behind me. I switched my focus to the gymnasium and the large number of inmates milling around there, all still oblivious to the drama up top.

It was just at that moment that I'd wiped my forehead and noticed my hands were damp even though the rain had long since stopped. As I looked down at my socks and shoes, I shook my head and felt on the verge of screaming. I was covered in that man's blood. I'd completely failed to notice how much blood and teeth and bones he'd spluttered on me when he'd taken that breath, or the extent to which my hands and fingers were now bloodied.

By this time I was coming into view of the other inmates, but I suddenly took a sharp left, to where the gymnasium, and critically the toilets, were housed. At that exact moment, the whistle went up – much to my further alarm. I was done with caring about the victim anymore and was just panic-stricken about my own situation. The alarm jolted me and I increased my pace, then gave in to the desire to run the last hundred metres or so to the gym. With blood smeared over my forehead and all over my hands, and a little on my knees and legs, other inmates saw me and moved rapidly away. I ripped my T-shirt over my head while still moving and wiped away as much as I could from my hands and brow. The T-shirt was quickly bloodied. I tried rubbing my hands and then my knees again, but that slowed my run which I could not afford.

'You fucking wanker!' I blurted out – to myself, to SlumDawg, to everyone – moving through the inmates like a storm was following me.

No cops. Yet. I guessed they'd all be running towards the victim, through the front entrance to the gym, while I was going in through the back. The other inmates were heading towards the gated area where everyone would slowly be processed and checked for cuts, blood and bruises or any other telltale signs of their involvement. I heard someone call my name, but I didn't look to see who. I stormed towards a cubicle in the toilets. I felt like I wanted to take myself out and beat myself to a pulp. How could I have been so fucking stupid?

I pushed the first cubicle door open to see two Hispanics standing there like I'd caught them smoking a joint. Their look of horror at my bloodstained hands spoke volumes. I shouted at them to fuck off and physically yanked the first one out. The second one held his hands up and scurried out as I quickly closed the door behind me. I dipped my T-shirt into the urinal then started to wash off my face and knees which were encrusted with a mixture of dirt and blood. The mess seemed to get worse as the diluted blood ran further down my legs while the sirens continued to blare 'lock-down', just adding further to my panic.

Just then I heard a light knock on the cubicle door

and someone whispering, 'Escosais . . . Escosais!' as he pushed a clean white T-shirt under the door. It was Polvora, my fellow stamp collector. At considerable personal risk, he was breaking the rules to help me, and the concern registered in his voice told me everything I needed to know about the danger we were now both in.

Surprised and grateful, I quickly grabbed the T-shirt but found that I couldn't speak; couldn't even utter the words, 'Thank you.'

'Fucking *rapido*, Escosais!' Polvora urged me, in a tone that betrayed his anxiety further, before I heard him moving off quickly.

I took my socks off and wiped down my shoes. They still had bloodstains on them, so I dipped them in the urinal, then stuffed my socks and old T-shirt behind the cistern which was wired down to stop anything being hidden inside. I took my shorts off and put them back on inside out. I paused for a second, the panic and noise around me still at its height. I took a deep breath, then tried to take a calm look at myself. My hands were fine, but since there were no mirrors I could only splash myself with more water from the urinal, and hope. When I got to my shoes, I could see blood and teeth and bone in amongst the laces, so I hauled them out, dipped the shoes in the urinal once more, then took my new T-shirt and opened the urinal door.

There was no one around – not good, as I didn't want to get isolated and find myself walking down towards the guards on my own. I ran through the gym corridors until I reached the exit. Everyone had moved towards the Ranges, and already the crowd was milling around the locked gates about 150 metres away from me. I would have to walk down there alone. I took a deep breath and moved swiftly towards the crowd.

The numbers were already backed up to the gate as the cops started the slow process of checking everyone's hands and bodies. I eased my way into the crowd in the hope of being more anonymous. We were packed together but I felt as if all eyes were on me as I checked and re-checked my hands and knees for any further signs of blood or bone.

It was only when I reached the periphery of that queue that I started to realise the enormity of what I had done, the danger I was now in, both from the Feds and the gangs. If they found blood on me now, I would be taken to the Hole then questioned by the FBI – I was the only one in the vicinity, after all. Any hopes of a transfer and getting home to England would be over.

A new wave of panic enveloped me as I thought of these consequences. They could put me down for murder or attempted murder, and who would believe it had nothing to do with me, that I was only trying to help? The Feds wouldn't care and no one else would ever know the truth. I would never get home. Never get back to Calum. Never find Cara. Even if I found her, they'd never let me near her. My panic deepened as I checked my hands once more. We were edging slowly forward and I could see four guards, with four separate lines building up in front of them as they individually checked each inmate. I recognised Malone from my first day and made a detour towards him, thinking my chances might somehow be better with him. Just as I did, I caught Polvora's eye and he motioned discreetly with his finger rubbing on his forehead just above his right eye. I wet my fingers and saw the telltale sign of a little blood as I wiped my forehead vigorously again. Polvora looked tense but he scrutinised me again for a second, then nodded it was OK.

As we kept moving forward to the right, I saw SlumDawg and the rest of his posse, laughing and joking and edging their way forward as if enjoying a pre-match ritual in a football crowd. SlumDawg looked directly at me and smiled his gormless smile. He'd be coming back for me soon enough, I knew. I wasn't afraid of him. In fact, at that moment I felt I hated him; that I would relish the visit. The beating started to appear in flashback and with that misshapen face dominating my thoughts, my revulsion overcame my fear and turned to anger. Still staring at me, SlumDawg raised his finger to his mouth in the sign of silence. Instinctively I nodded, my face still set hard as I stared at him. I wouldn't rat, of that I was certain, but at that moment I knew I would kill him if I had the chance. I had come full circle, past a watermark. The rules had changed – even for me.

I edged further towards Malone in the hope that he would inspect me. I made a final check as I approached the individual line forming in front of him.

'Mulgrew,' he said jovially as he prompted me to show him my hands. 'You been causing trouble again?'

'No more than usual,' I managed to respond, my head spinning. Malone laughed a little as he gave no more than a cursory check to my arms, my legs and my shoes.

'On you go, Mildew,' he said, turning towards the next inmate. I walked quickly back to the Range.

Back there, it was as if we were under attack. Inmates were filling up all the water containers they could as the talk raged about how long a lockdown it would be and how one of the cops had said some guy was dead, and how another had heard he was brain damaged, and another that he was OK. I felt physically sick, and I needed to wash my hands again, even though I knew they were clear of blood now. As I stood at the sink, Chief came to the one next to me, then New York to the other side.

'You dumb motherfucka, son-of-a bitch, dumb-assed Scot,' began Chief through gritted teeth as he looked straight ahead. I'd never seen him so angry. 'You stupid, stupid asshole,' he continued as I kept scrubbing my hands. I looked up and saw the concern on New York's face as Chief continued his tirade of abuse.

'Shit, Scotty,' added New York, more calmly but shaking his head. 'Shit.'

'I know,' I said looking right at him then turning to Chief, 'I know, OK? I know.' I tried to walk past him, but he put his hand out to stop me.

'Watch your back, Scotty,' he said. 'We'll cover you the best we can,' he continued as New York nodded, 'but you need to hope for a long lockdown and then you get your sorry ass transferred out of here as soon as possible. Either that or check yourself into the Hole, although you'll hardly be safe there.' He looked tired and drawn and sad, like he'd spent too much time in Big Spring. We'd all spent too much time here. He'd probably seen too many like me crash and burn.

New York put his hand on my shoulder. 'Joker likes you and he won't let anyone in here to try any shit, so you should be safe as long as it's lockdown. I'll do a shift, then Chief will do a shift,' he said, meaning they would watch me, 'and then we'll see if Angel can help out.'

'Look guys,' I began purposefully. 'I appreciate the support. But you don't need to get involved in my shit. It's my decision, my choices, I'll handle the consequences.'

'We're already in your shit!' said Chief angrily as he pushed past me out of the bathroom towards the bunk.

'Get your water bottles filled up, Scotty,' said New York. 'Let's hope it's a long one.'

I managed to fill a few bottles and clamber back onto my bunk, ignoring all the chaos and excitement around me. Ramon came over, patted me on the leg and said, 'OK, Escosais, OK,' as if he felt sorry for me. He knew; everyone knew. Mendiola looked frightened and sat on the bunk across from me, his rosary beads working feverishly – always a bad sign. I instinctively rubbed the beads and cross he'd given me, searching for some comfort from it as I sat up on my bunk. Mendiola kept looking at me, then launching ever more vigorously into prayer. I felt more of an outsider than I'd ever been, more foreign than ever. I'd crossed a line and there was no going back. I couldn't stay in Big Spring. I didn't fit in; I didn't belong. I'd just seen a man almost killed and I didn't want to play any of their stupid games anymore. I didn't want to be a part of any of this. Angel, Chief, New York, the shot–callers – all of them could fuck off. I wanted to go home; to curl up in the corner and be on my own. Or maybe I'd just sit here until they came and got me.

At that precise moment, AJ came in and headed straight towards me. He stopped about fifteen feet away. He looked angry, but I wasn't in the mood. For a moment he just stood and stared at me. Perhaps if I'd known it was the last time I would see him, I would have come off the bunk and hugged him, but I didn't know that and I stayed on my bunk, a distance between us. Maybe it was my expression, a look of despair or defeat, that softened his own. As AJ's face changed and he moved uneasily from side to side, he sighed heavily. Through all the continued noise and chaos, we had our own silent conversation. I lightly shrugged my shoulders as if to say sorry. AJ seemed to struggle with this – his backing of the wrong horse, all his training gone to waste, and the disgrace, he'd no doubt try and argue, that had been done to the librarians' profession, worldwide. He forced a smile and looked intently at me; I numbly stared back at him. We nodded briefly to each other as he turned to leave. 'Scottish shit,' he said with feeling, before swinging round, and then, for the last time, flashing me the 'L for library' gang sign with his thumb and forefinger. Minutes later the doors slammed shut and the lockdown began. It would be my last.

20

ONE SMALL STEP

The first few hours were a blur. I kept my back to the wall both literally and metaphorically and couldn't think straight. The scene at the running track replayed in my mind a thousand times and each time I'd either chastise myself for helping him, or at other times for helping out too slowly. 'Do your own time, Scotland' – that had been the golden rule; the one I could never seem to get the hang of. Faces haunted me. Julie chastising me for jeopardising my only chances of getting home, my mum, my brothers, Jamie, Issi, Calum and even Cara. Sometimes I even felt I'd let the shot-callers down, especially Angel. But the face that haunted me the most was a broken one, smashed beyond all recognition, lurching, reaching, spluttering towards me. Why hadn't I helped him earlier? What kind of man was I? What had I turned into?

Some of the most trusted kitchen staff were allowed out of the Range to work for a few hours, but other than that the lockdown was total: no mail, no phone calls, no exercise, no TVs – no nuthin', as everyone would groan. No one from the kitchen seemed to care much about what had happened, and each time I asked I got a deadpan response or a shrug of the shoulders. One guy told me he'd heard he was dead, another that he was stable in the local hospital in Midland/Odessa. No one cared either way. The only thing everyone could agree on was that it was a gang retribution because he had apparently been running with a different white gang in a state prison in Mississippi. No one seemed to know his name, but everyone seemed to feel this punishment was justified – that such was the order of things. No one switches gangs in prison. I tried to block it all out. I didn't speak much to Chief, but each time I almost fell asleep or would look over at him, he was there awake, watching me, or watching over me; Gabriel the archangel. He was an angry archangel too; he never spoke to me once over those first few hours.

After a restless night, the following morning New York and I played cards and sat around talking. The lockdown was already over but the government holiday meant there was no work and none of the prison's facilities were open. It was already hot and humid and the lack of things to do was making everyone edgy. There wasn't much talking and you could feel how flat the atmosphere was. I was in mental turmoil, dazed and unsure for the first time through all of this – through all the troubles of Enron, the indictment, my extradition, trial delays and judges, shoddy plea deals and then Big Spring – unsure of where my moral compass lay. I was edgy and kept watching everyone entering and leaving the room; wondering who would come for me. I didn't know what would be worse: the Feds or a gang visit. I could no longer tell right from wrong, good from bad. I couldn't think straight at all. I wouldn't rat on anyone, but if SlumDawg came near me or approached me, I wouldn't hesitate to extract my own retribution.

Around midday there was a scramble to the windows to see the first 'suspects' being led out for questioning. They were handcuffed and we pressed ourselves against the windows and watched them make a show struggling against the cops, aware of the audience of hundreds from the Ranges. I didn't recognise anyone among the first batch, although I couldn't be sure who else had been there. My attention had been on SlumDawg and his victim. A few hours later, to my surprise, they took out Angel, and he sauntered along the path that dissected the two buildings, taunting the officers, aware of his audience and supremely confident of himself. But they had not called me. Perhaps no one had seen me after all, I kidded myself; perhaps no one had talked. In the mid-afternoon, I relaxed a little and managed to catch some sleep, albeit with the images of that incident still dominating my thoughts.

Around 5 p.m., when we were beginning to get ready for chow time, two cops marched into the Range while I was sitting near New York's bunk, reading an old copy of *The New York Times*. There was a restaurant review in it, and the writer was complaining about the tepid water. I wanted to laugh.

'Mulgrew,' one of the cops bellowed. I sat upright immediately, all eyes turning to me as my heart began to race once more. This was it. They knew. It was over.

'Good luck, *amigo*,' New York whispered, looking at

me as I got up and giving me the obligatory fist bump. My eyes met Joker's and his finger rose to his mouth, making the silence sign. I nodded to him, realising at that instant that I was part of it all now, that I felt loyalty to him, to them, to all of them. I would never rat, even on people I detested. I walked towards my bunk to get my shirt. Chief was scribbling furiously, while Kola looked at me and winked. The room had gone quiet. I walked past Chief, then hesitated and fist-bumped his shoulder. Without looking up, he offered a fist back. We bumped and I walked forward escorted out by the two cops.

As they walked me out of the Range across the space between Sunset and Sunrise, I felt as if I was on a stage – a thousand eyes upon me. Why hadn't they handcuffed me? Everyone else had been handcuffed, I suddenly realised. That would look bad – as if I was collaborating. I put my hands behind my back – like a visiting member of the Royal family – hoping that some of my audience, up there in the Ranges, wouldn't notice the lack of cuffs.

After the last day and a half inside the Range, the power of the sun seemed greater than ever, but then the sun always felt greater than ever, every day in Big Spring. If the birds were singing, I didn't hear them and I moved along in a daze wondering how I was going to handle the Feds' questions, the interrogation. At least this time they might have the courtesy to ask me if I did it, I thought, as I picked up my pace to keep up with the two cops chatting happily in front of me.

We passed straight through the checkpoint I had stood at a day earlier, worried about blood and teeth, then turned right towards the lieutenant's office and what I used to think of as the dreaded Hole, solitary. It now seemed like a place of peace and respite – my only hope, in fact. I'd heard that they put you in there for a few hours before your interrogation; it might just give me a chance to work out a strategy.

But we walked past the solitary cells, towards the processing centre and the entrance, and when I saw Malone, looking partly at me and partly at something else, I felt deeply confused.

'Hello Mildew, looks like your lucky day!' he exclaimed, with a friendly smile. The other two cops ignored me. 'You've got friends in high places!' he added. I cocked my head questioningly. Who did he mean? The shot-callers? Had they somehow colluded with the guards to get me out of the heat?

Malone didn't elaborate, just escorted me to a holding cell, where a Colombian inmate was waiting. We made some small talk, and then I asked him if he knew what had happened to the guy that got beat up.

'What guy?' he asked.

'I don't know,' I answered tentatively. 'Some dude that got beat up in the Yard.'

'I don't know about that shit, man. I didn't see nuthin',' to which I nodded with bland acceptance.

'Why are you here?' I asked a little later.

My heart leapt as he responded, 'I'm being transferred.' Surely that could mean that I was too? Could it really be over? Could I really be starting a journey home? My mind was off and running again, but I felt drained. I couldn't take the ups and downs anymore. I felt beaten, emotionally sanitised.

'Do you think I might be getting transferred?' I stupidly asked, to a quick, disinterested shrug of his shoulders. Trying to keep the conversation going and needing to talk, after a few minutes I asked him another question.

'You don't look very happy for someone getting out of this shithole.'

'Because, *cabrone*,' he said carefully, 'travelling through the system takes many months, and they fuck with you the whole way. You will even miss Big Spring until these people deliver you to your transfer destination.'

Chief had told me this would happen, that it was terrible, but I barely listened. For me it was going home – the first part of it, anyway. But could it really be true? Maybe they were just holding me here before they questioned me?

After an hour or two, my temporary cell-mate was packed up and gone, then Malone came back to see me with a clipboard. 'Looks like you're being transferred, Mildew. I'm gonna be sorry to see you go.' I almost wanted to hug him. He kept talking to me, but I wasn't listening. The intense relief I felt was overcoming me, from being fearful for my life to suddenly realising that I was taking the first step towards going home. I wanted to dance around the room. I started listening to him again, and at that same moment a recurring picture of the events of the last few days came back to me.

'Mr Malone, do you know what happened to that guy that got beat up the other day?' I asked suddenly feeling very solemn.

'What guy, Mildew?' he asked, his squint eye peering off into the sunset.

'The guy that got beat up bad,' I responded, dreading his answer.

'You need to be more specific than "the guy that got beat up bad", Mildew. Guys get beat up bad every day,' he responded, way too cheerfully.

'The one we were locked-down for.'

'We wuz locked-down for quite a few things, Mildew. For one thing we were short-staffed, and it's a government holiday this weekend.'

I considered that for a moment before persevering.

'A white guy, handball player, medium build, moustache I think,' I said, desperately trying to think of a better description, knowing I'd just covered about 20% of the prison population.

Malone just smiled and shrugged his shoulders, 'Why do you care, Mildew? Didn't no one tell you to do your own time in here?' he asked without a hint of irony on his friendly countenance.

'Why you worried? You're going home soon – heading back to England. He wasn't . . .' then leaning close into me as if he had just realised something, 'he wasn't your boyfriend was he!?' asked a suddenly gleeful Malone.

'No, no!' I answered, irritated. 'Shit no. It's just he owed me that's all,' I responded, suddenly changing tack. 'I just wanted to know if I'll be collecting what's due, that's all,' I continued, trying to sound as indignant as possible.

Malone shrugged his shoulders again and I guessed his interest in what had happened was now fully extinguished. Nobody gave a shit; someone could have died and no one cared. I didn't even know the man's name.

I lowered my head and felt I was abandoning this nameless, faceless man once more, even though finding out about him wouldn't change what had happened or what was happening to him now. I had to let him go.

'Now, what do you want me to do with your stuff, Mildew?'

I looked up and focused on Malone once more. 'Give it to the Chief. Bed 8, lower bunk, Range 4,' I said, the sudden thought occurring to me that I hadn't said goodbye, that I might never see him again. I hadn't thanked him.

'All of it, Mildew? You're gonna need it. It will still take you months to transfer back to England and you're gonna be goin' to some pretty rough prisons. You know, not everywhere is as nice like here in Texas,' Malone added seriously.

'Give it to the Chief,' I re-iterated. 'He'll know what to do with it.'

I sat in the holding cell until night-time. My transfer bus was coming at 5 a.m. the next morning. Around 9 p.m. they moved me down to the dungeon-like quarters of the Hole, and with Malone having finished his shift, another guard took me to my solitary cell.

As we walked towards the cell I broke the silence between us.

'Do you know what happened to the guy that got beat up the other day?' I asked one last time, knowing my question was hopelessly vague.

'Which one?' was the gruff response.

'I don't know exactly,' I said, pushing my luck a little.

'Didn't see no body bags been used this weekend, so

guess whoever he was he weren't dead. Least not when he left here he weren't.'

I knew asking anything more was pointless – he wouldn't know and he wouldn't care.

'Why the fuck d'you care anyway?' he suddenly continued as we reached the cell door. 'You're from abroad, ain't you? You don't even belong here,' he said with barely concealed disdain as he undid my cuffs.

'The light don't work, so I hopes you're not afraid of the dark,' he said in a southern drawl, as he prodded me into the darkened cell.

Ignoring him, I walked in and sat down on my bunk as he slammed the door shut with too much enthusiasm. I sat for a moment as my eyes adjusted to the darkness, then I kicked off my shoes and lay back on my bunk. I knew I was damaged, wounded and hardened. I knew I would carry the emotional remnants of those last few days, of the last few years of turmoil with me, wherever they sent me next. I knew I'd changed, normality would evade me and that there would be a price for me to pay at some point, maybe in two months; maybe in a year, maybe much later. But at that moment I also felt I was lucky, truly blessed.

I pulled your picture out of my pocket and tried to scrutinise it in the dark. It had been 841 days since I'd seen you, but at last I was beginning my long journey home. 'I'm coming back to find you Cara Katrina, I'm coming back to Calum,' I whispered as I closed my eyes and thought that whatever tomorrow brought, I could deal with it. I was coming to find you.

It was dark, but I wasn't afraid.

Cara, aged 5, buying flowers for her granny Crail,
Scotland, May 2006.

POSTSCRIPT

JUST OVER A YEAR LATER, AFTER four more prisons in the United States and two in England, Gary Mulgrew walked free to return to his son Calum and to continue the search for his missing daughter, Cara Katrina. That search continues to this day.

A minimum of 60% of the author's advance and royalty from sales of this edition will be donated to charities on Calum and Cara Katrina's behalf.